ECOLOGIZING EDUCATION

ECOLOGIZING EDUCATION

Nature-Centered Teaching for Cultural Change

Sean Blenkinsop and Estella Kuchta

COMSTOCK PUBLISHING ASSOCIATES

AN IMPRINT OF CORNELL UNIVERSITY PRESS   ITHACA AND LONDON

First published 2024 by Cornell University Press

Library of Congress Cataloging-in-Publication Data

Names: Blenkinsop, Sean, author. | Kuchta, Estella, author.
Title: Ecologizing education : nature-centered teaching for cultural change /
    Sean Blenkinsop and Estella Kuchta.
Description: Ithaca [New York] : Comstock Publishing Associates, an imprint of
    Cornell University Press, 2024. | Includes bibliographical references and index.
Identifiers: LCCN 2023039431 (print) | LCCN 2023039432 (ebook) |
    ISBN 9781501774713 (hardcover) | ISBN 9781501774737 (epub) |
    ISBN 9781501774720 (pdf)
Subjects: LCSH: Education—Environmental aspects. | Education—Experimental
    methods. | Ecology—Study and teaching. | Outdoor education. |
    Educational change.
Classification: LCC LB1027 .B544 2024 (print) | LCC LB1027 (ebook) |
    DDC 371.3/84—dc23/eng/20230912
LC record available at https://lccn.loc.gov/2023039431
LC ebook record available at https://lccn.loc.gov/2023039432

To all-our-relations and to those educators
working hard to ecologize their practices

Contents

Acknowledging

Many parts of this book have been written in the temperate rain forest of Canada's West Coast, amid their soggy and vibrant communities. Specifically, many pages have been crafted alongside the Alouette River itself and surrounded by Water Strider, Step Moss, Sword Fern, Pacific Wren, Rough-Skinned Newt, Red Huckleberry, Douglas Squirrel, Skunk Cabbage, Red Cedar, and Chum Salmon, to name just a few. Many more pages have been conceptualized and penned in the presence of Harbor Seals, Pink Salmon, Glaucus Gull, Bald Eagle, Purple Sea Star, Gooseneck Barnacle, Bull Kelp, Hermit Crab, and the generous Pacific Ocean. These places and beings brought us inspiration, gifted us with ideas, and made possible other ways of knowing and understanding our responsibilities to writing this book. They are our co-teachers and collaborators throughout this book.

In similar ways, this book has also been created in companionship and collaboration with Cypress, Golden Ears, and Steele Mountains, Hardangerjøkulen Glacier; in the shadows of Red Cedar, Hemlock, Broad-leaf Maple, Red Alder, Douglas Fir, and Sitka Spruce; and amid the gifts of Sword Fern, Deer Fern, Lady Fern, Licorice Fern along with Salmon Berry, Black Berry, Huckle Berry, and Blue Berry. We are grateful for the microworld teachings of mosses, lichens, and fungi and to all the twittering, strutting, slipping, and hopping feathered beings and amphibians and reptiles—too vast in number to name. We are grateful to all the four-legged and furry ones who have left tracks, scents, inspirations, and lessons for us along the way. And we express gratitude to all those whirring, fluttering, plodding, scurrying, sliding smaller beings of earth and sky and the stones, soil, Sun, and weather that hold and protect them and us along the way.

Our engagement with these beings has occurred on the territory of Indigenous Nations, in particular the Coast Salish and we are so thankful to the Elders, teachers, and community members who have spent time with the students and patiently listened as we fumbled around in search of moments of understanding. Without their stewardship, guidance, and incredible generosity in terms of patience, shared story, time spent with learners the work and these lands in fact would be the lesser for all. As authors, we write from our perspectives as white settler scholars and educators trying to live in better relationship with the unsurrendered and traditional territories of Shishalh, Katzie, Kwantlen, and Snuneymux peoples in the place colonially known as British Columbia, Canada.

We recognize the complexities of relating to land in this role and our ethical responsibility to disrupt and unlearn colonial ways of being and teaching. Through our sharing of who we are, we establish the parameters of what we may know and what we may not know. We also acknowledge our limitations in understanding these territories, Indigenous Knowledge systems, and ourselves in the context of this work—work in which we strive to recognize, hear, and uplift the voices of Indigenous peoples, the land, and the myriad beings that make up the larger more-than-human world. We acknowledge that we have a responsibility to nurture sacred, reciprocal relationships with the land and its inhabitants, to learn about what it means to be a good relative to all beings, and to educate in ways that foster mutually beneficial flourishing for all.

We are indebted to that amazing, humble, openminded, curious, and courageous group of founders—Jodi MacQuarrie, Clayton Maitland, Mark Fettes—and researchers—John Telford, Laura Piersol, Mike Datura, Michael Caulkins, Veronica Hotton, Chris Beeman, Yi Chien Jade Ho, Naomi Steinberg, Tom Green, Chloe Humphreys, Stephanie Block, Gillian Judson, Lara Harvester, Anya Chase, Carleigh Smart, and others. We appreciate your amazing energy, teacher talent, and all-around brilliance and are so happy you are in the world doing the work you do.

We thank all the teachers and principals (especially Clayton, Sally, and Randy) who joined and continue to join the ecologizing journey. Your willingness to literally "step outside the box" of public school; to decenter yourselves and allow space for nature, children, and other humans to share space as teacher; to continue to strive for rich learning and align it with the demands of public education and a culture in crisis; and to be humble enough to continue to change the work even when the direction is unclear is inspiring. We hope this book does justice to everything you do and inspires others to take it up and take it further.

We also thank all those who surround any school. This includes the superintendents, trustees, union leaders, and employees of the ministry of education. Your role in providing space, in flexing the assumed rules, in allowing nascent ecologizing projects to set down roots and build strength cannot be understated. The process of change cannot occur without you. Our appreciation also extends to those parents and guardians who support, cherish, feed, clothe, and house all the learners we have had the opportunity to work and learn with. Your willingness to take the risk with your most precious of loved ones and enter into an untried educational program is something that still touches us most deeply. But we are also grateful for your willingness to step in when needed, to start visiting your children's and grandchildren's special places, to trust the place and process, and even to camp out the night before school starts.

Our gratitude extends to all the community members, organizations, local groups, and neighbors who have supported this long process. Many community members (especially the Alouette River Management Society, the CEED Centre Society, the District of Maple Ridge, Big Feast, Blue Mountain Woodlot, Malcolm Knapp Research Forest) have offered resources, expertise, places to meet, helped build greenhouses, honored highway crossings as classes headed for the park, helped make outdoor spaces safe for learning to those who stepped in to teach about birds, local medicines, and the stories of the land and on to those who just expressed interest and came out to support the learners and the projects and huge thanks and let us keep talking.

Importantly, several individuals worked with, cared for, and supported us, during the writing process by staring at pages and offering thoughtful and essential feedback. Stan Rushworth, Jesse Haber, Bob Jickling, and Donna Grand read various versions and portions of the manuscript and offered important and even challenging feedback. We would be deeply amiss if we did not thank the Social Sciences and Humanities Research Council of Canada for taking the risk to support the research end (remember, these are publicly funded schools) of these projects for without that support it would have been impossible to make this book happen. A great many others—human and more-than-human—have contributed directly, indirectly, fleetingly, flittingly, quietly, and humbly to this work. We hope you know who you are, feel your impact on these pages, and hear our thanks.

Sean adds: I have deep gratitude to my parents and son, Quinn, for indulging my crazy need to be "on-trail" all the time, for without a rich home to return to the adventure changes quite a lot. And my forever thanks and love to Jane, for being the best human teacher I have ever seen and for sharing my deep love of the natural world. I would not be who I am if you weren't here and as any who know us will attest, I am definitely the better for it. Estella adds: Thank you to my first teachers—my mother and father, from whom I learned the joy of curiosity, the pleasure of spending time in the trees and by the tidepools, and the importance of respecting the furry, winged, and wiggling creatures of the world. And thank you to my children, Maxwell and Celia, whose deep and protective love of the natural world inspires the work I do.

ECOLOGIZING
EDUCATION

IDENTIFYING THE PROBLEMS OF STANDARD SCHOOLING

Imagine a public school without walls, desks, blackboards, or buildings of any kind. When children arrive, they follow a dirt path down to a small clearing, surrounded by Douglas Fir, Western Hemlock, and Red Cedar. Steam rises from rain-soaked trunks as water drips onto Salal and Huckleberry leaves. A few hundred feet away, a shallow River chortles and washes over gray stones.

A School with No Walls

On the Alouette River's edge, a teacher and a group of younger children follow a fresh set of bird tracks. They talk thoughtfully about tracking, movement, silence, and who left these messages in the sand. Meanwhile, older children sit on fallen logs and write in weathered journals. Some reflect on an evening exploration with their families, others are reworking yesterday's poetry, and still others are drawing the scene before them. The benefits of this way of educating can be measured, observed, and appreciated not only by children's educational achievements but also by their sheer enthusiasm for learning and care for those around. Parents and caregivers report that children don't want to miss a day of school, even for a holiday. The humans at this school are coming to understand themselves as being in community with each other and with the flora, fauna, and River of this place.

The sensory environment of this school engages students and provokes their curiosity. Gone are the shuffle of papers, loud bells, and the scrape of chairs on

1

tiled floors. These children study without the low-grade buzzing of electric lights, projectors, and computers. Here, Moss springs underfoot. Chickadee, Crow, Mourning Dove, and other birds trill, caw, and coo from all around. River churns, shushes, and trickles, a rhythm that changes depending on seasons and storms. Dappled light patterns the wet ground. When the children talk, cry, yell, or laugh, their voices are softened by the expanse of trees and sky. Nature speaks with a resonant voice, and everyone is learning to listen.

It doesn't smell like a standard school either, where classrooms are infused with the scent of styling gel, art projects, old lunches, and off-gassing linoleum. These pervasive smells are punctuated by the odor of books, whiteboard markers, and various cleaning products. In other words, the air in a regular classroom is filled with the scents of human-made substances. But at *this* school, this school with no walls, the scents of rich, damp dirt; rotting leaves; and verdant Fir combine with the cold twinge of winter. The heady tang of oxygen blends with the mineral scent of moving water and the earthy fragrance of Moss steaming in the light.

And hold, dear reader, before throwing the naive, privileged, overly romantic book at us. For you are right: there are ancient and ongoing stories of deep injustice here, ones that these schools continue to reckon and wrestle with. There are failures, problematics, and ongoing difficult learnings that all must engage with—and we will get to them in short order. Yet there *are* successes, celebrations, works being done, quiet moments of rich learning at River's edge, and small ripples of potentially seismic change. And it behooves us to notice these as well, for to judge a book by its opening is to possibly miss its complex contents.

Picture "the standard North American school." What do you see? Typically, it's an unimaginative rectangular box set on a patch of level ground, surrounded by manicured grass. Inside the box sit other boxes. In these classrooms, students might learn about plants, animals, and weather, even while the building itself physically separates them from those things. A child who gazes too long through the window at a passing crow or cloud might be considered "distracted." Construction of the standard school likely required the ejection of birds and animals and the eradication of many plants. In some cases, wetlands were filled, creeks diverted, and rocks exploded. As a by-product of these processes, not only are local flora and fauna lost but so too are human—in particular, Indigenous—histories, including those that archived ecological knowledge and the shared narratives of humans, plants, and animals. Often, evidence of these losses is erased, while at the same time the colonial processes of construction and "standard education" itself are made invisible.

In contrast, the ecologizing school seeks to name and respond to these erasures and to facilitate sensory, relational flourishing between humans and the myriad other beings that make up this world, promoting well-being for all. For children, the complex aesthetic experience of being outdoors—wind, water, falling leaves—is a pleasure to be enjoyed, learned from rather than a mundane experience to be tolerated, survived.

Parents and caregivers report that the outdoor children tend to be calmer and happier than they were when "in" school. This is not a surprise. A sense of discovery, of possibility, and of activeness helps children thrive. The more academic among them can chase their own interests and are challenged and supported by place and teachers. Rana, a bright, inquiring spirit, found the repetitive style of classroom lessons difficult to endure. Here, she is immersed in a discovery project related to Fungi and has already located twenty-seven different species she wants to track. More rambunctious students can find rich and productive outlets for their abundant energy. Adrian, with boundless energy and passion, has become an important gatherer and builder in the village, often moving what seem to be cords of wood every day, and their skills with lashing are second to none. Those children with myriad and diverse needs tend to find connection, support, and therapeutic possibilities. Jamie is a neurodiverse child who used to run out of the classroom because of auditory overload. Quiet time was equally hard because of the unbearable silence. At the outdoor school, he self-regulates his delicate auditory needs by positioning himself closer to the white noise of the river or the hush of the woods. This diverse locale supports his subtle needs without setting him in contrast to his peers.

Almost all the parents and caregivers have reported to our researchers that their children now love school. "They explain things to me about insects, slugs, and snails that I didn't even know," one comments. "She doesn't realize she's learning because it's all fun to her," another remarks. "Last year he hated school. This year, he said school is the thing he's most grateful for," says a third. Deep immersion in the natural environment supports, restores, and promotes the child's instinct for relationship with all beings. These relationships nurture the child and support the ecological health of the area while at the same time allowing rich learning to occur and the prescribed content to be covered. After all, this is not a laissez-faire, kids-running-in-the-woods schooling. Without human teachers working in partnership with place, community, learners, and the mandated curriculum, none of this would come to fruition. Responding to the possibilities offered by the place and its denizens, witnessing and recording the learning outcomes as they appear amid the action, facilitating experiences in robust directions, asking good questions that further wonder and curiosity, listening to and including the variety of teachers who exist in an given place, all while scaffolding, growing, and deepening learning and enacting a curriculum that is responsive, equitable, expansive, experiential, and robust—these can only be achieved through the deliberate, mindful, thoughtful efforts of dedicated and devoted educators.

More critically, ecologizing education fosters a culture where the plants, animals, and wild beings of the world are actively and respectfully engaged. Cranefly maneuvering long legs across Moss stalks might teach an observant third-grader more about self-awareness, goal setting, and the mathematics of motion than a teacher with a chalkboard could manage.

The Seeds of Change

When parents and other adults first hear about these ecologizing schools, their reaction, voiced or not, is often: "That's not a school." For most, a school is a building, an institution, a set of organized rooms with tables and desks. It's bells, timetables, exams, carefully crafted work leading to learning, and lineups. It means doing what you are told, giving them what they want, and waiting for adulthood. This sentiment is so engrained that many of us reflexively resist the idea of a building-less school. We struggle to picture how it functions. We have difficulty imagining our way into such a different form for schooling. As such, the actuality of ecologizing schools seems to teeter at the edge of reason and possibility. Skepticism ignites. *We can't just stage* Lord of the Flies *and call it "education." Children are supposed to go outdoors at break time, for fun and play, and come inside to settle down, to turn to the hard work of learning, and to become educated. How can children learn to write and study with no desks?* And more deeply, more subconsciously, we may be wondering: *Why do these children get to go outdoors when we did not? We too yearned to run in the grass, climb trees, and balance on river stones, but we stayed inside because classroom education is better. It must be, or else what did we suffer for?*

While visions of education remain intransigent, institutions cannot easily be changed either, largely because of the powerful metaphors, languages, ideas, and imaginings upon which they are built. We and our imaginings are shaped by our experiences, our culture, and the contexts—including buildings—in which this all happens. The Brazilian educator and liberation theorist Paulo Freire explains, "The oppressed, instead of striving for liberation, tend to become oppressors. . . . The very structure of their thought has been conditioned by the contradictions of the concrete, existential situation by which they were shaped."[1] Thus, if change is to happen, we are going to have to consider the contexts in which education occurs. In fact, in our experience, abandoning the physical bricks and mortar of the school is the easiest task of ecologizing education. Disassembling hierarchical, professional, psychological, structural, and epistemological barriers is the much harder job.

After all, what does it mean to teach when knowledge is understood to be a shared endeavor and not the sole purview of expert humans? How do we decide what and how to teach? What is the scope and sequence of this work? How does one teach in ways that honor the learner and the world around as having knowledge and a stake in our shared future? And how does one aid the development of children into becoming deeply relational and ecologically connected adults when there are precious few examples and theories to support this work? Exceedingly few ecological educators have escaped standard schooling themselves, and we know that the experience of one's own schooling embeds deeply in the psyche. Even when the conscious layers have been shed, the subconscious still carries implicit structure, weight, and, for many, trauma.

It seems that we might begin by reminding ourselves that education is a tool for replicating culture, a way of instilling and cultivating adult values in children. Indeed, the word *culture* derives from the word *cultivate*, with all the agrarian connotations of seeding, growing, and harvesting for the benefit of the community. But what cultural "ways of being" are imparted therein? Modern North American schools typically emphasize the mind over the body, thoughts over senses, rationality over emotion, factuality over imagination, truth over uncertainty, stasis over change, independence over connection, and human over all else. These values link to Western ideologies that prioritize competition, a particular form of rationality, factuality, independence, progress, and an unshakeable belief in human supremacy. And these are the values that underpin the current industrialized culture that has brought the world to the brink of environmental ruin. Our view, then, is that education offers both perilous and hopeful possibilities for a world facing ecological devastation: it can remain a normalizing mechanism for the status quo, or it can move to redress the harm that has been caused and help transform culture, returning to the idea of culture/cultivation for the benefit of the whole community.

Indeed, this transformative role is what we envision for our ecologizing education project. Contrary to some misconceptions, however, we do not indulge in the fantasy that North Americans can live in a preindustrial past—such a mission is undesirable to most and impossible anyway. Nor is the goal to merely imitate beliefs and actions of more ecologically sustainable cultures—although, certainly, Western cultures can learn much from many, particularly local, Indigenous cultures. While we may engage with, be challenged by, see possibilities in, and learn from certain processes and concepts, dominant North American culture—like all cultures—must evolve from its own unique and complex interactions among history, geography, genetics, and the world around.

Culture is inherently, though not easily, transformable. Western culture has repeatedly illustrated that fact as assumed ways of being, such as imperialism, genderism, racism, ableism, and classism, have come under scrutiny and been slowly devalued. The current juncture in history presents another crisis-opportunity for deep cultural assessment and positive transformation. We can imagine our way into a healthier social, emotional, and environmental future. By dismantling humancentric ideologies, we can evolve into a more ecologically conscious, more equitable culture. The path ahead is lit with an environmental and social ethos and greater justice for all.

Ecologizing Education

This book is about ecologizing education, a term that positions education differently, not only from mainstream schooling but also from outdoor adventure education and "green" schooling programs often contained within the boundaries of standard classrooms or understood as minor addendums thereof. Those programs offer improvements to standard pedagogy but usually fall far short of the root-level cultural change that we understand is needed at this time. They may, for example, focus solely on building student confidence in the outdoors and increasing physical fitness. Or they may allow children to roam and run free, to be led by their curiosity, and to discover their own education but without attending to deeper cultural biases.

Ecologizing education is a project that places education at the center of the radical transformation of culture toward a more eco-socially just world. Ecologizing education recognizes that the very foundation of the globalized, industrialized culture is environmentally and socially problematic and unjust. It must change. Humans within these cultures must *be* differently in the world, and ecologizing education is about teaching in concert with that goal. Change needs to occur at the cultural level and not simply at the individual and/or behavioral levels, and education is central to that project. The process is creative, active, unfolding, and always in process rather than complete.

Ecologizing education moves toward richer, more diverse, mutually beneficial flourishing. By pushing against the colonial viewpoint, it works to right the wrongs of implicit and ongoing marginalizations, such as those created by anthropocentrism, species elitism, binaries, and individualism. Ecologizing education is in alliance with the natural world, understanding nature as filled with a myriad of vibrant, agential, and intrinsically valuable beings. Our kin. These beings have been and continue to be systematically marginalized and destroyed for the sake of a certain way of being human in the world, a way that current systems of education often continue to encourage, both explicitly and implicitly. Ecologizing education is about taking greater responsibility for redressing the eco-social tragedies of the past as well as greater responsibility for the future we gift to our descendants.

Ecologizing education is not a quixotic attempt to return to some imagined, idyllic past. While valuing the beauty, abundance, diversity, and relationships the more-than-human world offers, it also acknowledges that same world's potential for danger, discomfort, and apathy. Ecologizing education is not a process that requires the dismantling of all school walls. It is not meant only for those with privileged access to forests and oceans and other wildernesses. It is not a one-size-fit-all formula, where boxes can be checked on a form and—*voilà!*— education is ecologized! Rather, this process responds to the needs of particular locations and circumstances, including those of the local ecosystem and of the individuals involved. Furthermore, the capacity for ecologizing education doesn't begin with a chunk of wild land. It begins with a radical shift in orientation, values, and understandings, and from that shifted perspective, education unfolds differently, regardless of the locale.

Many educators find that in creating an ecologizing pedagogy, they are, in fact, working alongside nature as an active and able co-teacher. The human educators are coming to understand themselves as being part of a cultural change project. These educators recognize that if people are to *be* differently in the world, they must be supported in the endeavor. They must be helped and challenged to move from where they are, how they currently exist, to somewhere different. This is a learning process, one that requires different kinds of educators with a diverse and divergent range of skills.

This book does not approach the subject of pedagogy lightly. Rather, it views education as a process for reenvisioning culture. We take the stance that Western culture requires a seismic shift and that a radical new approach to education may be the most meaningful chance we have for real change. No reworking or reimagining of culture can occur without degrees of discomfort, reassessment, and realignment. But ultimately, the ecologizing education project is profoundly hopeful. Reenvisioning culture may mean sacrificing some comforts, conveniences, and material goods, but those sacrifices will make possible significantly improved social, psychological, and ecological health for all.

Ecologizing education is a promising growth process that includes both past and future into a more complete present. The industrialized world's current agenda, by contrast, looks suicidal. Yes, we'll need to make sacrifices, recognize traumas, and reevaluate responsibilities, but the ultimate vision is that of a healthier, more balanced world. This evolving culture will be better harmonized with the needs and rights of the natural world. Its citizens will refuse to perpetuate the environmental atrocities of the past. As Stan Rushworth, an activist for Indigenous rights and an educator of Indigenous literature, notes, "We begin to be liberated from the pain by *seeing* it, not by denying it."[2]

Ecologizing Education: Schools and Research

At the outdoor school, low-hanging clouds release a cool rain in pattering ripples across River, sand, and the children's raincoats. Raindrops bend moss capsules covering a log. Moss on another log is being systematically ripped off by an eight-year-old boy who balls it up and throws it at another boy. Another student interrupts, explaining that moss is an important habitat for spiders and insects and that the capsules provide food for mice. One child shrugs, but he does stop and then wanders off. The other, head down, hesitates and then tries to press Moss back onto the bark. He has been at the school longer, has been reminded more often. But he won't need reminding again. His understanding of and relationship with Moss, the ecosystem, and himself have deepened, along with his sense of responsibility.

This book draws from several schools but two in particular that have emerged from, engaged with, worked with, and walked alongside the ecologizing educational theorizing work done by a team of researchers at Simon Fraser University in British Columbia, Canada. The first school, now twelve years old, is a kindergarten to grade 7 school consisting of almost one hundred and fifty students. This school has no building at all and moves among several forested, meadowed, and riverine sites on the edges of a suburban community. The second, another K–7 school, started ten years ago as a school within a school. Here, the ninety students spend significant amounts of time engaged in curriculums of the nearby Ocean, estuary, and forest. Both schools have come to see themselves as sites of activism and resistance—places of cultural change. They recognize that part of their work is to respond to the colonization and oppression of people and nature while working alongside a dynamic natural world with agency of its own. Here, the human teachers are decentering themselves and allowing the students to be co-taught by the world around.

At its core, this book is a call to action. Many people already recognize the urgency for environmental action on all fronts and will turn to this book for resources to support and challenge their practices going forward. We hope the many others who open these pages will be convinced along the way that ecologizing education presents an opportunity for more joyful, authentic, connected education for children and is essential for the depth of cultural transformation necessary to restore planetary and, by extension, human health.

Our book is framed around five central chapters. Each chapter is titled with a single gerund—that is, we have chosen for each a *moving* title, not in regard to its emotional content but because everything about ecologizing education is processional. Things are in flux, spreading out, turning in, spilling over, enfolding, and so on rather than complete, static, resolved, or determined. Chapter 1 describes the origins of the ecologizing schools and then focuses in particular on the Maple Ridge Environmental School and the Nature Education for Sustainable Todays and Tomorrows (NEST) program.

Chapters 2 and 3 explore two of the biggest pieces of the change conversation that we in ecologizing education have encountered over the past ten years. In chapter 3, we respond directly to some of the aspects of the modern Western world that challenge and block our ability to connect with one another and with the natural world—alienation, isolation, individualization, colonization, resourcism, privilege, and human elitism. Rather than spending time elaborating on these problems, we point in their direction through these responses. It has become clear that eco-social cultural change is not going happen without building rich, diverse, and more trusting relationships, and that will require much healing. Chapter 3 explores how mainstream culture undermines our own health and that of the planet and offers hope in the gifts of healing that the natural world provides.

In chapter 4, we turn directly to the question of education by exploring philosophical perspectives in order to examine the structural challenges of ecologizing education and potential responses to these challenges. In chapter 5, we set aside the theoretical and return to practice, thinking through some of the "hows" related to actually ecologizing education with real students in real places alongside nature.

The conclusion, rather than offering a sense of finality, focuses instead on change itself and on the skills and orientations needed to begin an ecologizing education venture—for the project is in no way completed. Here, we come back around, in a way, to our discussion of *culture/cultivate* by offering the metaphor of a small-scale, sustainable farm and the seeds needed to make it all work. The idea here is to provide a form and some potential places for readers to start the project of ecologizing education. Start wherever you are, in whatever way makes sense and works for your community.

What follows hereafter is a little more setup on relating, healing, and changing in order to prime the pump, grease the wheel, or—perhaps more apropos—prepare the ground. But first, a brief note on language.

It is challenging to find appropriate language for the range of beings that exist outside the human. This is because that language often "others" (used as a verb here)—consider, for example, the terms "nonhuman" or "other-than-human"—which is problematic if we are trying to build equitable relationships. Sometimes we test out these terms by applying them in human situations: for example, what would it feel like to be referred to as "nonwoman"—or "nonman"? Then again, it seems that certain words confirm an artificial separation between humans and all else (for example, nature or the environment), which in turn leads to ignoring, backgrounding, then hierarchizing, and more. And yet the fixes—such as "nature/culture" or "we are all nature" or "post-nature"—don't really work because the language itself doesn't undo the politics of the divide/binary that currently exists and in fact can obscure it. Again, if we try it out in the human context, does it work? Would we be comfortable with "we are post-race" or with the term "genderless"? Such terms may be aspirational (although it seems they are most often uttered by the more privileged side of the binary), but they certainly are not in line with the lived reality.

Consequently, in this book we have made two choices regarding language. First, we tend to use the term "more-than-human," a turn of phrase suggested by David Abrams when he wrestled with these same challenges.[3] This term seeks to undo both anthropocentrism and human alienation from all other beings by suggesting that humans are part of something bigger than themselves. The term "more-than-human" is not, then, a reversing (and thus a reiteration) of the hierarchical binary; instead, it sees humans as incorporated as an equal part into this larger group called more-than-human. The term is certainly not perfect, but it does attempt to negate the hierarchy, and it not only honors the physical "others" but also can be seen to go beyond the physical to include spiritual and emotional elements. Second, we have messed a little with how members of the more-than-human are named. When possible, we have focused on the particular, to undermine the general categories so common to colonial frames of mind, and we have capitalized their given English human names. So, when we are speaking about known particular individuals or small groupings, those we are working with or have spent time alongside, they are capitalized (for example, Cedar, Crow, and Moss), just like our own names, as a sign of respect. Groups of particular species we also try to name, but without capitalization, as with the word "humans" (for example, birds, trees, clouds, and sand). These linguistic shifts are largely symbolic, but they are an attempt to push back on invisible biases within language, and we hope and anticipate that future educators, students, and nature's many other beings will present new suggestions.

The Need for Relationship

Before children begin their formal education, their actions appear to be guided mainly by internal curiosities and impulses, with caregivers stepping in only as needed to moderate dangerous or unsociable behavior or to pattern the day with meals and sleep. These internal impulses include all the destructive, unbounded, and brilliant instincts and intuitions associated with young children. For most preschool-age children, the curious self is still mostly whole and vivid, and the relational self is still active. A sense of wonder and of being part of the world guides the child to follow Butterfly, trying to imitate and communicate with her. It leads the child to commune with and understand Tree while sitting on its limbs. It leads the child to walk into a room and, before even glancing at their mother, ask why she is sad. In other words, young children seem to have an instinctive connectedness to themselves and others. Many have not yet fully adopted the detached individuality and rationality-above-all attitudes promoted by the culture and often sustained by the education system despite teachers' best efforts.

This intrinsic connectedness is now evidenced through cognitive and neurobiological research. The Harvard neurologist Matthew Lieberman and the Oxford psychologist Sue Gerhardt have determined that infants and children are predisposed to shared cognition and communal emotion.[4] While standard schools tend to refocus students on their individualized and rational self, ecologizing education seeks to attend to the ecological self—this more immersed and connected self—by supporting children's seemingly wonder-full and relational impulses.

After having spent twelve years in mainstream education, most adults in modern Western culture seem to have lost touch with their more relationally able selves. They do not notice and wonder at Butterfly, cannot listen to Tree, and have limited sense of how a loved one feels if they can't see them (and, sometimes, even if they can). Detached from ourselves, we detach from others. Having lost the taproot to relationship, adults often find the process of connecting and caring for others—human or otherwise—frustrating and time-consuming rather than instinctive and rewarding. For most North Americans, the culture of separation surrounds and permeates daily life. Having succumbed to what Robert Stolorow and George Atwood call the "myth of the isolated mind,"[5] individuals project their own sense of alienation onto the world, seeing other people as threats or as means to particular ends and looking upon forests, rivers, and mountainsides for shallow personal gain and material advancement. The question then becomes: how do we respond to this alienation, loneliness, and isolation? And can we teach toward and for relation?

The Need for Healing

In the consumer mindset, people look upon stuff, the environment, and other people and ask not "How are we related?" but "What can you do for me?" Such a mindset upsets what Matthew Lieberman calls our deepest and most fundamental need: connection.[6] This unmet need—this lack of connection—actually causes pain, a sense of loss, and even trauma. And so, as we teach toward and for relation and restored connection, the question of healing has also become an important discussion in the project of ecologizing education. In fact, as we explored this topic in more depth, it became clear that healing needed to be considered from multiple perspectives.

First, healing is needed in the relationship between humans and the earth's other beings. Second, healing is needed for the pain of severed relations and for the mental and emotional health struggles arising from a range of alienations— from other humans and from the more-than-human. Third, healing is needed in order to recognize the interconnected and inter-influential space between human and more-than and to acknowledge that some of the suffering that humans are incurring is *because* the earth is hurting. And finally, healing can emerge from the naming and changing of the colonial, oppressive, violent, and destructive ways modern cultures have treated the earth and its myriad denizens. This latter form of healing might, for instance, take the shape of a truth and reconciliation process, where the truth is about privileged humans naming their roles in and the advantages gained from the colonization of peoples and planet.

Today's children are coping with epidemic levels of mental and emotional health problems. The researcher Jean Twenge reports that, already by the 1980s, the average child was experiencing more anxiety than child psychiatric patients had in the 1950s; since then, the rate has steadily climbed.[7] The nonprofit organization Mental Health America reports that teen depression is "increasing at an alarming rate," with one in five teens now suffering from clinical depression.[8] The psychologist Thomas Verny warns:

> The latest research shows that we are creating so many violent children so rapidly that we will never be able to treat or rehabilitate them all. And the alarming statistics of infanticide, delinquency, and criminality are just the tip of the iceberg. Underneath the water are the invisible scars on each child's soul, subtle changes that will, depending on the presence or absence of certain protective factors, lead to a life assailed by anxiety, depression, failed relationships, lack of motivations, addiction, or suicide.[9]

In classrooms, there is a growing need for support and for the expansion of various social-emotional learning programs just to be able to start on the project of learning. The medical doctor Gabor Maté argues that the deterioration of mental and emotional health among North American children is "a threat as deep and ominous in its future implications for society as the well-recognized environmental/climate change crisis."[10]

In fact, the two—human health and planetary health—are indelibly related, and the mode of thinking that insists they are not is a big part of the problem. Children in ecologizing education programs are more likely to have rich relationships with the places where they live—and successes with a diversity of students suggest that these relationships are important for health and well-being. These children recognize that they are the air they breathe, the water they drink, the food that has come from this earth. These realizations lead to an experienced understanding of their interconnectedness. They understand that their own health is dependent on the wellness of the world they are immersed in. It becomes difficult to see oneself as healthy when the rest of the world is sick.

Rapacious cultures are ones that attempt to function within imagined categories and prioritize economics above all else. In contrast, for many Indigenous cultures, science, spirituality, gender relations, the environment, and economics are all related. Attempting to function within one of those facets without regard to the others is illogical, immoral, and ultimately implausible. In the same way that standard schools break learning into smaller disconnected pieces—subjects, tests, developmental stages—our approach to environmental problems also tends to be segmented, with saving the sharks, prioritizing climate change, and curbing pesticides comprising separate environmental pursuits. The ecologizing education project recognizes the need for a more contextual, communal approach—a radical shift in the fundamental ways we conceive of the world and our relationship in it.

Many diligent, conscientious teachers and educational administrators recognize that even well-designed standard schools reduce creativity, critical thinking, primacy of experience, genuine personhood, and care for the environment. Due to the constraints of the system's conception, design, and fundamental assumptions, the sincere efforts of these educators to redress these concerns often amount to no more than a bit of tinkering: the adoption of a school recycling program or student-created skits on sustainability. We worry that this work might actually obfuscate the more significant challenges that exist. In *The Cancer Stages of Capitalism*, the philosopher John McMurtry argues, "Disconnection of disease epidemics from the social-system determining them is an account blind-spot."[11] In other words, people must recognize the disease-causing systems (for example, lack of relationship, a colonial orientation, the poisoning of the planet, alienation, and propensity toward profit and plunder) deeply embedded within our culture in order to enact effective changes. Rushworth notes that the plagues of medieval Europe came about because humans were living "in filth"—that is, living with their offal thrown in the streets and with infestations of rats—and then he adds, "We're still living in filth, but the filth is real shiny and pretty, so we don't see it as filth."[12]

Like many teachers, parents and caregivers are increasingly frustrated with status quo education. One parent recently lamented to us, "We wanted our children to go into outdoor schools too, but the only ones available were too far away, or private and too expensive. It wasn't possible." One of the goals of this book is to provide interested parents, caregivers, administrators, and educators a means of thinking through education from an ecologizing perspective—whatever their current circumstances. Cultural change does not happen overnight. It's a long, slow process filled with uncertainty, reassessment, and hard, creative reworking. It might begin, for example, by investing in a school vegetable garden instead of another new playground. Trees, songbird shrubs, and a butterfly habitat might be planted to replace one of the school's fields. Outdoor field trips might become regular events for every class. When building remodeling takes place, creating more natural spaces—or protecting existing ones—might be considered in earnest. And when brand-new schools are needed, some collections of parents/caregivers, teachers, community members, administrators, and representatives of the larger more-than-human world might opt to create a building-less school, like the Maple Ridge Environmental School, rather than digging up and building over another local ecosystem.

Alicia Kear, a high school English teacher in a standard classroom, illustrates the kinds of shifts that occur when one has been deeply engaged with ecologizing education ideas for some years.[13] She regularly takes her junior English classes outdoors to walk in the nearby nature trails. There, they might practice rhyming ("tree," "bee"), study alliteration ("bark," "brook," "bearberry"), or develop ideas for a short story based on their observations ("The Hungry Beetle"). She also introduces them to the concept of ecological literacy—the skill of understanding the processes of ecosystems that sustain life. Although Kear has received the support of her administration, her students, and the students' parents/caregivers, she notes that her formal teacher education provided no training in this kind of pedagogy. Consequently, she has few models to turn to and expends significant energy creatively rethinking each aspect of the curriculum.

Can standard schools—with all their physical infrastructure and dominance over the land—ever become truly ecologizing? Perhaps not. Yet the largest barrier is not the physical building but the cognitive infrastructure that persists in its biases toward human elitism, competition, educational hierarchies, separation of nature and culture, and an isolating sense of the self. It is those cognitive barriers that this book works hardest to identify and dismantle. As we point out, since these barriers tend to sever the relational self, they often cause pain to the human as well.

Deep and meaningful pedagogical transformations are a necessary part of addressing these challenges of understanding health and finding ways to heal. But those steps can only happen if we acknowledge and find ways to address the links between environmental degradation, divided and alienated selfhood, truncated relationality, the colonization of nature, and the deep cultural errors of the past. Can education be part of the healing process in all its complexities? What skills, pedagogies, ways of being might the ecologizing educator need to be a part thereof?

The Need for Cultural Change

Many people are looking around today and questioning the passed-down values of the industrialized world that have led to our current environmental catastrophe. Amid the tsunami of bad-news stories citizens have become inured to, concepts like the Anthropocene have become household language. This term, coined by the atmospheric chemist Paul Crutzen in 2000, refers to an epoch when human activity has so dramatically altered the functioning of the entire planet that it will be recognizable forever in the geological record.[14]

On the one hand, this term "Anthropocene" and the chilling facts it suggests provide a solid wake-up call—an icy glass of reality splashed in the face. But many theorists identify cultural biases within the term because it suggests that "humans" are the problem, an assertion that doesn't take into account, for instance, that not all human cultures have participated in and "benefited" from post–Industrial Revolution capitalism and resource use (at the expense of the planet), nor does it take into account that humans lived across the globe very successfully for thousands of years prior to the settler arrivals and colonization.[15] Indeed, the Ika and Kogi peoples of Northern Colombia, the Tarahumara Nation of the Mexican high desert, and the Sami peoples of Norway have not dangerously altered the functioning of the earth. Thus, the term "Anthropocene," while somewhat helpful in activating attention to the crisis, ultimately perpetuates the cultural myopia responsible for it. Additionally, with this term, humans still get to play center stage. Besides, this nascent and as yet unreliably defined epoch is not the result of *human* behavior—it's the result of *particular cultural* behaviors.

People in industrialized nations have varying reactions to the dreary news about the environment. Admittedly, many have given up. "I know the situation is catastrophic," an elderly friend recently admitted, "but I won't be here in twenty years, so—maybe it's selfish—but I don't care." Other people say, "It's all part of a fated design." This is the "everything happens for a reason" argument. Still others claim the problem isn't *that* bad—even when faced with overwhelming evidence to the contrary. Among the more honest are those who acknowledge, "I care about the environment, I just can't abandon my whole life—my car, my job, my shopping habits—to go live in a tree. There's only so much I can do personally." Others go to exhausting (and expensive) lengths to buy biodegradable dishwasher detergent, an electric car, and solar panels, often sensing the insufficiency of their efforts. Amid corporate and government inadequacies and cynicisms, too much burden has been placed on the individual.

This book resides on the premise that there is a moral imperative to do what we can to change and heal this alienated and rapacious cultural relationship to the earth and to seek greater balance. Indeed, an ecological ethos acknowledges that human relationships to the natural world are woven together through care, responsiveness, and responsibility. Enacting the necessary changes will involve a seismic cultural shift for many, though not all, and, we think, not necessarily for the worse. This means rethinking our place in any ecosystem, our rights to consume the other, and, perhaps most significantly, what it means to be human. In reality, no one knows with certainty how our ecological crisis will unfold. That uncertainty underscores the imperative to prepare young people for greater attunement to their more-than-human kin while developing greater adaptability, creativity, comfort with uncertainty, and diversity in ways of knowing.

In its current form, Western culture's impact on the natural world is most aptly described by the language of colonialism.[16] Sitka-Sage, Piersol, and Blenkinsop describe urbanization, for example, as a process of "silencing, dehistoricizing, and violently dislocating Indigenous and other marginalized populations."[17] We believe the brokenness of the environment is experienced on conscious and subconscious, social and personal levels by all of us. Enacting violence upon that which we deem lesser and insignificant results from a mindset of separation and superiority.

Even those who insist they are untouched by the planet's ill health frequently suffer inexplicable ennui, the malaise of inner vacancy, and a distinct loneliness that may course through the entirety of life, from birth to death. Denying the voice of nature requires denial of personal responsibility, the wellness of being-in-relation, and the privileges and implied violences that come with being human—and it results in much suffering and mutual alienation. Everything within our universe—from water systems to atoms to light waves—evidences connection. Loneliness is, therefore, an illusion. The notion of our personal existence as separate from the varied entities of this earth is also a misconception. The belief that polluting the local river, putting poison in the soil, and extinguishing the wolf habitat doesn't also affect us is unscientific, irrational, and misguided.

But change is possible and necessary. A movement is bubbling, a vibrancy percolating up through layers of concrete and alienation. Our kith and kin and even our consciences are reaching toward one another and seeking to find ways to be different together, to mitigate suffering, and to increase flourishing and possibility. In order to do this, learning must happen, education must be involved—and this book steps into that project.

BEGINNING

Envisioning and Creating Eco-Schools

Clouds settle over the forest like the ghosts of old boulders. They shed sheets of rain over Thimbleberry, Lady Fern, and Hemlock. The air is sweet from the bright green growth sprouting from branch tips and lumpy carpets of moss. The Land is its own entity, yet humans looking through the lens of cultural values conceive of it in vastly different ways.

Various sources tell us that long ago—before the school existed and the settlers arrived—this specific site flourished with the kind of rich, interspecies culture that develops over millennia. Patterns of flora revealed long relationships between weather and seeds. Old-growth, juvenile, and fallen conifers engaged in slow-moving cycles of birth, death, opportunity, accident, mutual support, competition, and, especially, interdependency. As Suzanne Simard, a forestry researcher from the University of British Columbia, tells us, "A single tree can be literally linked up to hundreds of other trees." She explains that what we see aboveground is only "the tip of the iceberg. . . . Under a single footstep, there are 300 miles of fungal cells stacked end on end."[1] Those fungal cells help transfer carbon in the form of sugars—tree food—as well as minerals, water, and chemical messages throughout the forest in endless exchanges, often on a needs-based system, that are undetected by the human eye.

The humans who have lived in the Coastal Pacific Northwest since time immemorial experience the land as a sentient being, conscious of and able to influence the humans upon it.[2] The Kwakiutl Band Council describes these lands as "a living world that has provided for generations the spiritual and physical foundations of our culture."[3] The place names they assigned to geographic locations and features across a vast region were reminders of their cosmological origins and history, were markers of territory, and were indicators of activities associated with those places.

The first settlers established a different relationship to place. Many found the land inhospitable and profoundly unwelcoming.[4] This place and its original people, they determined, were in urgent need of civilizing. While a few settlers built relationships with more-than-humans and cared for the land, the vast majority looked upon land as an object, something to be owned, a resource, a potential profit, and a place to enact colonialist ideals of "progress." In fact, these European settlers belonged to cultures that had already razed the last old-growth forests at home to build the ships that launched colonial expansionism and further empire-building. With the kind of ignorance that assumes superiority, they believed the First Peoples' notions of interconnection and obligation to land were backward. It would take hundreds of years for settler populations to begin to acknowledge that notions of sustainability and ecological interdependence were not cultural whims but facts—critical not only to planetary health but to human health as well. As the educational researcher Michael Marker notes, "Modernist social systems and knowledge taxonomies have too often followed a colonialist recipe for seeing the landscape as an inanimate surface for extracting, shaping, and constructing the artifacts of progress."[5]

Prioritizing individual and material prosperity, European settlers soon began logging for profit. Ancient old-growth forests were carved up. A clearcut is a destruction that ignores human responsibilities to an interdependent relationship. The few surviving trees struggle to overcome such a leveling, as some modern foresters have come at last to acknowledge.[6] Eventually, old-growth forests in North America were reduced to only 7 percent of their former size, and 80 percent of those meager remains are currently scheduled for logging.[7]

Nowadays, a gray gravel logging road cuts through the forest. On one side is a young, planted forest of Douglas Fir and Red Cedar; on the other, an infant Hemlock forest of four-foot trees. This is now the location of the University of British Columbia's Malcom Knapp Research Forest, an area of more than 5,000 hectares devoted to multidisciplinary research. Over the last fifteen years, Malcom Knapp projects have begun to shift focus from growth, harvests, and yields to the ecological health of forests. This new trend in the field of forestry examines the complex interdependencies and exchanges that occur within forests, both new and old.

Old-Growthing the Mind

Here, on this site of colonialization of Indigenous culture and land, this place of changing forestry practice, the children of the Maple Ridge Environmental School are partaking in a way of learning that is at once old and new. Lorna Williams recalls that in the nearby Lil'wat First Nation community, education has always involved storytelling, community, responsibility, free play, and a deepening relationship with "mother earth."[8] Lil'wat people, Williams explains, "believe that each child comes into the world with gifts to share."[9] The Maple Ridge school seeks to weave into these traditions while still attending to federal and provincial curriculum guidelines. It also embraces cultural diversity and technological tools, such as iPads. In essence, this style of schooling is a way of remembering forward. As Joe Sheridan and Roronhiakewen Dan Longboat suggest, "The status of being and belonging that is reconciled on Turtle Island is not to be someone *new* but to remain someone ancient and to learn the lesson of being from time immemorial—that one cannot be beyond one's Indigenous self without devastating effect."[10]

Sheridan and Longboat also suggest that, from a Haudenosaunee (The Six Nations) perspective, human imagination is "understood to be animal and spiritual helpers manifesting their presence in one's life."[11] In other words, what we tend to think of as our own ideas, our own creativities, our own discoveries of what is possible, are, in fact, gifts from ancient others and our natural kin. Human immersed in the more-than-human. The relationships required for this gifting do not emerge quickly, as Sheridan and Longboat explain: "Old-growth minds and cultures mature, emerge, and encompass the old growth of their traditional territory."[12] Further, they consider that settler cultures have not yet had time to develop these old-growth relationships and that settlers are still "learning to think as the continent thinks."[13]

We raise this point to suggest that perhaps part of the ecologizing education project is to allow for gifts to be offered and received. That means giving space for learners, teachers, and community members to build the right relations so that a "gift economy"[14] culture grows and we can properly receive the rich range of gifts being imparted by the land itself. It means acknowledging these important sources of knowledge and moving away from epistemological egoism that situates all knowing, imagining, and thinking in the mind of a singular individual.

In fact, one way to view ecologizing education is to see it as an ongoing effort in maturing our relationships to the natural world. Ecologizing schools is a way of engaging in the *old-growthing* of the human mind. This effort seeks to reach out to learners, families, and communities within the immediate generation but with an eye toward former and future generations as well. The cultural change project of ecologizing education is a multigenerational vision toward old-growthing. Decisions about the development, style, and daily activities of these schools are taken with greater responsibility when seen with this value perspective.

Responding to Injustices

All the humans who initiated the development of the Maple Ridge Environmental School have deep and personal relationships with land. Clayton Maitland, the school's first principal, used to take student groups down to the creek site once a week at his former school. These were often the "problem students," nonconformists, and rebellious young people who couldn't get on board with traditional school.

But the definition of "problem student" is more rigid in standard schools. There, the definition may include the unmotivated, intellectually gifted student who rarely completes homework and "spaces out" during tests. Or the exceptionally creative student whose penchant for completing tasks in alternative ways has earned them the descriptor "rebellious and uncooperative." Or the Black student who was sent to anger management counseling after years of subtle and not-so-subtle racism from their teachers led to outbursts of anger at systemic injustice. Or the student whose deeply kinesthetic learning orientation makes them reject the stacks of paperwork required in standard classrooms. Or the student who refuses to attend school because they sense that standard school appears to be more about control of children, maintenance of hierarchies, and lack of actual choice. Some seemingly "troubled" students are, in fact, engaged in active political resistance. Schools often use deficit model thinking in response to students who don't fit the efficiency model: Sit, be quiet, do what you're told. Educators who are in a position to choose how students should behave and what they should be capable of inevitably fit into particular sociocultural positions. Unwittingly or not, they use the deficit model in reference to people not fitting *their* expectations—essentially, that is, not being like them.

Clayton could relate. By the time he graduated from high school, he felt like an idiot. His particular kind of intelligence, in addition to his talents and emotional nature, had been deeply undervalued. Now, as the adult in charge of "delinquents," he was given specific instructions: "Do whatever you need to do to get them to love learning." In fact, the creekside park offered all kinds of engrossing learning opportunities. Clayton's students welcomed the weekly outings, gained more confidence, and began to express natural curiosity. This teaching experience allowed Clayton's own relationship to the water, forest, insects, animals, and weather in this location to unfold over several years.

He had become a school vice principal by the time he met Jodi MacQuarrie, a teacher librarian. Jodi's childhood was typical of Canadian settler children a few decades ago. She spent enormous amounts of time outdoors, playing in the woods, riding bicycles down the trails, collecting tadpoles and garter snakes, tobogganing in winter, and generally roaming free until the "whistle" for dinner sounded in the distance. As a young adult, she developed a passion for social justice issues. Her parents were South African immigrants to Canada, and she hated the racism she saw there. She was drawn to support kids who struggled in school, and this led her to working with gifted and ESL students. After a year teaching in scenic Norway, she returned to British Columbia to pursue further studies at Simon Fraser University. At that time, she had the sense that everything in her childhood home was disappearing—the creeks, the hillsides, the forests. She knew the smells of the trees and creeks, the turns and bumps in the trails, but they were being disappeared to make space for human needs. The land was being turned into sprawling subdivisions and expansive strip malls. It was being covered up, polluted, and destroyed.

Jodi became involved in advocacy projects for social justice on campus. There she met Sean Blenkinsop, a professor at Simon Fraser (and coauthor of this book), and that's when "everything coalesced," as Jodi says. Sean had adopted the term "eco social justice" for their advocacy work, and this frame gave Jodi a way to reflect on and talk about these entangled issues.

How Far Are You Willing to Go?

Deeply unhappy with the state of education and deeply concerned about the local environment, Jodi and Clayton started to daydream. What were their wildest dreams about education? How could education be an answer to a vanishing landscape, a dysfunctional educational system, and a world in need of social justice? Jodi invited Clayton to Simon Fraser University to meet with her professor, Sean, his colleague Mark Fettes, a professor of imaginative education, and several other interested graduate students. There, they began earnest and illuminating conversations about what might be *possible*.

Sitting under Cherry Tree on campus, Sean asked, "How far are you willing to go?" He wanted to know how serious they were. Change can be difficult, painful, and challenging, and people need to have the energy and the willingness to suffer through the process. Sean was already thinking along the lines of a new model for public education. By the time he sat on Grass with Jodi and Clayton, he had already been an outdoor, environmental, and justice-oriented educator for nearly thirty years. During this time, he had watched rivers he used to paddle and drink from become polluted and die. He had been feeling the pain of disappearing ecosystems, discussing potential changes with colleagues, and devoting all his free time to being with and learning from the myriad denizens that make up the natural world. He had also witnessed the educational power of the natural world for the hundreds of students he had shared time with on the trail. And he had watched many attempts, within both the formal and informal education systems, to tackle growing environmental problems; in so many cases, these attempts resulted in insignificant, insufficient gains. It was clear that environmental education was losing ground to environmental destruction, and he knew "this tinkering shit isn't going to work anymore."

In fact, a number of other environmental educational models had already sprung up and were leading struggling existences or, in some cases, had already failed. Despite enormous efforts and commendable intentions, many of these educational programs, some schools even, had not attended to the need for deep-level cultural change. They tended to approach environmental education from a behavioral perspective, focusing on things like not harming nature, building relationships, and learning more information about local flora and fauna— none of which was in any way wrong per se. However, if the goal is to actually change the deep-seated problems that are part and parcel of the culture, those steps alone were apparently insufficient.

It takes an enormous amount of time, creativity, willingness to risk, and experience in nature to imagine and then pedagogically and curricularly implement new ways of relating to the natural world. One by one, idealistic programs either close down or spend all their time trying to find the money to survive. Innovative schools teeter toward obscurity or are forced to change by the very systems they are critiquing. Eco-imaginative teachers burn out and leave the field, and garden boxes fill with more weeds than possibilities.

Creating School Differently

Clayton, Jodi, Sean, and Mark knew that if they were truly going to create change through education, their model had to be different from the very beginning. Even the development, even the planning, even the coordination would have to recognize the leading role to be played by the natural world and the need for wide collaboration at all levels. From the first day, they made a choice to only have meetings in the presence of actual nature. The team spent enormous amounts of time outdoors in Maple Ridge. In winter, when meetings had to be held at night and coastal British Columbia was being drenched in cold rain, the team found parks with covered shelters, and their discussions were serenaded by falling waters. Even when meetings had to be moved indoors, they placed Willow or Spider Plant on a seat where the meeting took place so nature could not be so easily backgrounded. In addition, they each took time to be alone outside prior to these meetings in order to open themselves up and attune themselves to a growing sense of relationality.

Relationships with humans needed to be built differently too. The original quartet quickly bloomed into an ever-shifting group of graduate students, professors, and teachers. They knew that, from the perspective of the community, new schools tended to "appear" after a few years of closed meetings among administrators, trustees, and civic government. So, in contrast, the environmental school deliberately involved community members in many meetings, right from the start. The team understood that the school was not going to work unless they could help parents and caregivers not only understand their own ideas about what a school is but also imagine what else school could be. Over the course of several years, they built relationships with school board trustees and the superintendent by inviting them to events, having meetings, sharing information, updating them on developments, and gathering resources. They made community allies in the horse club, fish hatchery, city library, Seed Centre, and Alouette River Management Society.

Meanwhile, relationship-building needed to occur in a different way with the local Indigenous community too. Ecologizing education, such as at the Maple Ridge school, has a responsibility to partake in truth and reconciliation processes by acknowledging and honoring those communities and cultures who lived on this land first and who are inextricably woven with the land. Over millennia, they have ensured and continue to ensure the care and sustainable relationships with the land, even as settlers have usurped these ancient geographical homelands. Building relationships within the local Indigenous community means respecting important cultural differences. The Western propensity to silo relationships into either personal or business and the priority to get things done quickly can be understandably met with suspicion. Indigenous peoples have experienced a long history of European settlers grabbing what they want and making off with it, whether it be land, cultural artifacts, information, or easy solutions.

Thus, over the course of several years, Clayton and others built lasting friendships within the local Indigenous community. They brought gifts, such as tobacco, and went out fishing together. These are not business relationships established for the sake of the school but genuine and multidimensional friendships. A couple of the Elders are regular, paid visitors to the school—they tell stories, help children make drums, do Salmon ceremonies, or just sit and develop relationships with the children. The bonds go deep and have lasted beyond Clayton's retirement, both for

Clayton and for the new principals. Understanding that land and language are deeply interconnected, several school community members are currently studying *Hǝṅ̓q̓ǝminǝṁ* (*Halkomelem*), the local Indigenous language. When tragedy, such as a flood or the death of a community member, strikes the Indigenous community, everyone at the school bands together to send meals over. Jodi describes it as "a strong reciprocal relationship."

Physical and Cognitive Structures of Standard Education

For a while, the group toyed with having some sort of physical structure, a building of some kind, that could be used at least part-time. After all, coastal British Columbian winters are soggy, muddy, and cold. In the end, through extensive conversation and ongoing engagement with their more-than-human cocreators, they decided that any kind of structure would limit the imaginative possibilities. A physical school reinforces the imagined structures of what school is, making it harder to redefine what a school can be. It can be helpful to avoid having reminders of the previous notions, structures, and inherent metaphors contained within human-designed square structures that occupy previously wild spaces.

Indeed, the building itself carries ideas of how power works (tables and desks pointed toward the teacher) and imparts expectations of behavior (sitting, listening to authority, containment in rooms). The desks, chairs, large gyms, and ringing bells all channel teachers, learners, and caregivers into particular ways of being and confirm particular understandings of how education and schooling works. We know where we're supposed to sit, how we're supposed to behave, and when learning is supposed to start and end. We see the teacher as "expert" and knower, books as containing knowledge, and the vice principal as the enforcer of rules. Even a typical building's commitment to straight lines promotes linear movement, social order, and specific thinking processes.

When the group met with the superintendent, they asked for two things: First, no building. And second, a year to work with the school's teachers to give them new options and space for developing new eco-teaching habits so when the stress of working with students started—and it always does—they didn't fall back into the troublesome and anti-eco habits of previous practice. The superintendent was fine, with obvious reservations, about having no building. (Of course, one of the advantages to this is that costs are quite substantially reduced—no cleaning, no upkeep, no electricity and heating!) But the second request was tricky. How could the school board afford the expense of letting teachers do training for a whole year? Even more complicated were issues of seniority. In British Columbia, the most senior teachers have first pick of assignment. Logistically, that meant a few near-retirement teachers might choose to "ease out" their last year or two in what some might perceive as a relaxing, alternative setting.

In truth, though, ecologizing work is emotionally, cognitively, socially, and culturally challenging work. It involves introspection, humility, and uncomfortable processes of growth. It entails identifying the ways one has personally acted from a stance of human exceptionalism and then making an effort to dismantle that complex, ingrained machinery. It means having the humbleness to notice when a lesson is being offered by the more-than-human world and deliberately sidelining oneself to let it unfold. It means recognizing that a five-year-old child who has not yet been indoctrinated in Western-style education may viscerally relate more intimately with, as part of, the more-than-human. Learning is not about comfort, and fundamental changes cause pain. Hanging out by the creekside all day may seem like a relaxing venture, but not when part of the project is to radically alter the foundational beliefs that structure the dominant society.

Western engagement with the natural environment—indeed, any techno-industrial culture's engagement with the environment—amounts to systemic oppression of ecological systems and the diverse entities that exist therein. Since systemic oppressions operate at the level of implicit forces—structuring all cultural decisions while floating mostly just below the level of conscious thought—they are not easily overturned. We need time to learn new habits—and time for these new habits to become instinctual. When facing twenty-five children in a downpour, it is easy to revert to old patterns unless new habits have been thoroughly established. Furthermore, those with more power and privilege in these situations can be reluctant to change. Efforts to dismantle systemic racism and systemic sexism, for example, have been engaged in by multiple generations over hundreds of years, and they continue as painful ongoing processes. Instructors, researchers, parents/caregivers, and administrators undertaking an ecologiz-*ing* pathway in education must learn to view the process as an ongoing, complex, mistake-filled, and layered experience with no finish line. The gerund "ing" acts as a reminder of this.

For all these reasons, the team needed not only a full year to support potential teachers but also the ability to work outside the seniority system. (Our position was that even one year isn't really enough time.) Eventually, the superintendent and the union agreed to a certificate program, called "Place Conscious Ecological Practice" (PCEP). The PCEP was a requirement for teachers at the outdoor school, which, incidentally, circumvented hierarchical hiring. This free, one-year certificate training was open to anyone who wanted to take it. It allowed the team to see who was interested, who had the skills, and who might be a good fit. But now that people were starting to grasp the scope of the project, how many of them would really want to teach outside in the rain all year while participating in a massive shift of cultural values? In fact, quite a few.

Hungry for Change

The team was continually surprised by how many people were hungry for change—and how hungry those people were. Over and over, parents, administrators, union specialists, school board trustees, and teachers expressed their frustration with standard schooling. They knew the old system wasn't working. It was stuck in the inertia of preparing students for a world that no longer exists. It wasn't successful in reaching most kids and wasn't responding to the diversity of needs, challenges, cultures, and gifts that fill twenty-first-century classrooms. And it certainly wasn't answering the call toward a more just social and ecological world—a call heard through Black Lives Matter, Idle No More, the MeToo movement, and the environmental student strikes. Many parents, teachers, and administrators yearned for an alternative to standard education— even if it was to be a radical one. Some adults were still wounded from their own schooling traumas; some teachers were frustrated by their inability to change their own classrooms; some parents were watching their children lose motivation and grow despondent inside standard schooling.

Of course, not everyone understood the aims of this new alternative schooling. Thinking back to a couple of specific administrators, Clayton recalls, "They think we're playing in the dirt out there." But even those administrators got on board with the plan when they saw the great push—a tsunami, really—toward that type of education. There was even federal support, as Mark and Sean had just secured a government grant (from the Social Sciences and Humanities Research Council of Canada [SSHRC]) to facilitate the development of the school and subsequent research.

While the team had initially anticipated that just a few outdoor enthusiast teachers or parents would attend meetings in the small town of Maple Ridge, often twenty to twenty-five people showed up. The Place Conscious Ecological Practice program included a lot of time outside at different sites, participant-designed lesson plans, curricular evenings, and philosophic discussions on the deconstruction and reimagination of educational theory. It also included workshops on the experiential learning cycle, plant identification, and outdoor safety and risk management. These events gave adults the opportunity to experience for themselves what ecologizing education might look and feel like in action, which is important since people typically don't adopt pedagogical practices unless they have actually experienced them.

Much of this time, the work appeared to be at the limits of people's imaginations. People had difficulty visualizing this kind of education. They simply couldn't see it as possible. *No building? No bells? No hierarchy? Natural world as teacher? What?* This wasn't really a surprise. People need time to imagine, time to learn, time to experience different ways of being and teaching in the world, and, ultimately, time to transform. They need a community of support to help them through the process. Where some institutes have offered three-day workshop intensives, the team understood that people need months, if not years, to have deep-felt experiences with nature and with these new concepts. In fact, brief periods of training may end up being worse than nothing because they give people a false idea about their own preparedness. Superficial preparedness most often leads to failure. Furthermore, those whose goal is to secure profit and power through the trend of "greening" education can emerge from these short workshops with all the right language and none of the right intention.

Guiding Principles and Values

Influenced by various eco-philosophers, nature writers, critical eco-thinkers, eco-feminists, and Indigenous theorists,[15] the collective team slowly and carefully developed five values, or principles, for the Maple Ridge school that were guided by an ecological worldview and that shared a number of common characteristics. First, they were understood to be open-ended—not the final word or commandments or in any way the end of the discussion. Second, they were meant to serve as guidelines, much like a rope guides hikers through a dangerous mountain trek: the rope acts to support while also pointing us in a direction. (In this situation, likely many other tracks could be chosen for this climb.) Third, these values served as explanatory tools that could be offered to parents, caregivers, and educators to reflect on. Lastly, they were reminders of what this school community deemed important—which can be helpful because once immersed in the actual doing, especially if it is *doing differently*, it can often be difficult to remember. Thus, these principles can become a heuristic, something to walk with and push against, a kind of corrective, a reminder, and a commitment to change as well. They also may offer some direction, inspiration, or a push-off point for others in thinking through their own educational projects.

Maple Ridge Environmental School Principles and Values[16]

We seek to grow relationships and nurture practices of learning and teaching that embody the following principles and values:

1. Place and community. *We cultivate learning in, about, with, and from local places. This includes spending extensive time immersed in the outdoors, dialoguing with the diverse people connected to these places, and exploring the meaning of places in the context of the broader community associated with them, its past and future. Our hope is to nurture and develop an inclusive educational community deeply rooted in place.*

The pairing of place and community may seem redundant. However, one of our specific aims was to respond directly to what the eco-feminist and philosopher Val Plumwood has called the "backgrounding"[17] of the more-than-human world—the way nature and its many beings disappear from view and care as soon as humans gather. The goal of this principle was to find ways for the more-than-human world to be constantly present and playing an active role in the students' learning. If the natural world was to be one of the active co-teachers, then the aim was to create a place where learning could happen not only *in* and *about* place but also *from* place. The goal was to remind everyone at the school that nature has an active, cocreative role in the process of learning.

2. Nature, ecology, and sustainability. *We cultivate learning in natural settings, where we listen for what the more-than-human world has to teach us. Through the cycle of the seasons and the years, knowledge of ecosystems will be built gradually so that diversity, complexity, and sustainability become part of our understanding of the world. How to live sustainably in this place is an ongoing question in everything we do.*

Part of the goal here was to continually make the natural world a presence and a partner in the project. We chose the word "ecology" rather than the more recognizable word "environment" for several reasons, but primarily to sidestep some of the metaphorical baggage. "Environment" has tended to be understood as an entity set apart from humanity. Using the word "ecology" instead did two things. First, it positioned the teachers and learners within, as a part of, the ecosystem, and second, it sought to remind the community not only to look to ecosystems as examples of sustainable communities with much to teach but also to remember that the whole concept goes back to the Greek word "oikos" ("home"), which is the root of the word "ecology," the study of and care for home. For the school, "sustainability" was troublesome as a concept because it had been, in some ways, co-opted and overly generalized. Yet there was a sense at the time that it was a recognizable term in the general public and that those involved in the school could redefine, re-vivify, or reject it as made sense.

3. Inquiry and possibility. *We cultivate a spirit of inquiry involving everyone: The natural world, students, parents, community members, teachers and researchers alike. We are committed to exploring multiple pathways of learning and teaching that engage many different ways of knowing and forms of knowledge. Meaningful, authentic, locally-inspired individual, group, and community projects play an important part in this process.*

For the school, the spirit of inquiry was an important guideline, not only for the obvious reasons that appear previously but because inquiry is about exploration, openness, unfolding, growth, change, and possibility. Western education often seems to suggest that by looking in books, pulling out rulers, and theorizing, people can know the world. But ecologizing education acknowledges that nothing is ever *completely* known. Here, the point is that knowledge is not the sole purview of the human; rather, it is a shared endeavor among all beings and, as such, is necessarily incomplete. There are so many varied knowers that meaning and knowledge can always be added to and changed. In the inquiry model, a constant process of questioning emerges. And in the ecologizing model, this process decenters the human and isn't necessarily building toward a complete knowing. One is pushed to ask how Cedar understands Sun and to contemplate whether Salmon makes sense of Water in a different way from Human.

The choice of the word "possibility" was made because of its reference to existential philosophy. For the existentialists, the notion of possibility invokes the seemingly endless number of choices available to each of us, to our familial groupings, to our communities. Through the act of *choosing*, we are, in Sartre's words, both creating value and creating the kind of world we want to live in.[18] We need to allow each other and ourselves to make those choices, live with the possibilities and the accompanying responsibilities, and accept the challenge of change rather than passively adapting to an imperfect world. The big addition the school made to these existential ideas was to seek to include the more-than-human, not only as entities to be considered when humans are choosing and enacting possibilities but also as beings with the same rights to choose and become as well.

4. Interdependence and flourishing. *We cultivate an appreciation of people both as unique individuals and as members of nested families, communities, and places. We seek to understand the complex ways in which we can help each other flourish, and how to build relationships and systems that contribute to such flourishing. We aim to foster respect, care, and health in everything we do.*

Linking interdependence and flourishing at the school clarified that one of the pivotal roles and moral responsibilities of humans was to support the maximization of diversity, complexity, and flourishing for all, human and more-than-human alike. The purpose of this principle was to remind all of the danger of trying to sustain a way of living that is currently inequitable and destructive to many while also reminding the community to help one another reach their potential. This conjunction of interdependence and flourishing had interesting implications for the assessment of student learning. For if interdependence is a basic principle, how might something like contribution to the flourishing of others and the community be assessed? Or, maybe, how might assessment help learners move toward interdependence?

5. Imagination and integration. *We cultivate imagination in teaching and learning as a key to deeper understanding, creativity, and responsiveness to place and community. We look for ways to integrate learning across the curriculum, bridging language arts, sciences, histories, geographies, mathematics, and physical and social skills. We develop educational practices and materials that nurture a sense of wholeness in learning and teaching.*

The school was committed to a more integrated curriculum, in line with a more ecological orientation and a sense of knowledge as being shared throughout community. The imagination component was added with a particular focus upon the educational ideas of *imaginative education* (an educational theory developed by Kieran Egan[19]) and a sense that exploring possibility and deep change, at the level of the individual or the community, depends on the ability to employ the imagination. One must be able to imagine themselves *being* differently in the world, for example. Intriguingly, as the project progressed, it became clear that our human imaginations were limited.[20] Contrary to the popular belief that the imagination is completely unfettered, the school had myriad encounters where it became clear that the imaginations present were limited culturally, linguistically, and experientially. These limitations were often very difficult hurdles to overcome with regard to the challenge of cultural change.

The First Weeks of the Maple Ridge Environmental School

Finally, after three years of preparation and the involvement of Indigenous neighbors, administrators, parents, community members, and dozens of researchers, along with the Alouette River, Douglas Fir, Raven, and other beings, the Maple Ridge Environmental School officially opened. On the first day of school, eighty-eight students were cared for by four teachers, one resource teacher, three educational assistants, several researchers, and a temperate rainforest ecosystem. It might have been a momentous day, a grand achievement that evidenced years of hard work . . . but none of the original team remembers. That fact might be chalked up to busyness or to the plethora of memorable events that came later. More likely, it speaks to the values of the team. As Mark explains, "I've learned from working with Indigenous people that it's more important to have a good process than to have good goals."[21] The opening of the school wasn't as important as community-building and relationship development in the local more-than-human or the ongoing process of learning how to be a human differently in relation to the natural world.

Besides, the start of the school wasn't exactly smooth. While the children were joyful, one educational assistant quit after two weeks of being drenched by rain. The remaining teachers tried to figure out how to manage stacks of sopping wet notes before largely abandoning paper altogether. Also, learning didn't come entirely easily—at least not for the teachers, who struggled against their own preconceptions and ingrained experiences of what education looks like. Perhaps because they expected a radically different kind of pedagogy, they often didn't trust their teaching instincts. They figured they couldn't do what they had done in the past, but they also had no clear idea of how to move forward. They struggled with mixed messages when the school's principal told them to "forget every-thing they know" while researchers pointed to rich learning opportunities being offered by the local kin. Their love of the outdoors did not necessarily translate to a creative and attuned sense of how to learn with and from more-than-humans. Mark adds, "The teacher certificate training was an introductory set of lessons and fell far short of what is needed to change practice. It was a consciousness-raising program but fell short of what teacher training might look like." With eighty-eight kids to suddenly attend to, teachers fell into habits of hiking, playing games of chase, and building wooden structures in the ever-expanding student village.

In those early days, parents struggled to understand what their children were learning. Several parents told researchers their children claimed they were learn-ing nothing. In fact, many children who had already been in standard school-ing did not associate learning with "fun" and so didn't realize that measuring raindrops in vials, reciting limericks about weather, and hearing Indigenous his-tories *is* learning. Some nervous parents wanted documentation of their children's learning—familiar things like completed math handouts. For the most part, though, the children didn't do math practice on paper. They did it on wood while building an outhouse, or they recorded it with a stopwatch while racing twigs and leaves down River. These immersive, embodied learnings can be harder to evi-dence than practice on paper, particularly if your experience has come solely from one way of learning. Two families pulled their children out of the school after a few weeks out of concern that "real" learning—that is, measurable, pen-and-paper, abstracted learning—wasn't taking place. And in many ways they were correct. Teachers were still trying to get their feet under them, and this new kind of educa-tion wasn't readily recognizable *as* education.

Sharing Learning and Expanding the Teaching Pool

One interesting discovery for all involved was how easy it was to overlook the range of learnings that can happen—that *were* happening—and how hard it was to come up with good systems for recording, displaying, and even just convincing others (and ourselves) of these learnings. Early on, the teachers landed on two successful modes of communicating with parents and caregivers. First, teachers began reporting "learning stories" for the children. That is, teachers wrote down stories about each child that illustrated their learning and advancement. This break from traditional documentation proved to be more work for educators but was well received by parents. Secondly, educators began reporting on student progress using an online site for parents. Here, they uploaded photographs of children studying salamanders, measuring river currents, and discussing the history of place. They also uploaded photos of the many artifacts that evidenced learning (but were not the usual paper handouts), such as wooden structures lashed with sophisticated knots, ephemeral natural art projects made of ice and leaves, and temporary calculations drawn in the sand with sticks. As part of the school's commitment to break down "professional" barriers between teachers and families, parents and caregivers were also invited to add to these online spaces by documenting the kinds of learning children were doing at home, such as reading a novel, listening to Grandma's stories, and counting change at the grocery store.

A further, more expansive strategy developed by the school was to actively bring parents and caregivers into the teaching ranks. Being naturally porous, the walls of the school made this invitation more possible than in typical educational settings and allowed for a kind of pedagogical transparency: one could always see what was happening at any given moment in a child's "classroom." Also, given the more inclusive nature of the educational project (that is, adding nature as a co-teacher and decentering the human), it made sense to explode learning beyond where it is often positioned, inside a school.

This invitation to have parents/caregivers actively engaged in the educational process was extended for a series of reasons. First, it makes learning a more seamless and ongoing process. Second, it was a conscious step toward breaking down some of the hierarchies that currently exist in schools, where one group of adults is professionalized as educators/experts and another group remains separate from learning while doing drop-offs and making lunches. Third, it was a way to educate the community: it not only helped all involved to understand about this unusual form of education but also served to further the project of cultural change. If the aim is to change culture by working with children, it is helpful for parents and caregivers to recognize this and even further it outside the school. The fourth reason—admittedly less on the radar when the school opened—was to help parents and caregivers step into learning gaps that might be occurring for their children because of such a radical change.

Many caregivers could see and were heartened by the effects of this educational approach: the building of deep relationships with peers and community, rich knowledge of the place and the more-than-human, and sophisticated language and concepts with regard to their own positionality. They could also see that their children were more confident, happier, much more physically and politically engaged, and using fine motor skills exceptionally well. However, when measured against standard schooling, some educational experiences were missing. Rich, more wholistic, integrated, place-based, and experiential learnings take time, and as a result, choices have to be made about priorities. In this case, things such as ongoing focused scaffolding and even numeracy and literacy drills were getting shorter shrift than they would in a more standard classroom. So, even though an expansive culture of orality, diversity in the ways of reading the world, and practical immersion in numeracy existed, some children were not getting enough support at the school to bring particular skills together. They were having trouble becoming literate and numerate. Ultimately, most parents, caregivers, and even teachers have accepted that they will have to do things differently in order to best "cover" the standard curriculum because they also understand the rich benefits of this kind of education. In this way, the active invitation to be involved, the enacted openness of the school, the online platforms, and the many parent meetings allow the children's many teachers to come together to meet the fullest range of needs and possibilities.

One final note: the parents and caregivers were not, in general, an overly privileged group such that they had the time, fiscal ability, or education to provide these extras. Rather, they were seeking different opportunities for themselves and their children and making choices and sacrifices in support of that. Historically, while schools were responsible for doing literacy and numeracy, families were responsible, either explicitly or implicitly, for all the other stuff that might or might not be considered important. At Maple Ridge, some of those "other" things were prioritized to the level of school, which left families with different options for their own learning time. In some ways, ecologizing education asks those involved to engage in a cost-benefit analysis when it comes to learning and to consider whether to include learning possibilities that are not currently part of most schooling. For many families and children at Maple Ridge, the social, emotional, and ecological benefits of the environmental education far outweighed the disadvantages. The choice was easy.

Reading in the Rain

Nonetheless, the Maple Ridge Environmental School has struggled, still struggles, and will continue to struggle to meet some of its curriculum expectations. How does one scaffold toward rich numeracy in a drizzling rainforest? How can children grow their literacy while also deepening relation to place? How does learning get organized and ordered so that older children are ready for the depths and complexities of literacy and subject matter study?

Of course, improvements occurred over time, as teachers better understood the places where school was happening, what could be done in the rain, and the many affordances that the natural world provides as the human teachers have become more ecologizing. The students do practice creative writing and scientific reporting in journals that work in the wet and the dry. During winter, they regularly visit the library and sit for reading hour. Additionally, as teachers have considered the trajectory of learning across the school—from kindergarten to grade 7—they have begun to recognize that engaging, meaningful, and kinesthetic lessons tracing river currents, reading tree rings, and tracking animals also, in time, build out skills of tracking letters of the alphabet within words and onward to a rich literacy that is more than just interpreting words on a page.

Children can also develop the deep foundations for print literacy that floats on a sea of talk (to paraphrase James Britton[22]) through reciting local or famous nature poetry, engaging in analytical discussion, telling stories, hearing stories from Elders, and recording oral stories on rain-protected iPads. Both younger and older students begin to understand literacy as being related not just to words on paper but as *semiotic,* a world filled with signs and symbols and their interpretations. In this situation, semiotics becomes *eco*-semiotics because it expands beyond just human signs and symbols. It includes sophisticated ways of reading the world through weather patterns, animal tracking, soil analysis, and the whys and wherefores of flora growth. As for numeracy, which has been a hard nut to crack in ecologizing ways, the challenge includes rethinking the street-level understanding of math that permeates public schooling in North America—a subject that always has a right answer, that can resolve any trouble, that is somehow perfect in its implementation, that straightens the lines of the world and abstracts the encounters of its beings. Oddly, the creative, entangled, poetic, and incomplete nature of math doesn't tend to appear until one reaches university, and by then, for many, the damage is done. Ecologizing education is still wrestling with how to "do" numeracy, but conversations in Waldorf and in posthumanism offer some intriguing avenues as we start to consider what a posthuman-entangled relational math might look like in practice. Some of these ideas have yet to become steady features of the Maple Ridge school, and parents and caregivers have, at times, stepped up to play important teaching roles as partners, particularly in the literacy and numeracy projects. Most of those engaged with the school, including some of the original founders, are still critical of how these are understood and experienced and are working on developing better strategies.

Success and Enacting the Vision

Two students are standing near River. It is fall, water levels are rising, and the whole school has been waiting expectantly for the first Salmon to appear in this ancient home and rich spawning bed. But they are late, and the word from scientists is that the entire migration this year is in trouble. Overfishing, rising water temperatures, and summer droughts are all part of the problem. And these students know it, feel it, and understand this crisis at a very deep level. For if Salmon fails to return, then, as one student points out, "Orca can't be Orca." To which the other responds, "and Kwantlen [the local First Nation] can't be Kwantlen."

Ten years after its opening, the Maple Ridge Environmental School is still evolving. On the bright side, the students are thriving. They love the immersive, imaginative learning style that centers less on teachers and more on plants, place, animals, elements, and the children themselves. Parents/caregivers, still hungry for alternatives to outdated standard education practices, have flocked to the school as well. The current waitlist is three times the size of the current student population, and they have already added two more classes. When British Columbia eased its COVID-19 restrictions in May 2020, children at all BC schools had the option of returning to school for the remaining month of the school year. According to Jodi, 80 percent of the environmental school children returned to school, compared to only 20 percent in the rest of the school district.

More important than the numbers, these children have a deep ecological understanding of where they live. They comprehend and have respect for local water cycles, salmon life cycles, seasonal changes to flora, and the impact of weather patterns in visceral ways that most college students couldn't fully grasp. They understand that the Land beneath their feet is the ancient and current home of the Katzie and Kwantlen First Nations and that there is a bond between people and place that is ontological. (Remember: "Kwantlen can't be Kwantlen" without Salmon.) Students have been regularly gifted with some of the stories and traditions that have bound humans to these waterways, this forest, and this landscape since time immemorial. By listening to and learning from local Indigenous Elders, they have become active in the slow reconciliation processes so necessary—and so overdue—in this country. One day, when an Indigenous Elder, a regular contributor to the children's education, was drumming for the children, Jodi recalls that she looked at Clayton and smiled. So far, this was the closest enactment of the school they had envisioned together.

And yet the school still grapples with significant challenges. Changing the larger culture is another nut that has yet to be cracked, even though changes at the level of individuals have been in some cases quite dramatic. And although the school has succeeded in the undoing of some of the troublesome tropes of a system that tends to be anti-environmental in its orientation, many other habits have yet to be located and undone. At times, the radical positionality as an "out there" school can foster complacency and a self-congratulatory feeling that is both good (for respite and honoring all the hard work) and worrisome. Yet maybe the real successes of Maple Ridge can be seen in its ability, at the national and global level, to inspire others into ecologizing education in their own places, not as replicas thereof but by inspiring whatever form of ecologizing makes sense in a particular place.

Struggles and Successes for Graduates, Parents, Educators

Ecologizing education is not easy or quick to implement and is not a panacea to everything that ails us. Challenges exist within the process; these include, for example, finding ways to do literacy in more ecological ways, changing teacher practice such that it honors the natural world as a co-teacher, and recognizing and responding to the limits of our own imaginations when it comes to changing culture. Challenges exist as well between the ecologizing program and the larger culture—where trees still don't have rights, where all voices are not honored and listened to, where humans, some humans more than others, are still the absolute center of everything. We envision a culture where the more-than-human world is a partner not just in ongoing learning and teaching but also in what the world is to become going forward.

Some graduates of the school have struggled upon leaving. Their educational experiences at the environmental school may have completely transformed them, but education at standard schools has not transformed in their absence, nor has society at large. Transitioning back into high school has been a confusing, disorienting, and sometimes unbearable step for which some were underprepared. Two students dropped out of schooling altogether. Another took up the superficial values on offer at her new school and eventually became hooked on drugs.

In contrast, some graduates are having great success while still critiquing the standard education system itself. One student became a nursing major at university but continues to express concern to her teachers that the program requires an unhealthy amount of sitting. Another student, dismayed at the lack of experiential learning and creativity, dropped out of standard schooling in grade 9. Later, he returned and completed grades 10, 11, and 12 in a single year so he could fulfill his goal of becoming an environmental scientist. Clearly, graduating students need increased preparation and ongoing support for whatever they transition into.

Part of this preparation might also include skills useful to the entire ecologizing education community. At Maple Ridge, the changes in language, in ideas around schooling, and in relationships and responsibilities toward the natural world are not immediately recognizable by or acceptable to the larger culture. This suggests that ecologizing education community members will need thoughtful training and support in order to translate these experiences and ideas for the larger culture to understand, to maintain those changes in the face of potential pushback, and to become politically able to advocate for change. Some of these skills might include finding allies, building community, thinking critically, developing a sophisticated understanding of rights, and more. These skills, then, become "tools in the toolbox" of critical change agents, helping them both advocate for their vision of a changing world and protect themselves from the challenges they will confront. After all, the broader culture might not understand what is being suggested and is, at the very least, not totally amenable to the changes being advocated.

Of course, children aren't the only ones learning at the environmental school. Because of their children's coaxing, many families now spend more time outdoors and have become more actively concerned about environmental protections. One parent of three boys at the school has also become a teacher there. For many parents, the school hasn't been just about building relationships with the environment—it is also a part of their own healing process. More than one parent at the school has reported that their childhood school experiences left them feeling painfully unvalued, deficient, and even traumatized. However, at the environmental school, several have reported feeling valued as knowledge holders and seen as individuals, and they experience a meaningful sense of belonging with the school community.

Even researchers have been transformed. The researcher Yi Chien Jade Ho reports that her personal sense of identity and belonging have shifted. Having spent her childhood and young adulthood living in numerous countries, she says she has often felt that she doesn't belong anywhere. After three years at the environmental school, however, she is experiencing a "heightened place sensibility." She explains, "I am the embodiment of all the places I've lived, not just physical place and land, but the cultural and social encounters that I've had, and my own connection with the natural world."[23]

Expanding the Possibilities

This book is not really about a single school. In fact, schools all over North America are experimenting with pedagogy, spending more time outside, and working to prepare children for the world to come. The COVID-19 pandemic has many recognizing the value of the natural world and realizing that being inside is not as safe as previously assumed. Nonetheless, the Maple Ridge Environmental School is a pretty sweeping example to consider, and since ecologizing education is seeking to radically change the culture, it seems a good place to start. Every school engaging in this ecologizing work will have its own unique set of ecological, social, cultural, and political circumstances to negotiate; not every ecologizing school starts, or needs to start, in this more seismic way of Maple Ridge. A group seeking change doesn't necessarily have to start a brand-new school, conduct 100 percent of their education outdoors, forgo buildings completely, or have a research team present all the time. As such, we offer here a brief introduction to three other schools, each with its own unique origin story, with the intention of expanding our imaginative range as we continue to explore ecologizing education.

NEST: Risk Management and the Half-Indoor School

A little more than 100 kilometers away from the Maple Ridge school, the Nature Education for Sustainable Todays and Tomorrows (NEST) program is operating as a school within a school. Composed of four classrooms, ninety students, four teachers, and several educational assistants, NEST operates side by side with a more traditional stream of four classrooms; together, they make up Davis Bay Elementary.[24] Since its commencement in 2012, NEST children have spent 50 percent of the week outdoors at the beach, estuary, and forest and 50 percent indoors reading, writing, and pursuing other activities often better suited to dry, indoor settings. The NEST program has two portables for kindergarten through grade 3 classes and a separate annex outbuilding for grades 4 through 7. The school is located in a fantastic spot with regard to access to natural sites. The ocean front, a strip of deep Rainforest, and a salmon-bearing Creek are all within a fifteen-minute walk—even for very short legs. Also, early on, the school community supported the building of a greenhouse that, under the guidance of two gifted gardeners and committed community members, has become an additional important space of instruction at all levels.

The school was, for the most part, the result of the savvy visioning and long-term planning of Davis Bay's principal at the time. Having learned how to navigate the politics of the school board and facing a potential school closure due to declining enrolment, she found the right conditions for launching an idea she had been preparing for years: an eco-school. She worked hard to engage two groups of local community members: those who were concerned about losing their school and those who were interested in more environmentally focused programming. She sought input from Sean and the researcher Laura Piersol, who both live near Davis Bay. She focused on finding the right teachers, negotiated with senior leadership, and provided space for all the involved groups to come together and create a vision for NEST. Importantly, the creation of NEST was quite different from the process employed by Maple Ridge. Although the teachers took the ideas of nature as a co-teacher seriously, they also, in contrast to Maple Ridge, very quickly adopted a sense of being activists and agents for change (an idea we will return to in greater detail later).

Response to the idea of an eco-school was tremendous. Soon parents, caregivers, and community members were holding regular meetings, a little bit of money was located to support planning time for the incoming teachers, and work commenced on developing a comprehensive risk management plan. Perhaps because one of the teachers at Davis Bay already had an extensive background in outdoor education, the safety and risk component was much more highlighted at NEST than at the Maple Ridge school. The NEST team approached the local government and successfully compelled them to install a crosswalk with flashing lights at the bottleneck where students crossed to Ocean and Estuary. Classes at NEST often pair up when heading outside: this allows for shared planning, wider learning opportunities, and the abidance of safety rules with regard to the number of adults present. Neighbors are accustomed to seeing gaggles of small humans carrying their safety packs (including rain gear, sweater, hat, lunch/snack, water bottle, and school supplies) and heading down the trail and across the road to their outdoor classrooms.

Gabriola: Truth, Reconciliation, and Gardening

Across the Salish Sea from Davis Bay, nestled against the shores of Vancouver Island, sits Gabriola Island, a small community of 4,000 humans that has long been a landing place for artisans, small-scale back-to-the-land farmers, and those seeking slower, more community-focused lifestyles. As such, the elementary school on the island has long played a central role in the community. Here, a thirty-year teaching career means working with multiple generations of a family. It was into this situation that Mark and Sean were invited in 2016 by Kate, one of the school's most experienced teachers.

With a background in Waldorf education and a commitment to the natural world, Kate was a well-respected educator known all across the island for her schoolyard garden, her connections throughout the community, and her habit of taking students outside no matter the weather. Thus, different again from Maple Ridge and NEST, here was an established school that, under the auspices of a particular teacher, began moving in an ecologizing direction. Many pieces were already in place. Kate was known for getting her classes into the community and for her work in the garden. She had built a sizable and energetic group of local parents and caregivers. Most crucially, the faculty actively sought advice and change in this direction. Importantly and understandably, the vision began to flex and change as more people became involved.

Initially, at Kate's invitation and as part of a larger plan to become a more community- and place-based school, she and the then principal cooked up a partnership with Simon Fraser University's eco-research team. The first year involved several professional development days, including back-and-forth between and among the faculties at Gabriola and NEST, and initial grant applications to get some seed money with a focus on building out the community alliances and connections while also supporting the desires and skill sets of the teachers. With a change in administration, there was a bit of a lull in energy, but the process took off again when three things happened. First, Kate retired from teaching, which meant she could spend more time focused on the work of building community relationships, expanding the pedagogical and curricular capacities of the faculty, and educating parents and caregivers rather than being subsumed by the ongoing process of teaching full-time. Second, the community, the faculty, and, in fact, the province and nation became much more engaged with questions of Indigeneity, traditional lands and educations, local stories and languages, and the questions, challenges, and possibilities of truth and reconciliation. The third happening was that the research team had further grant-writing success and received a larger, longer-term grant. This allowed the project to pay a community coordinator (Kate), several graduate students (focused on teacher training and curriculum development), and local Elders whose knowledge and expertise have become invaluable. Gabriola continues to work to make its curriculum more place-/land-based and to better integrate the stories, language, and ways of being and educating of the local Indigenous community on whose traditional land the school exists.

As a community school, Gabriola is a wonderful place to work from. Access to the forest is directly behind the school, and across the road is a large community garden and kitchen area alongside an eldercare home and a lowland Pond. Also, the school can actively draw upon a rich and diverse human community. This includes many small-scale and market gardeners who have been active in helping develop a gardening plan for the school. The completion thereof has been lying fallow for the last few years as the plans grind their way, at a glacial pace, through the machinations of the larger school district, but the go-ahead looks close at hand.

Yueming Elementary: Citizen Science and a Local Ocean Curriculum

Ecological schooling, of course, is not just taking place in British Columbia, Canada. A little farther afield—10,000 kilometers, in fact—Yueming Elementary School in Northeastern Taiwan emerged as a result of principal Huang Jian-Rong's savvy business sense and deep ecological attunement.[25] Huang spent his childhood strolling through rice paddies, catching crabs and elvers, playing in the riverbank mud, and swimming—experiences that led to a decades-long career teaching in an "ecologically oriented elementary school program." When he heard about the closure of a standard school in a small rural village in Yilan county, he looked at the "concrete jungle" of that campus and immediately saw an opportunity to transform it into "a large sustainable classroom" that might attract new families. He removed concrete and changed the wastewater system and then added an "ecological pond," a recycled rainwater system, and plants that attract bees and butterflies. He also worked to create more harmony and integration between indoor and outdoor spaces by setting up outdoor hallways, finishing walls with natural colors, and planting climbing vines around the concrete building.

The school sits right next to the ocean, and children trek through one of the largest bird sanctuaries in the nation to reach the beach. Huang recognized the unique educational resource this environment offered. Yi Chien Jade Ho, who spent several weeks at the school as a visiting researcher, describes the "nature orchestra" of bird calls and crashing waves as truly awesome. She reports, "They deconstructed the national curriculum to integrate the local history into the school."[26] Indeed, at Yueming Elementary, they have developed an entire curriculum around oceans, and they emphasize hands-on, experiential learning with a particular focus on sailing for "personal growth and development." Parents who were initially concerned about the safety risks of sailing were put at ease when they were invited not only to witness children's sailing trials but also to try out the experience themselves.

Principal Huang's efforts have been enormously successful. The school has won multiple awards for environmental education and has attracted award-winning science teachers. The children are highly enthusiastic about their education and articulate about its purpose and design. They are used to trekking past flocks of tropical birds to suit up in life jackets and spend the day practicing sailing, snorkeling, bodyboarding, and other ocean arts. Other learning opportunities emphasize food and agriculture, wetlands exploration, life skills, and the outdoors in general. The school has attracted so many families that one of the primary ongoing concerns is gentrification of the village.

But many readers may be wondering—*what about children's safety? This outdoor learning sounds fun, but isn't it just too dangerous? Maybe this kind of thing may be possible in a "rules-flexible" world on the west coast of Canada, but how realistic is it elsewhere?* Too many wild animals, too many dangerous people, too little nature, and way too much paperwork in an overly litigious backdrop—all of these are comments, critiques, and "yeah buts" we have heard over the years. To be fair, we still hear them and also feel them ourselves at times. In the following section, we respond to the safety issue, but in our experience, sometimes the "yeah buts" appear to be quick ways to excuse ourselves from even trying. Starting the Maple Ridge Environmental School and the NEST program wasn't easy. Getting a class outside, even for half a day, is going to take some work and planning. Parents/caregivers, colleagues, and administrators may sometimes question and look askance, but ecologizing education calls for stepping into uncertainty and, perhaps, reassessing risk, danger, and unseen rewards.

Risks: Cougars, Needles, and Strangers

Inaudibly, Cougar pads onto the road a short distance from the children at the Maple Ridge Environmental School. He weighs as much as a full-grown human, is twice as long as the giant Alaskan malamute, and can sprint at 70 kilometers an hour. Undoubtedly, Cougar represents the worst fears of many parents. Indeed, parents who pulled their children from the Maple Ridge school cited the lack of physical boundaries, such as fencing, as one of their key complaints.

But the environmental school has carefully prepared for such moments. Although cougars are very rarely seen in the area, teachers, parents, students, and researchers know to keep an eye out for them and are trained to recognize their tracks and respond appropriately. When he was principal, Clayton would arrive early every morning to do a small gratitude ceremony, monitor for bear and cougar tracks, and check for damaged tree branches that could fall. And at NEST, students are actively brought into these assessment and decision-making processes, which helps them develop the comfort and awareness needed to be outdoors. As a result, for example, children know to stay within certain boundaries despite the absence of fencing, and they know why.

On this particular morning, Cougar traveled down the road and thus left no tracks for adults to observe. Initially, he wouldn't leave the road. Clayton reports, "Nobody panicked. Everyone knew what to do, even the kids, because we had rehearsed that scenario many times over."[27] After one of the parents spotted Cougar, the forestry service was called, the children were corralled into a tighter space, and several adults went up and banged pots very loudly to scare him off. Then they tracked him into the woods to make sure he wasn't lingering nearby. They moved school to a different location for the following week. Meanwhile, the forestry service located and removed a deer kill nearby, motivating Cougar to clear out of the area.

The dangers of outdoor schooling are real and need to be carefully assessed and prepared for. However, the story of Cougar speaks to successful preparation and an ultimately peaceful negotiation of space between humans and indigenous more-than-humans. Cougar was not harmed, merely deterred from the area. Presumably, he returned to the nearby forest and mountains. The children were safe—and felt safe. Established protocols were followed and proved successful.

Not every school or family has access to forests and mountains containing cougars, and there are risks and challenges to being outdoors in urban centers, where most schools are, as well. Many ecologizing teachers confront issues such as traffic, trash, needles, meddlesome humans, and a lack of "wild" space. Yet, if this work is going to be successful in its mission to radically change education, it must be where most learners are. Wild Wednesdays or Freedom Fridays or Nature at Noons have become an accepted part of many elementary classrooms across Vancouver and Southern British Columbia, and teachers have become adept at finding tiny pockets of green in parks, ravines, empty lots, and hedgerows, where encounters with nature might happen for their incredibly diverse charges.

Risk management work has evolved too. Advance completion of paperwork allows teachers to more spontaneously decide when to head outside, and information sessions prepare parents and caregivers for these occasions. Many schools have collected appropriate clothing from donations and the lost and found to properly outfit all students. Because of the ongoing nature of some of this work, teachers have also built relationships with the local human community. For example, locals come in to help with the gardening or to be on the lookout for exciting encounters with nature that they can share or to assist teachers in cleaning the areas in a well-used park where trash and drug paraphernalia are quite common. The work and risks may be different than those inside the classroom, but learning how to build community and developing the ability to assess local risks are important not only for the ecologizing educator but for the students as well.

The Unseen Risks of Indoor Schooling

Upon hearing that Cougar came near the Maple Ridge school or that urban educators are having to remove hypodermic needles before every visit to a park, some parents may dismiss outdoor schooling as too risky. But, in an odd way, outdoor schooling may in fact be *less* risky, since the risks are better known and, as such, can be better prepared for.

In *Slow Death by Rubber Ducky: How the Toxic Chemistry of Everyday Life Affects Our Health*, Rick Smith and Bruce Lourie point out that seemingly ordinary objects in our indoor worlds pollute the human body and that exceedingly little research has investigated the consequences.[28] In their 2014 study, Philippe

Grandjean and Philip Landrigan note that a few common industrial chemicals often found in paint and fluorescent lights and used as wood preservers cause "neurodevelopmental disabilities, including autism, attention-deficit hyperactivity disorder, dyslexia, and other cognitive impairments, affect[ing] millions of children worldwide."[29]

All of these authors lament the lack of research into thousands of everyday chemicals that may be putting children at risk. What chemicals have been sprayed on the school lawns? What chemical varnishes have been used on the school desks? What is the impact of years of exposure to off-gassing linoleum floors? These are some of the more urgent questions, but one might also wonder about the impact of light and noise pollution or the long-term health implications of reduced physical activity in indoor settings. Humans and their ancestors have lived alongside cougars for hundreds of thousands of years. But humans have only ramped up the intensity of indoor spaces replete with artificial chemicals and other hazards in the last century or so.

The risks of indoor schooling may be poorly understood and analyzed, and this lack of knowledge and awareness may induce a false sense of security. An interesting activity that we have developed for graduate students in our ecologizing programs is to have them do full risk assessments for their indoor classrooms like the kind demanded of them for any outdoor time. The results are illuminating.

In fact, the general public's whole notion of safety may be ill-informed. In the past decade, only two people have died from cougar attacks in all of North America. Meanwhile, toy balloons are considered the number one cause of choking deaths in young children.[30] There are noticeably greater dangers—from falling down a flight of stairs, from school shootings, from being crushed by a piano,[31] and from getting into a collision while being driven to school—than the danger from wild cougars and supervised visits to the local park, even in places where children regularly play in cougar habitat.

Additionally, as the educational researcher Chris Beeman argues, outdoor ecological education may be safer than standard education when considering long-term benefits to mental, emotional, and physical health.[32] Beeman points out that the predictability of standard, indoor educational settings does little to prepare children for the unpredictability of life—a life that is clearly getting even more unpredictable as we venture into the Anthropocene. Wild spaces foster embodied learning and quicken reaction times. Children who live almost entirely indoors have significantly reduced opportunity to practice balance, coordination, problem-solving, responding to uncertainty, and strength-building, Beeman notes. In the indoor classroom, students sit at tables while the teacher explains how worms aerate the soil. For the moment, their bodies, whether squirming or still, are irrelevant objects. During this same lesson in the outdoor classroom, one student balances on a rock, several others squat, and a few others are learning that a fallen tree branch seat will support only two of them. As Beeman suggests, short-term "cuts and bruises" may usher in greater self-awareness, ability, and responsibility that prevent more serious injuries later in life.

Being cut off from the more-than-human world may also lead to lifelong difficulties for children because a "potentially healing relationship and a place of growth is also lost," Beeman argues. He recognizes that Indigenous students, in particular, may experience this loss as devastating. Furthermore, students in standard education may simply have fewer opportunities to *truly live*, to fully experience what it means to be alive and human. Who wouldn't want to enrich their life by listening to an Elder recount ancient raven stories as actual ravens chortle from the breeze-blown treetops overhead? Who wouldn't want to race leaves and twigs in a mathematics game down the rushing spring river while nibbling on nearby salmon berries?

Learning in wild spaces is an experience of being more immersed and involved while engaging all of one's senses and capacities. Beeman summarizes, "Despite the difficulty in doing so, care and concern for the welfare of students and teachers, and a minimization of *all* kinds of injury, especially those that may be more difficult to discern initially, may emerge later in life, or may persist throughout life, ought to be at the forefront of policy and practice." The critical question is: What are we risking if we don't act to change education as it currently stands? Maybe the answer is: Much more than we think.

Right Action and Overcoming Obstacles

Despite their careful management of known risks, the Maple Ridge team understands why some parents are reluctant to send their kids outdoors all day. Indeed, the fact that so very many parents over the previous decade have sent their kids is a testament, in part, to the degree of suffering that standard school has caused their children and themselves. While the schools mentioned here continue to address areas of concern—in literacy learning, in safety management, in reconciliation processes, in changing culture, in co-teaching with nature, in gentrified school districts—they all offer immersive, embodied, experiential, and ecologically responsible and attuned learning that is unmatched by standard schooling. The creation of these schools required careful attention to complex sociocultural, educational, and geographic conditions. The Haudenosaunee might say the Land itself is helping in this endeavor, by gifting humans with insights, goals, and creative solutions. The Maple Ridge school team repeatedly noted surprise at their ability to overcome so many seemingly insurmountable obstacles. Anishinaabe Elder Alex Mathias revealed to Beeman that when the hunter brings right manners, right respect, the animal will present itself.[33] Perhaps because the Maple Ridge school emerged out of thoughtful, respectful practices, the world presented what was needed to turn vision into reality.

RELATING

Overcoming Isolation and Alienation

In the temperate rainforest, Raven chortles high in the treetop. Glassy-gray River rolls over rocks, chattering in crests and pools of white bubbles. A slow breeze lifts Hemlock's branchlets. Tiny feet of Gall Midge touch down on the uneven terrain of Moss in tactile dialogue before it lifts off into the breeze. These multisensory forest conversations never cease.

The communications occur through sight and sound, like most human communication, but also through movement, touch, chemicals, pheromones, temperature, current, and many other means. A changing breeze alerts Mouse to the presence of Owl. Dew falls onto stone, and flora register the temperature change. American Dipper ferries into the eddy line and snatch insects from River. Fungi spores drift about, and Seed splits open beneath soil and heads for Sun. Shadows shift slowly over the forest floor, and Lily of the Valley reorients to maximize connection. River Microbe caresses sedimentary rock, pulling calcium and gathering larger predators. These dialogues—whether they be fleeting, cyclical, or unending—pattern the day, bringing flora, fauna, and the elements into constant communication, whether auditory, visual, haptic, chemical, or otherwise.

As architects, interior designers, and social geographers know, the physical environments we place ourselves in communicate as well. Spaces and landscapes can impact our actions, shape our interactions with others, modulate our sense of belonging, and affect the way we experience the world. They can even direct how we behave and who we are. Consider your response to seeing a set of desks in a classroom when you visit a school. What are they telling you about the expectations, limits, and opportunities of that space? The quality of light and sound, the visual stimuli, and the social ergonomics of place impact behavior and attitudes in subtle but important ways. The geographer Yi-fu Tuan explains that our experience of place is formed by multiple overlapping factors. Firstly, we are, he writes, influenced by the sights, sounds, smells, tastes, and haptic experiences of environments and the activities these environments invoke ("perception"). Secondly, those "perceptions" form cumulative memory and combine with our cultural outlook ("attitude"). Together, these "perceptions" and "attitudes" about place form our "worldview," the "attitude or belief system" that is "partly personal and largely social."[1] In other words, the experience of *place* and what it communicates has a tremendous impact on one's worldview, but the experience of place is also colored by the values and practices of human culture.

For example, often the first time a teacher decides to take their class outside, it is chaos. Children scatter, run screaming in multiple directions, and appear to have a hard time listening to instructions, being quiet, and even learning. This is because, for the children, the *place*—the outdoors—is understood, culturally and experientially, to be a site separate from learning (learning happens *inside*, in schools, in a particular fashion and order). Outside is the world of recess, of self-direction, of freedom even, and for this to change, the educator needs to undo these social assumptions. This includes not only changing their students' ideas about what learning is and where it happens but also creating new learning structures and scaffolds for being outdoors that do the work of those that are implicitly built into schools and classrooms. Additionally, it means watching for how children are replicating dominant, often problematic cultural practices and values in and toward natural spaces and beings.

In a temperate rainforest, the constant interspecies dialogue reveals a world of complex interdependencies, antagonisms, or symbioses—and, above all, connection. The world is always and already in relationship. Standing between Hemlock, River, and Gneiss, one begins to understand how the field of ecology emerged. Theodore Roszak explains: "Ecology does not systematize by mathematical generalization or materialist reductionism, but by the almost sensuous intuiting of natural harmonies on the largest scale. Its patterns are not those of numbers, but of unity in process; its psychology borrows from Gestalt and is an awakening awareness of wholes greater than the sum of their parts."[2] From an ecological perspective, wholism reigns. Life is connected to life, but with a paradox of individuals and interdependencies, separate and entwined at the same time. This ecological philosophy runs contrary to the West's ceaseless focus on individualism. The dominant North American culture generally regards dependency as weakness or as a tax on personal freedom that should be reduced to minimal and temporary levels.

However, ecologizing education recognizes that independence, at least in the ways it is promoted culturally, is largely an illusion and creates alienation, painful disconnections, and unecological habits. If Tuan is right that our worldview is created due to both place and the cultural values experienced in place, then ecologizing schools in North America run up against an immediate conflict: Is the world primarily a place of individuality or a place of relationality? The awareness of this conflict and the ecologizing educator's ability to address it can determine whether an outdoor school merely duplicates mainstream culture in an outdoor setting or it expands and changes experiences and possibilities, with the potential to radically and positively shift mainstream culture.

A History of Enforced Individualism

Research that informs Western education has often been oblivious to its own cultural biases and messaging about independence and disconnection. Research in the social sciences, for example, has tended to start with the premise that the independent, autonomous adult is the standard for healthy humanness. Thus, adults have been encouraged to prepare children for this goal. For example, the American psychologist Abraham Maslow greatly influenced the way generations of parents, educators, caregivers, and policymakers attended to children when he asserted in the 1950s that a child's most basic and fundamental need is for air, water, food, and shelter. In his famous hierarchy of five needs, "love and social needs" rank in the middle.[3] By placing love as a more distant priority than food and shelter and by ignoring the natural world altogether, Maslow prioritized the individual over the social, independence over interdependence, the human world over the relationship between humans and the natural world. By operating from an autonomy assumption, Maslow's ideas aligned with other North American experts of that era who argued and often continue to argue that children should be trained for independence, often the earlier, the better.

Beyond psychology, other Western authorities promoted individualism from other angles. The philosophers who underscored our education systems, such as Descartes and Rousseau, oriented from a fundamental belief in the isolation of the individual and a separation of mind and body. Meanwhile, in medicine, some doctors in the nineteenth and twentieth centuries believed that parents were the carriers of potential diseases and thus encouraged mothers and fathers to maintain distance from their children and avoid physical affection.[4] With good intentions, they warned that kissing an infant could lead to death because of the risk of passing along "tuberculosis, diphtheria, and many other grave diseases."[5] Sterility and a lack of physical contact in orphanages, children's hospitals, maternity wards, and family homes were lauded.

Aligned with this thinking, some psychologists also worried that too much motherly love might corrupt a child's character and health.[6] "When you are tempted to pet your child remember that mother love is a dangerous instrument," John B. Watson, the president of the American Psychology Association (APA), cautioned.[7] In Watson's 1928 book, he claims that too much physical affection in childhood leads to "aches and pains" as well as insomnia in adulthood, conditions that interfere with the all-important ability to be a useful worker.[8] He instructs mothers "not to talk in endearing and coddling terms" and to "[n]ever hug or kiss [children], never let them sit on your lap."[9]

Like many specialists of the time, Watson misinterpreted children's despondency and resignation for confidence and autonomy.[10] But these children weren't actually confident or autonomous at all—their attachment systems were utterly broken. Contemporary psychology suggests that they likely grew into adults who had learned early to compensate for lack of connection by seeking to rely only on themselves and finding reward in work and culturally sanctioned achievement rather than relationships.[11] Experiencing empathy and forming emotionally intimate relationships may have been difficult for them. In fact, this aloof parenting style trains the neurological and hormonal system of the child's body, creating a biological propensity to focus on the self. The ethical psychologist Darcia Narvaez writes, "Within a culture of detachment, adults view humans as selfish and competitive by nature. Because of this, little attention is given to humanity's and, especially, children's basic needs."[12] When the culture provides little support for caregivers, when caregivers in turn are unable to provide tender, loving, consistent, and relationally responsive support for infants, children can develop into adults who feel half-alive, numbed to the world and to others.[13]

At the same time as these shifts in infant and child-rearing were taking place, societal changes were creating ever more distance between children and the natural environments. Today, 82 percent of North Americans live in urban settings.[14] As the delights and temptations of electronics compel them, each generation of children is spending less and less time climbing trees, searching for tadpoles, and throwing snowballs—and more time indoors staring at screens.[15] Increasingly parceled off to after-school classes and no longer considered safe to walk to school on their own, children are now more likely to watch trees, birds, and dandelion puffs pass by automobile windows and glimpse them from classroom windows. Collectively, the electronic boom, urban densification, perceptions of safety, and educational advancement combine to plant young humans in increasingly anthropocentric environments, that is, environments designed by humans for humans and stocked with human-made objects.

How might our more-than-human relations contribute to the development of human biological attachment systems? It's a question in need of more answers. Narvaez helpfully suggests that we expand notions of attachment development to include "ecological attachment."[16] She points out that throughout our evolution, human babies were ensconced in natural environments, which they explored through crawling and toddling. In other words, they developed early relationships through experiential and multisensory modes of interaction. Noting that the more-than-human offered additional "partners" in child-rearing—entities that stimulate, support, comfort, and provide for children—Narvaez reminds us that many Indigenous cultures acknowledge these familial partners with kinship terms, such as identifying Juniper as grandfather or Piñon as grandmother.[17] While these relationships may be spiritual in nature, their impacts are also biological. Time spent in natural (as opposed to human-made) environments positively contributes to cognitive, emotional, physical, and social well-being through a host of biological, neurological, and psychological mechanisms.[18]

What happens when nations are run largely by the policymakers, CEOs, school principals, and educators who experienced emotionally isolating child-rearing and notable nature separation? The severing of relationality between caregivers and children in settler culture has resulted in generations of increasingly isolated adults. Perhaps it's a little less surprising then, albeit horrific, that these settlers separated generations of Indigenous North American children from their families, communities, and ecological homelands as they forcibly moved them to residential schools. The psychologist Sue Gerhardt argues that we "are living in an impoverished emotional culture, the end product of decades of individualism and consumerism, which have eroded our social bonds."[19] The erosion is not only reflected in our inability to bond with other humans. It is also evident in our diminished capacity to bond with the rest of the denizens of the more-than-human. Indeed, the very architecture of our attachment systems has been altered by—what is in evolutionary terms—drastic, sudden, and severe changes in lifestyle. Yet this ubiquitous sense of isolation has been taken as proof that autonomy is the paramount condition of existence. Scientifically, this is akin to starting fires and then pointing to those fires as proof that fires are pervasive. Emotionally isolated and ecologically detached adults are not evidence that the isolated individual is an inherent feature of existence. They are evidence of isolating cultural practices.

Contemporary Life and Ongoing Isolation

In North America today, parents are facing challenges unlike those of previous generations: the middle class has been hollowed out, the unstable gig economy has overtaken steady lifetime jobs,[20] house prices in desirable locations have sky-rocketed, and multibillion-dollar porn, drug, and gaming industries compete for their children's attention. Overworked and exhausted parents, chronically stressed about paying the bills, being evicted, and securing the next short-term contract should not be tasked with revolutionizing culture to better support children's needs (although, remarkably, many are trying). The term "parenting" is, in fact, a misnomer, a misleading directive. In fact, children are "communi-tied" into adulthood, but today that "community" consists of a potentially dubious mixture of humans, social media influencers, and international corporations and fewer and fewer more-than-human kin.

Faced with impossible demands on their time and energy, many North American parents may be unable to respond to their infants' and children's needs in the ways that our species evolved to expect.[21] For example, they may maintain markedly less physical contact with their infants and children, as strollers, play-pens, and baby monitors take over the roles humans used to have. Yet physical affection between mother and infant, the neurologist Michael Meaney has dis-covered, beneficially stimulates particular regions of the brain.[22] Physical affec-tion also contributes to advantageous sharing of microbiomes, the "trillions of bacteria and fungi" living symbiotically inside us, as Narvaez reminds.[23] In other words, caregivers have historically been a means of mediating and introducing infants to the communities of the microscopic more-than-human that has played essential roles in human survival and evolution. Today's parents are also likely to maintain less eye contact with infants and children, as cell phones and screens capture our attention. Yet eye contact, along with other forms of responsiveness, is essential in helping a child grow their communication and social skills, ac-cording to the Harvard University Center on the Developing Child.[24]

The point here is not to guilt-trip caregivers and parents for their child-rearing practices but rather to point out how cultural forces pin us all into roles where our child-rearing options are limited. Indeed, we are all limited in how we *are* the world and how we express ourselves more generally. We may lack the op-portunity, support, or time to reflect on our own upbringing or to consider whether we want to align with the driving North American values of hyper-individualism, materialism, and nature separation. We may lack models for a more relational and supportive form of parenting, for a more connected way of being in the world. Due to the demands of our work, we may lack the physical and emotional energy and economic stability to care for children and ourselves in a different (read: more diverse and emotionally nurturing) way.

Parents and caregivers, of course, are just one aspect of the complex web of values, lifestyle choices, and beliefs that comprise culture. Narvaez reminds us that infants "are born into an existing *ecology*."[25] In other words, everything—

from the air the mother breathes to the microbes and pesticides she ingests in her food to the unseen biases of culture—impacts her baby before the baby is even born. Narvaez concludes that babies raised in the typically North American manner have a physiologically underdeveloped relational capacity. As such, the neurological underpinnings of empathy and care have been understimulated. But, in a supportive environment, the brain, we now know, *can* change.

The biological infrastructure of an individual's attachment system is not limited to human-to-human relationships. Cultural practices can erode our capacity to bond with our more-than-human relations too. Today, billions of humans reside in dense urban centers, a habitat composed largely of metal, glass, cement, angular lines, and human crowds, not to mention noise, air, and light pollution. For centuries prior, our ancestors largely lived in rural settings. Affected as they were by the vagaries of the natural world, these lifestyles could be difficult and sometimes grueling, but they did provide abundantly more and richer relationships with land and its more-than-human inhabitants than does urbanity. The sounds of farm animals, the sight of birds in flight, and the scent of earthy soil were regular features, offering comfort, stimulation, and relationship to generations upon generations of infants and toddlers.

Some researchers, like the environmental scientist Ming Kuo, suggest that perhaps humans were never designed to live walled, cemented, and fenced off from much of nature in urban settings.[26] She notes that "habitat selection theory" is the idea that "we're wired for whatever habitat we evolved in." Just like animals at a zoo, she explains, human health and psychology may suffer when we're situated in artificial environments, separated from greenery, trees, and moving water.[27] E. O. Wilson and others have taken these ideas further, suggesting that humans have a proclivity toward—even an innate love for—our diverse relations; that part of being human is to care for—and be cared for by—the more-than-human world; and that we, as humans, are wired in this direction. They call this biophilia.[28]

One wonders, though: How well can those who have been cleft from their relational instincts by alienation and urbanization provide the ecological care, give attention, and take up the responsibility urgently needed? Urbanization—compounded by isolating child-rearing practices—and limited exposure to the more-than-human are likely to intensify the dual issues of anthropocentrism and individualism over time.

The End Results of Isolated Individualism

Despite their deep concern for the environment, the average American or Canadian is forced into being largely preoccupied with their own survival and material priorities. Operating from the centrality of the self, we prioritize our own needs and those of our families first. Likewise, mining CEOs and corporate lobbyists likely consider their own needs first, followed by the needs of their shareholders, colleagues, and employees. Some questions are rarely asked: Whom *else* should I care for? How is my existence, my expression of self, made manifest—and at whose expense? How does my action impact *everyone*, including the myriad and diverse beings of the natural world? Who is caring for me who I am not acknowledging or even noticing? Instead, most North Americans ask the question that rings like a kind of cultural tinnitus: What can *you* do for *me*?

When Beaver creates a dam on a desert creek, it forms an oasis that invites myriad beings for whom the hot and dry is unworkable. Ultimately, that industrious rodent raises the overall level of flourishing for surrounding flora and fauna, for the whole community. In contrast, the American dream primarily aims to raise the overall level of living for oneself and possibly a few additional humans. And, unfortunately, that dream is largely manifesting as an ongoing nightmare for the majority of earth's inhabitants, both human and more-than-human. Might the whole thing be rewritten in Beaver's image, where the dream is to raise the whole community?

If the child is disconnected from the earth, their caregivers, and themselves yet still seeks to belong—as we all do—they may find comfort in and settle for reduced forms of connection—the ones sanctioned by the dominant culture: consumption, competition, commodification, supremacy. Alfie Kohn writes, "First we are systematically socialized to compete—and to want to compete—and then the results are cited as evidence of competition's inevitability."[29] The growing child can ignore and rebel against their mother, compete for position with peers, and take what they want from the earth's resources—all the while aching to belong. Even though children are pushed toward independence, they are often granted the most superficial kind of individuality, manifesting mostly in their mundane consumer choices, such as the coolest toothpaste or wildest hair color. They have been inundated with messages from industry and even government and schools to put their own needs first, that it is their right and goal to satiate their material desires. *Shop till you drop. Don't settle for less. Dress for success. Have it your way. Because you're worth it. He who dies with the most toys wins.* Even popular modern psychology underscores the doctrine of individualism by urging young people to love themselves first and, only when and if they accomplish that, love others. Their parents, teachers, and peers may likewise be trying to incubate self-love within the isolating bubbles of hyper-independence.

If we turn our attention beyond this sense of individualization and human isolation, we can see the parallels happening between human and the rest of the more-than-human. For if the "I" is most important in the human world—and the human takes that same position among all species—the obvious result is the shunting aside or deeming problematic of relationality toward those whom Winona LaDuke calls "all our relations."[30] Eco-philosophers have long talked of this separation between the human and the rest of the world, with many suggesting that this alienation is an artifact of the move to lessen the value of all our relations,[31] to instrumentalize them and make their value utilitarian—rather than taking on the responsibilities that would be required if we were to be in genuine relationship, acknowledging that they exist independently from us and have rights, possibilities, and values intrinsic to them.

Despite this orientation toward the self, the individual is not exactly thriving under these ideals either, as increasing mental illness rates, shortening life spans,[32] and plummeting social trust attest.[33] Many researchers have documented increases in childhood depression, loneliness, neuroticism, attention disorders, and anxiety,[34] and have pointed to disconnectedness as the cause.[35] Toddlers are now being treated with psychotropics for depression and bipolar disorders.[36] These conditions now common in North America are exceedingly rare in traditional cultures around the globe where connections to others are central.[37] Adults evidence these problems as well, but, worryingly, each generation seems to be faring worse than the previous.

In fact, the deterioration of childhood mental health and the degradation of the environment have deeply entwined roots. Environmental degradation decreases human emotional, social, and physical well-being.[38] For example, recent epidemiological evidence suggests that urban pollution increases ADHD, anxiety, and aggression,[39] and slows cognitive development[40] and emotional regulation.[41] Similarly, the human-made chemical BPA, common in food and beverage containers, has been found to change and repress the social functioning of mice over multiple generations.[42] Viewing the world through the lens of individualization prevents acknowledgment of cultural practices that both exacerbate problems and obstruct potential solutions (such as the solution offered by the process of ecologizing education).

Humans damage forests, pollute rivers, and disrupt delicately balanced ecosystems. Reduced environmental health, in turn, reduces human health in complex, far-reaching, and potentially lifelong ways. The root injury to both, however, comes earlier and involves subtle and persistent cultural messaging to children about disconnection. BPA damage and water pollution are mere symptoms of a larger blight within Western culture. Banning BPA helps in the short term, but what will be the next BPA? Environmental destruction will continue until modern Western culture goes to the deeper root of the problem: its flawed and limiting core beliefs about connection to fellow humans and our more-than-human kin.

Systemic Isolation in Standard Schooling

Personal and human supremacy is also messaged through the physical spaces that contain childhood. The anthropologist Felice Wyndham says that in modern Western cultures, we live, work, and go to school in "dead boxes."[43] Our days are filled with dead things: desks, computer screens, walls. Our tables and papers are flattened dead trees. In fact, we humans make these dead things and shape them for our own use—and they, in turn, are shaping us. The message is powerful. Pick any classroom in North America and it will look roughly the same. It is not a place filled with living things, and although many teachers work hard to make classrooms as lively and inviting as possible, there are limits to what can be achieved within these spaces, limits often enforced from unexpected quarters, such as when the teacher is told to remove natural materials by the fire chief for reasons of safety. Yet the classroom window may reveal a small forest, a frigid snowscape, and beings engaged in their own projects. In these homogenized classroom environments, people logically adopt a worldview wherein they are the "subject" and everything else is an "object." Worryingly, this relationship to human-constructed inanimate objects is then transferred to those that are animate, living, and vital. All-powerful humans act upon an "inferior" environment and its myriad objects, using all for their own benefit. By the time they enter the ecologizing school, most kindergarten children have been exposed to this subject–object dynamic on a daily basis in homes, community centers, indoor preschools, libraries, play gyms, and relatives' and friends' houses for five years. Equally important, so has the teacher—and for much longer.

Schools, as a whole, have worked hard to turn attention toward social and ecological wounds, but their very structure tends to send anthropocentric and individualistic messages, albeit unintentionally. The physical space of standard schools reinforces this subject–object dynamic and the separation of humans. Furthermore, because educators may be offered little time for deep and sustained reflection or the opportunity to step outside the box of culturally based schooling expectations, many pedagogical practices have limited room for change. Understandably, the internalization of these subject–object and hierarchical paradigms results in some students—or perhaps *all* students some of the time—feeling objectified, inconsequential, lesser than, or used by others. They may treat others in this manner too. Perhaps this internalized worldview is why standard school systems tend to fall short on emotional flourishing.

Many adults readily confirm this fact with their own anecdotal memories. Surface complaints include meaningless, tedious, and disconnected curriculum. Deeper retrospection often recalls lonely and isolating social cliques, laced with the anxiety of incessant competition and even trauma. Furthermore, since the standard school is primarily a place of a quite singular form of rational learning, successful children must find ways to sideline emotion, relationships, and yearning for sensory experience. Brief trips outdoors, mindfulness moments, and more "emotion" talk in classrooms cannot resolve these issues because the foundations of the system and, by extension, the pedagogical approach itself are built on problematic notions.

Despite countless thoughtful teachers working to oppose these conditions, most students feel on some level that their larger nature—as whole and interdependent, emotional, sensual beings—has been quashed. Belonging to the system seems to come at a cost. To truly succeed in the eyes of the teacher, the cooperative child must become competitive. The relational child must promote the self. The emotionally gifted child must concentrate on the rational. The diverse knower must narrow the allowable fields of meaning-making. Myriad possibilities, ways of knowing, and some spark of life—of the core self—must be relinquished in order to adapt to the demands of the classroom, the curriculum, and the culture.

Prior to school, many young children start asking questions about how trees feel when they're cut down or what it means for whales to swim with so much plastic or where garbage goes. Many adults are as uncomfortable with these questions as with ones about Santa Claus: we don't want our children (or ourselves, for that matter) to know the truth. We don't want them to know about the daily destruction of the planet, and so we separate the child and ourselves from that relational instinct by repeating the lies that were told to us. *Trees don't care if they're cut down. The ocean is huge. The garbage just goes "away" in a truck.*

Children who spend abundant time in more complex natural spaces are pushed to crush their desire for environmental engagement, that part of themselves that cares for the natural world. After all, the "voice" of culture inside them insists that such a disposition is crazy, overly sentimental, and even wrong. The child who felt truly loved when sitting in a favorite maple tree now remembers the experience as "childish," private, and embarrassing. The child who attentively watched and cared for spiders now stomps on them in the schoolyard to make the other children laugh. When we no longer feel encouraged to be relationally aware and responsive selves, we move toward superficialities and find ways to protect ourselves from pain. Eventually, we may succumb to shallow forms of relating to ourselves, others, and the diversity of beings that make up the more-than-human.

Concerned educators labor in vain to counteract these tendencies because the system is rigged in one direction. Despite their often extraordinary efforts toward collaboration and community-building in the standard classroom, the direct and indirect messaging systems embedded in centralized learning outcomes, architectural designs, and competitive grading models tend to reinforce autonomy, thus obscuring relational impairments in students. Where the forest imparts a complex ecological philosophy—an enlivening and humbling paradox that everyone and everything matters and is simultaneously insignificant, that everyone and everything is in relation and yet distinct—the standard classroom typically presents, with limited complexity, a world of detachment, separation, objectification, and individualism.

This messaging is evidenced in the materiality of the space itself, in social expectation, and in curriculum design. Children's freedoms are restricted by classrooms, bells, desks, and other actions imposed by a system, a teacher, and a physical space where efficiency, commonly a buzzword for control, is a primary goal. Industrial lighting, worksheets, standardized exams, rows of desks or rows of tables—all promote a code of conformity, even when a particular assignment or instructor aims for creativity. Lessons are broken into chunkable parts and further fragmented into test questions. The educator John Holt explains that contemporary education compels children to work for "petty and contemptible rewards" and "the ignoble satisfaction of feeling that they are better than someone else."[44] Importantly, children are trained to look outside themselves, often toward human "experts," for instruction, discipline, and reward at the expense of their own internal knowing, in what often amounts to forced learning at an inappropriate pace. They are told what they should experience and what they should learn. As the environmental leader Vandana Shiva articulates, "We've moved from wisdom to knowledge, and now we're moving from knowledge to information, and that information is so partial—that we're creating incomplete human beings."[45]

In 1986, Alfie Kohn reported that 65 percent of sixth-graders prefer a cooperative style of learning over a competitive one.[46] However, standard North American education prizes students for obedience and encourages the kind of competition that fosters it. Kohn explained, "Children who are set against each other are easier to discipline."[47] The result is reduced cooperation and connection between peers and a more limited relationship between teachers and students. Today, even though many teachers focus on relationships and earn trust, inspire, or become confidants, those roles are optional and hard to accomplish for an entire class of twenty-five to thirty diverse students. The combination of class size, centralized mandates, the downloading of larger systemic responsibilities (for example, mental health care, responding to needs of complex families and learners, etc.), and increasing demands on the teacher's role makes the obedience-authority paradigm, so critiqued thirty-five years ago, a continuing presence in many schools.

The standard North American educational design places humans at the center of existence—with Brown Bear, Peat Moss, River Stone, and Chestnut Pollen positioned as extraneous, sidelined *objects*. This implicit curriculum teaches children that the more-than-human world can be ignored and is of minor educational and cultural importance. The typical classroom makes it difficult to foster relational feeling between students and, for example, the schoolyard tree. Self-identifying male children often feel particularly embarrassed by their instinct and need to care for others and the desire to remain connected to others. In fact, the student who cries for the tree that has broken in a storm will likely be laughed at by peers. What is a tree for? The culture, and often by extension the curriculum, says a tree is for making paper. The curriculum imparts false truths: that the world is known, that knowledge can be broken into bits, that learners are consumers of knowledge and are lesser-thans in the educational process, and that everything is served to them only by human experts—teacher, parents, Google, or book authors.

In sum, typical North American pedagogy does little to encourage an ecological instinct in children. While teachers may *tell* children to care for one another and the environment, the day-to-day contexts continue to prioritize the individual and the human. Thus, while high school students may acquire knowledge, for example, of the complex chemical interactions that turn sunlight, air, and water into food for plants, they may have no experiential reference for the process. When they look at a leaf in the sunlight, they may never consider the processes occurring between them. They have learned the *theory* of photosynthesis from textbooks without learning the *reality* of leaves in sunlight. They have spent little time encountering trees or leaves and, consequently, feel little relationship with or connection to them. They may see themselves as utterly disconnected from the leaf's processes, even though they may have just breathed in oxygen the tree has released, cut a living branch to create a paltry fire, or ripped off a leafy bundle to fiddle with.

Standard pedagogy has remained essentially unchanged in this way for more than a century. Thus, the centrality of the individual and the importance of the human are replicated from one generation to the next—or perhaps, as Narvaez warns, the centrality of the individual is not just replicated but intensified. With the relational instinct significantly impaired, individuals who believe themselves to be kind, aware, and respectful have been and continue to be proxy to and even privileged by the pouring of toxic chemicals in rivers, the plowing up of forests, the paving over of unique habitats, and the exploding of whole islands without a thought to the loss of lives. Those rarer individuals who grow to adulthood with a relatively intact relational and ecological capacity struggle with the complexities, feel the pain of ongoing violence, and have generally spent enormous amounts of time outdoors in nature—*despite* the indoor school system.

The Relational Instinct

The Harvard neuroscientist Matthew Lieberman, one of the world's leading experts on prosocial development, states simply: "Maslow had it wrong." The infant's "most primary and urgent need," he claims, "is bonding."[48] The newborn infant knows what many scientists have been culturally trained to overlook: connection and ongoing connection come first. Their very life was conceived through the physical and, hopefully, loving connection of their key caregivers, who are themselves defined by their social and more-than-human environments and by their ancestors and the ancestral environments before them. Human life is made possible by the fertile interactions between microbial, atmospheric, and other connections. And further, it is enriched, depleted, or altered by psychological and biological impacts, such as the expectant mother's peaceful and abundant garden or the father's exposure to harsh chemical agents. Who among us would choose a life with plenty of food and shelter but no love or connections to anyone, human or more-than-human? It's not just that survival depends on relationships: indeed, life has little meaning without them.

Indeed, evidence of interdependence is so omnipresent in the natural environment, one wonders why Western scientists imagined humans to be exempt. Ivy climbs because of Maple and Sunlight. Maple spins seeds into the breeze. Thimbleberry awaits Bear. Even our bodies are not our own, as Narvaez reminds us: "The human body cannot function without the trillions of other organisms that conduct a host of symbiotic functions that keep it alive."[49] The cause of the individualism fallacy is one thing, but the result is quite another. How different might the last half-century of parenting advice, pedagogical practice, and environmental policy have been if love and bonding were recognized as the world's most urgent need? And if relationship and cooperation were understood as fundamental?

Researchers have only fairly recently studied the extent to which humans are physiologically cocreated by other humans. However, research remains distinctly lacking on the subject of the involvement of more-than-human beings in human physiological development. For example, what important neurological, microbial, or sensory processes occur when an infant feels the breeze on their face throughout the day? What processes or physiological development may be reduced when an infant is kept almost entirely indoors with static air? How is an infant's neurological development altered by shifting patterns of outdoor light, as opposed to relatively constant and artificial indoor light? And more directly, how does one come to understand the color green when immersed in the nuance and subtlety of a temperate rainforest versus in the uniformity of the lime-green walls of a classroom? Anthropologists who study traditional peoples around the world consistently remark on the precociousness and social skills of those children.[50] To what extent is that maturity attributable to the influence of more-than-human beings? More pointedly, how might a lack of exposure to all these relations reduce a child's well-being, their range of experiential encounter, their imagined possibilities (for example, one child, when asked about what they wanted to be when they grew up, responded "Salmon"), and their ability to empathize with and care for others, including care for the natural world?

In the 1970s, the developmental psychologist Carol Gilligan pointed out that "the relational bias" in women's thinking was viewed as a deviation or deficiency rather than as "a different social and moral understanding."[51] She explained that women at that time frequently expressed values of compassion, inclusion, social harmony, and empathy and used those values as the basis of moral decision-making. Although Gilligan wrote of women's values, evidence suggests that a "relational bias" is the norm for all children of any gender. Contemporary North American culture fractures the psyche, creating a kind of eco-double consciousness:[52] one part feels innate compassion and connection to all living beings, while the other part criticizes that impulse, believing it to be a sign of weakness and inappropriate dependency. Children who manage to maintain a strong relational self often feel quite alien from their peers, experiencing a kind of double life—outwardly displaying the culturally accepted self and inwardly maintaining the hidden, relational self, which, if not addressed, works to seed doubt and complacency regarding the oppression of the natural world. It can lead to a sense of insecurity and a fear to express especially if one of the selves continues to be denigrated. Our contention is that this tension is widespread; there are many of us who are caught between what we understand to be the cultural norm and our own relational and experiential connection to the natural world.

Reduced relational capacity need not be a life sentence, but it can impede a child's ability to care about others, including the diversity of the more-than-human. It may be altogether unreasonable to expect a child to embrace their relationships with Gall Midge, Hemlock, and River if they are carrying the psychological wounds of enforced independence deep in their psyche. They may respond with resentment, feign boredom, react with hostility, or be excessively interactive, evidencing their anxiety rather than mutual engagement. At ecologizing schools, all the teachers, human and otherwise, gently and patiently encourage emotional connections while valuing interdependence. Evidence from these BC schools suggests that students have often begun to heal from emotional and relational wounds. Sometimes, they find their own therapeutic interventions, which are often under-recognized by their teachers and unnoticed by their peers, such as seeking out comforting nature sounds or bonding with a particular tree. And for those who come from situations where the dangers are clearly human, finding and building safe relations with natural kin and places can be an important salve, antidote, or just respite.

Returning to the Relational in Ecologizing Education

Outdoor environmental schools are born into an existing cultural ecology. Ecologizing educators may find themselves reflecting on the patterns and messaging of isolation in their own childhood as well as those of their students and their caregivers. Some of the work of radical cultural change is about acknowledging and psychologically untangling from wounding aspects of the current culture and bringing subconscious damage to light. But another aspect of cultural change involves opening doors to new opportunities for connection and belonging. This process is a *returning* to the relational because, we argue, the relational orientation is inherent in the human species despite its having been suppressed and diverted.

In most cases, children arriving at the ecologizing schools have just exited standard schooling and its embedded and enforced messages of isolation. Understandably, therefore, these students may be unlikely to notice, for example, that dialogue within the forest changes when humans step into it. Human voices may drown out River's story and scatter Sandflies. Song Sparrow's trilling goes unnoticed. Flying Squirrel scampers high up the tree. Shyer creatures go into hiding completely. And what of the more subtle conversations? The ones between sunlight and leaves, worms and soil, water and roots?

Most North Americans are unaccustomed to noticing these languages, this multisensory dialogue that brings flora, fauna, water, and weather into communication. Nonetheless, many children readily sense the vitality of the forest. By discussing ecological dialogue and by making space to listen, the ecologizing educator creates an experiential and possibly conceptual bridge for the student in the hope that they may cross over and discover—or rediscover—genuine relationships with the other members of the more-than-human. During this process, students are reunited with a hidden, sometimes self-repressed part of themselves. The Jewish philosopher Martin Buber explained that all children are born with the relational instinct and that teachers carry the responsibility for recognizing and supporting opportunities to relate.[53] In Buber's view, all of earth's beings— horses, the element mica, children—contain a divine spark, and he believed in the importance of connecting these sparks through multisensory, experiential, and spiritual "dialogue."[54] Doing so creates a coming together of self and Other as well as an expansion of self, since the self is incomplete in isolation.

The Language of Relationality

To the Western mind, "talking with the trees" might sound metaphoric, a bit of poetic whimsy and personification. This is one of many subtle cultural biases that is often carried into the outdoors. This assumption primes children for shallow or dismissive relations with the natural world. In fact, what we think of as "language" is itself a metaphor. The words, grammar, and syntax that we utter from vocal cords, tongues, and mouths are representations of things. Conversely, the gestures, communions, and communications in the forest are most often not representations at all. They are first-line communications. The word-languages that humans employ—though rich with possibilities and potentials for interaction, translation, and connection—are only one form of dialogue. They are also limiting in ways that reflect cultural values.

In terms of its ecological ethos, the English language is particularly problematic. One of the key issues is that English lacks the vocabulary needed to conceptualize relationships with the natural world. A number of other languages do have vocabulary for the kinds of deep engagements humans regularly experience within those cultures. The Welsh saying *dod yn ôl at fy nghoed* has been literally translated to mean "come back to my trees" but is understood to suggest one's return to well-being or a balanced state of mind. The Japanese language maintains the concept of *shinrin-yoku*. The term, which literally translates as "forest bathing," means to walk through the forest for personal healing and restoration. In Norwegian, one can participate in *friluftsliv* (literally "free-air-life"), which means to go out into the great outdoors with a spirit of exploration and appreciation for the natural world. Thus, these concepts of well-being enable an emotional, spiritual, and long-lasting engagement with nature that is unmatched by, say, the concepts of "camping" or "outdoor adventure."

A second key deficit for the English language is its focus on nouns, that is, on *things*, rather than on actions, relationships, or experiences. This focus not only prioritizes objects but also positions them as static, which makes conveying ideas about relating, process, movement, or incompleteness more difficult. Where the English language categorizes stars, plants, and rivers as "things"—that is, mere objects—hundreds of North American Indigenous languages refer to star *spirits*, plant *spirits*, and river *spirits*.[55] In other words, rather than simply assigning labels for stars, plants, and rivers, Indigenous languages use names filled with vitality for these more-than-human entities, implicitly recognizing their agency.

While nouns are predominant in the English language, other languages rely more on verbs. Robin Wall Kimmerer reports, for example, that verbs comprise 70 percent of the Potawatomi vocabulary, while verbs account for only 30 percent of English.[56] Kimmerer explains that by using verbs instead of nouns, Potawatomi acknowledges the animacy of Water, Beach, and Mushroom. The words "Watering," "Beaching," and "Mushrooming" pulse with an aliveness of being and becoming, unlike the flat, inanimate objects implied by the English language. This question of the stasis of the noun can be influenced and altered in various ways. For example, in this book we have tried using gerunds in particular places to recognize and emphasize movement and process.

These seemingly insignificant details about the English language are, in fact, critical because, as Lev Vygotsky notes, "speech plays an essential role in the organization of higher psychological functions" and a child perceives the world "not only through his eyes but through his speech."[57] Vygotsky describes language as a cultural tool designed to help us understand the world. However, in using the tool, we are also shaped by it, and as a result, we come to make sense of the world the way our culture does. With its word limitations and object-orientation, the English language influences our conception of ourselves, our relationships with all-our-relations, and our receptivity to a wider diversity of communications.

In the case of ecologizing education, if the teacher employs the English language in standard ways, without acknowledging or accommodating for its ecological gaps, the child's ability to relate can be hampered. Expanding relational capacity while attending to linguistic limitations with twenty-five rain-soaked forest students can seem like a tall order. On the other hand, the setting itself can inspire invention and intuition for receptive students and teachers. For example, some teachers have begun to play a game called "ecologizing the troublesome cliché," where "killing two birds with one stone" becomes "feeding two birds with one hand." Other teachers encourage students to play with capitalizations across beings and to notice and name situations of nouning rather than verbing or of hierarchizing humans and marginalizing more-thans.

Despite its many limitations, the English language also has a particular strength in that it is a remarkably adaptable and flexible language that allows for playfulness, spontaneity, expansions, and cross-linguistic collaborations. That is why we can say things like "Octopus dreamed me" and "sometimes humaning is hard" and, despite never having heard these words used in this way, listeners and readers are likely to easily grasp their meaning.[58]

Listening to the Voices of Place

First-grader Lana's story illustrates the relational, cultural, and linguistic complexity involved in ecological mentoring. Lana often notices what other students, in their rush, do not notice: a feather, a piece of wasp nest, a slug. She approaches more-than-human beings with devotion and reckless enthusiasm. Left to her own instincts, she will literally love a creature to death. In her exuberance, she squeezes and injures Worm, stuffs Butterfly in her backpack for safekeeping, and manhandles Slug all the way home, slime oozing all over her arms.[59] She removes insects from trails and tree hollows to bring them home, believing she can "protect them best."[60] Lana's intense attachment supports her development as an ecologically minded human, but she relates to more-than-human entities only on her own terms. This orientation leaves her relationships one-sided. She may not feel pain when Butterfly is crushed, but Butterfly does. Here, the ecologizing educator has an opportunity to facilitate dialogue between Lana and the forest beings, to help her develop awareness of the paradox of being connected yet separate.

One way to facilitate dialogue and engage with this problem of language is by leading students on a sound walk or listening walk. The listening walk is a way of approaching the natural world with attentive receptivity.[61] Modern Western culture encourages assertive, dominant, and active control over the environment, and even when those qualities combine with appreciation and enjoyment, they generally exclude receptivity. Attentive receptivity, on the other hand, is a way of being in the world that emphasizes *being* over *doing*, since much of what Western humans *do* in the more-than-human realm results in destruction. Attentive receptivity relies on "long-term experience of living in conjunction with place and the conceptualization of such an experience."[62] In other words, attentive receptivity encourages cumulative experiences with *specific* more-than-human entities (for example, not just experiencing the presence of hemlocks, but experiencing a relationship with the same Hemlock over time). Attentive receptivity encourages child and Hemlock to develop a long-term relationship narrative. It also assumes that either child or Hemlock can initiate the relationship and that both have agency.

Like learning a foreign language in a different cultural setting, tuning into the dialogue of the forest requires effort. The teacher creates an opening for dialogue between students and the various elements of nature by talking about nonword language, by encouraging attentiveness, by critically examining particular notions of communication, and by providing opportunities to connect. But relationships cannot be built on coercion. More-than-humans and children must reach toward each other. To participate in the forest conversation, the talkative child must temporarily suspend chatter. The self-absorbed child must turn attention away from the self. The already visually observant and emotionally doting child might be encouraged toward an outward receptivity. In so doing, they potentially discover other more ecologically robust modes of relating.

The book *Wild Pedagogies* has described this process of relationship-building as a practice, similar to the way in which meditation or tai chi might be understood.[63] These are disciplines that take care and commitment and that are developed, ever deepening, over time. These practices take energy and effort as skills are discovered and developed. But like all relationships, these can expand one's sense of self, one's sense of community, and one's place in the world.

Parents report that children at Maple Ridge are showing increased confidence and better social skills. As the relational self is more fully accommodated, the world seems less dangerous. The students have greater capacity for learning and engagement now that energy is not wasted obscuring and denying the ecologically connected part of themselves.

Raven, a fourth-grade student who has been at the Maple Ridge Environmental School for three years, says "you hear" a plant "through your heart." She explains: "It's not 'speaking' it's more like energy or signals. You don't hear it out loud . . . you speak your way, they speak different ways, like thousands of different ways. Billions. It's like the birds with those signals, like when you see a bird flapping up in the sky and a flock of birds, how they all move at the same time, it's because they tell each other like through mental speaking."[64] The more our relational selves grow, the more capacity we have to connect with others, human and more-than-human. The Simon Fraser University eco-research team writes, "The world literally speaks to us, not in our language but in its own; we become, as it were, bilingual. No longer separated from the more-than-human world, we have become a part of it; an ontological shift has occurred."[65]

During these listening walks and related activities, the voices of the more-than-humans are not only heard; they are also, at least to some degree, freer to vocalize. Despite the whooshing of many pantlegs and scuffing of a couple dozen shoes, birds trill from the trees again. The Flying Squirrel comes out of hiding, peering down from a high branch with curiosity. A gust of wind picks up, sweeping the children's attention up into the many waving branches of the Douglas Fir. The environmental activist Steve Van Matre's description of this connection is remarkably similar to that of nine-year-old Raven: "Yes, the earth speaks, but only to those who can hear with their hearts. It speaks in a thousand, thousand small ways, but like our lovers and families and friends, it often sends its messages without words. For you see, the earth speaks in the language of love."[66]

Realities of the Relational Worldview

Over time and with mindful mediation from the teacher, activities like the listening walk begin dismantling ideologies about human centrality and superiority. Slowly, philosophies emerge that better support personal and planetary well-being. In the ecological worldview—where everything and everyone can dialogue—all beings have intrinsic value. Moss capsules feed mice, and moss greenery houses numerous insects. Wind expands the forest by sailing birch seeds and the tiny hemlock cones away from parent trees. Wasps pollinate plants and flowers and prey on fly and caterpillar populations. The exhalations of children are absorbed by local flora. Their fingerprints impart and absorb new microbes in beneficial exchanges. Children develop deep bonds with the river, the birds, and the surrounding families of trees.

The ecosystem offers a worldview wherein every being belongs. Every being has inherent value and is therefore deserving of respect. An ecologizing educator can help children begin to look at themselves and one another in a new way that aligns with these ecological principles. In a standard classroom, the child's unarticulated question might be *How can I belong?* In the ecologizing school, belonging is a more accessible worldview. The forest is a deeply connected ecosystem. As such, the internal query might shift to *How are we connected? And how can we explore these connections?* Each educational environment allows for certain questions and ways of questioning and at the same time is closed off to others. The child in an ecologizing education may begin to ask questions about their relationship and responsibility to others. They may understand themselves in a more expansive way than the child in an indoor setting can even imagine.

Of course, suggesting that entities within the ecosystem are deeply interconnected is not the same as suggesting that all connections are benevolent. The road out of modern Western culture's dominant and violent ideology toward the Earth can detour through other troubled domains. For example, some ideological refugees of imperialism maintain that people need only arrive in the forest and wait for nature to bestow blessings. These individuals expect more-than-human entities to live up to highly romanticized notions of interspecies bonding. Interspecies bonding can occur, but human expectation for bonding is problematic and perpetuates the centrality and privilege of the human.

A related problem lies in automatic and unthinking references to "Mother Earth." To be clear, many individuals, especially Indigenous peoples, all over the world have a profound feeling of mother–child relationship with the earth that confers a sense of responsibility, reciprocity, and mutual love. However, many non-Indigenous North Americans use the term "Mother Earth" as a kind of evidence to themselves or other humans that they care about the earth. In reality, the dominant culture tends to treat human mothers with the same dismissive, taken-for-granted disregard as it treats the earth. Without thoughtfully unpacking the term, some individuals treat "Mother Earth" as a helpful servant or self-sacrificing parent who performs all the relational work and is ever available to and interested in her human children. Such a person expects generosity but extends only need in return.

This view does not account for the position of humans within a complex web of interconnection. It is fundamentally dangerous to assume that grizzly bears and cougars appearing before us are seeking only spiritual bonding. (The documentary movies *Grizzly Man* and *Blackfish* bear tragic witness to this premise.) People too are part of the food chain. Moreover, while we hope to avoid becoming bear meals, we regularly engage with more-than-humans in distinctly unromantic ways, such as hosting, for better or for worse, mosquitoes, ticks, and viruses.

Children in ecologizing schools negotiate a multitude of relationships, each containing unique complexities. At the beach school, Seagull may be friendly one moment and snatching a sandwich the next. River is beloved by students at the forest site, but they respect the stinging cold of its winter waters and the fast-churning currents in spring. When we move out of the ideal, we make room for the real, ultimately deepening, relationships. During a wet walk in March, a teacher noticed a tree raked over by bear claws. In the spontaneous ensuing lesson, the educator recounted a Salish legend, discussed Bear's biological habits, and reminded students how to communicate respect and nonconfrontation to Bear through body language, staying calm, and giving Bear space.

Ultimately, ecologizing education seeks a profound cultural shift in the conception of humans' place within the world. The simplicity of classroom hierarchies and human supremacy is dismantled to reveal complex entanglements and fecund networks of interconnectedness. The relationships are dynamic, multilayered, meaningful, and sometimes surprising and challenging. Gall Midge becomes a mentor. The child hears from River and becomes an ally and interpreter. Wind is a clown one day and a precarious hazard the next. The obedience-authority system gives way to priorities of acceptance, respect, and interdependence. In ecologizing education, learning often appears to be more emergent, with lessons initiated by a child, a teacher, a falling pine cone, or a slow-moving banana slug. In this way, curriculum shifts from emotionally vacuous and sensually dry curriculum packages to sensory stimuli that support the presence of the whole child: heart, mind, and senses.

Many children will have suffered severed relational needs in infancy and in classrooms; nonetheless, in the forest and with an ecologizing human educator, they can begin to heal. And as their physiological capacity for relating improves, so too does their sense of belonging and the urge to care for the well-being of all-their-relations—and also the comfort, willingness, and ability to learn. The caring, cared-for, and embodied child can engage in dynamic dialogues occurring at multiple levels of awareness. This process is slow and arduous for children whose relational wounds run deep. Children who may have successfully outcompeted others in standard classrooms might relinquish control, centrality, and entitlement with ambivalence. Whatever their unique pathway, each child learns through deep engagement to increasingly comprehend, respect, learn from, love and be loved by, and work to safeguard all beings of the more-than-human.

HEALING

Facing Pain and Working toward Reconciliation

"I don't want to hear anything negative," a friend recently said. "The world is too full of negativity, negative news, and suffering already. I just want to be positive, and I want to be around positive people." North American culture has long valorized optimism and the pursuit of individual happiness. Evidence of these priorities can be seen everywhere around us—on advertising from soda ("Open a Coke. Open happiness"[1]) to chain restaurants ("Happy meals" for kids[2]) and in best-selling books like *The Secret*,[3] which promote the idea that you can take control of your life with positive thinking. It's true that, in general, having positive expectations and seeing the silver lining in hardships can improve well-being.[4] However, an unwillingness "to hear anything negative" or to experience negative emotions is ecologically and psychologically problematic.

Yet these days many feel pressured to perform happiness by actively repressing the voices—their own and others'—that disrupt joyful performances. Conforming to social expectations, exhausted parents mutter about the "joy" of parenthood. Downtrodden teachers reassure parents and administrators that their classrooms are happy places. Stressed teenagers curate their social media profiles with a bevy of smiling, sunny, photoshopped images. Indeed, North America's penchant for positivity has shifted over the last couple of decades. The cultural norm increasingly *insists* that people perform perpetual optimism. The communications professors Rosalind Gill and Shani Orgad note how people are increasingly called upon to take up a "mind-set in which negative experiences can—and must—be reframed in upbeat terms."[5]

Happiness, then, is no longer optional. It's mandatory. In the words of the psychologist Edgar Cabanas, "Happiness has become a new moral regime in neoliberal societies," and this messaging is "permeating every layer of the social realm."[6] American culture commands people to *look on the bright side* so they can *turn that frown upside down* and *live the dream*. Cabanas explains that happiness has become "a normative lifestyle which is specifically targeted, shaped, and achieved through the consumption of happiness commodities within a wider happiness industry."[7] Essentially, citizens are expected to uphold the corporate-capitalist model of society by maintaining enough positivity to participate vigorously as a worker and buy a lot of stuff to support the national economy. The requirement for happiness leaves many people denying unhappy thoughts, repressing negative feelings, ignoring the state of the world and their neighbor's lives, and secreting away their sadness and feelings of shame at, supposedly, being the only one who feels this way.

How does this pressure to be individually happy at all costs align with the goals of becoming more ecologically and socially just? If everyone is happy and the future is bright, what's the point of changing anything? Does the happiness mandate allow for the deep work of healing and cultural transformation called for at this moment? How does it impact the child whose need to "fit in" is at odds with their angst about climate injustice? How does it impact the parent activist trying to alert community members to the environmental catastrophe brewing on the horizon? Or the ecologizing educator aggrieved by the death of a local river and having to ignore this to teach to a nonenvironmental status quo?

Healing is often slow and complex. At times, it is discomforting. Mandatory happiness distracts people from facing personal and collective traumas, thus preventing the healing needed to attend to encroaching ecological catastrophe and other injustices tangled therein. It also prevents people from engaging in the sustained efforts needed to redress the systemic cultural roots of those traumas. To heal ecologically means addressing wounds in multiple interconnected domains—from human psychology and health to social justice, from Indigenous reconciliation to shifts in our philosophic understanding of the way the world works. It means tracing the threads that connect an unprecedented wildfire season to a teacher's intergenerational trauma to a child's ADHD and so on. Ecological healing necessitates recognition of the ways in which our educational system has reinforced anthropocentric and individualistic messages, has sidelined particular histories, and has obstructed particular ways of knowing.

In fact, in the context of neoliberal capitalism, the happiness fixation tends to promote—and sell—a culture of instant gratification, quick fixes, excess control, consumerism, and self-centeredness.[8] And while we are definitely supportive of happiness, self-care, and love, when any one of these becomes the singular focus, important complexities are lost, and change and healing are actually limited. Whether or not we recognize these tendencies toward superficial happiness and denial in ourselves or within the wider culture, it's useful to have some understanding of them, their pervasiveness, and ways of addressing them.

In fact, when the happiness mandate is scrutinized more carefully, it begins to look like its opposite: the push to be happy actually maintains our *un*happiness.[9] Many cultures around the world promote life satisfaction, such as through the Wabi Sabi appreciation of beauty in imperfection, the Buddhist transcendence of personal passions, or social traditions that bring people together in times of hardship. Yet the particular brand of happiness promoted in North America today is closely aligned with materialism and a desire for status—values known to reduce overall well-being.[10] Happiness, or so we are led to believe, means smiling beside your beautiful home, perfect family, and enviable car. Not smiling yet? There are a pill, a headgear gadget,[11] and dozens of apps and instructional books for that, along with a vacation package, a new automobile, and a better home. In their birth cohort study, Jean Twenge and her colleagues revealed that psychopathology in American college students is rising in tandem with "cultural shifts toward extrinsic goals, such as materialism and status."[12] Essentially, seeking meaning through collecting stuff (whether awards and accolades or boats and houses) reduces well-being. And if those purchases fail to improve well-being, one's sense of status may falter as well, leading to an even greater drive to appear well by making more purchases. This circular reasoning spirals many supposedly "successful" individuals into a state of ennui, anxiety, or depression.[13]

In their book *The Wellness Syndrome*, Cederström and Spicer explain that the "be happy" mandate is the psychological component to the more general wellness ideology that has "wormed itself into every aspect of our lives."[14] While wellness is a worthy goal, the mode and motive of today's externally imposed wellness are highly suspect. As Cederström and Spicer explain, "People who don't carefully cultivate their personal wellness are seen as a direct threat to contemporary society" because more happiness generally equates to more productivity in the workforce. According to the authors, more than three dozen colleges and universities in the United States now expect students to sign "wellness contracts" that ask them to commit to "physical, social, emotional, environmental, spiritual and intellectual wellness."[15] Alenka Zupančič examines the troubling philosophical implications of this trend: "Negativity, lack, dissatisfaction, unhappiness, are perceived more and more as moral faults—worse, as a corruption at the level of our very being or bare life. There is a spectacular rise of what we might call a bio-morality . . . , which promotes the following fundamental axiom: a person who feels good (and is happy) is a good person; a person who feels bad is a bad person."[16]

Yet these false assumptions pose obvious challenges, whether personally or socially, for all of us and in particular for those engaged in a seismic shift in cultural values. Although we believe that the ecologizing education path ultimately brings more joy and meaning, the fact remains that a willingness to face hard emotions such as grief, guilt, confusion, anxiety, and loss is necessary for facing the reality of our planetary health, for responding to the needs of our communities, and for attending to the deeper healing work of living well within this reality. A cultural fixation on positivity may push us to be good consumers while hiding deeper troubles beneath its veneer and limiting our ability to share, recognize, and get care for our "negative emotions." Its focus on the flaws of the individual can divert attention from the systemic forces involved in environmental degradation. And it doesn't allow us to step back and examine the sources of the negativity that drives the need for positivity.

In fact, longing for positivity—for the cheery metronome of upbeatness—may merely be a cover for deeper anxieties. The positivity trend may evidence societal denial, a mechanism that helps us to "not know" the actual state of the world. No one wants to feel anxious, helpless, and desperate. But much of the news about the state of the world's ecosystems leads to precisely these kinds of emotions. Although not yet defined in the *Diagnostic and Statistical Manual of Mental Disorders* (DSM-5), "eco-anxiety" is now a recognizable psychiatric condition that increasing numbers of therapists report treating.[17] The problem is that many therapists treat it as a personal disorder, an individual problem that can be treated through active denial, even repression, like a fear of meteorite strikes—rather than an understandable reaction to a terrifying problem that remains inadequately addressed by the world's leaders and the general public.

Eco-anxiety isn't the only uncomfortable emotion raised when one engages in ecologizing education. Mark Fettes explains:

> The norms of school, the hidden curriculum, get internalized at a deep level—about behavior, about authority, about what education is. If you want to challenge that set of assumptions, the way our learning is related to those things that are not human, it implicates the entire hidden curriculum of school. But it won't shift unless it is brought to consciousness. People are not adept at sitting with discomfort. It's easy to think of an outdoor school as being unproblematically a nice idea. But, really, if you take it seriously, it should draw you into a deep questioning about what school is for. What are we trying to accomplish here? For the adults it ultimately involves a kind of grief. If you ask those questions honestly, and answer about your own experience, you'll feel cheated and betrayed. You'll feel "it's too late for me." This is why people shy away from it.[18]

Chances are, if you're reading this book, you've already decided to brave the emotional content that attends this work. You're learning to lean in, to stay in the challenging conversations, because you are aware of what we are likely to lose if we don't find ways to act and respond and if we try to block out all our "non-positive" feelings. Numbing in order to not feel sadness, regret, guilt, and other "negative" emotions can mean numbing *all* emotions. There is no unidirectional emotional openness. As such, positivity alone can never be the answer.

Although it is sometimes painful to do so, it is better to feel, to bear witness to our authentic responses to the world and our role within it, as ecopsychologist Joanna Macy explains: "The refusal to feel takes a heavy toll. Not only is there an impoverishment of our emotional and sensory life—flowers are dimmer and less fragrant, our loves less ecstatic—but this psychic numbing also impedes our capacity to process and respond to information. The energy expended in pushing down despair is diverted from more creative uses, depleting the resilience and imagination needed for fresh visions and strategies."[19]

While hope is important, the happiness mandate doesn't allow us to examine ecological disasters well enough to address them. To do so, we need tools like critical and creative thinking, community building, honest assessment and evaluation, and emotional range. As Macy points out, denial diverts cognitive and emotional resources toward suppression that could be used in these efforts instead. The current cultural obsession with positivity turns out to be pretty negative for our own well-being, for the children in our care, and for the more-than-human world.

Discomfort and pain can be birthing, healing, motivating, and transforming forces. Part of the difficulty of acknowledging emotional suffering results from the North American habit of viewing emotions as separate categories: One can be happy or sad, not both—or so people tend to believe.[20] But just as the ecologizing effort calls for more wholistic learning, so also it invites a fuller sense of emotional reactions than currently allowed by positivity gurus. We grieve because we love. We are anxious because we care. We feel helpless while simultaneously grappling with how to respond. We greet our old friend—dying River—with joy, guilt, care, grief, and anger. Emotions lean into each other and can be experienced together.

Although each person's journey is unique to their own cultural background, educational history, and lifestyle choices, educators in this process will likely find themselves confronting unsettling emotional experiences. Children entering into ecologizing schooling need support too. In our work at the eco-schools, this has meant finding ways to name, bear witness to, and acknowledge the emotions the students are feeling. It means offering space for them to feel while deepening relationships to the more-than-human and to themselves. It means helping them notice options for living differently while also finding places where their voices and opinions can be heard and have an impact. Students have done a great deal of ecoservice work, have negotiated different school-based standards of practice and values, have been involved in local climate rallies (along with their teachers), and have engaged in local politics in various ways. In these ways, emotions neither are suppressed nor remain stuck; rather, they are transformed into meaningful action.

To a certain degree, feelings of grief, despair, and even guilt are natural for those embarking on these explorations. It's necessary to support each other and care for oneself—not by denying and avoiding difficult emotions but by being willing to acknowledge and experience them. In failing to make room for negative emotions, we thwart personal healing processes and limit our cultural capacity for positive transformation. Real change requires deep work. It involves untangling deeply embedded thoughts and conceptions about the functioning of the planet and our place within it. We need our whole selves present to take up the task. The sections in this chapter offer a few examples of the kind of emotional, judicial, and ontological healing people might encounter on their ecologizing journey. We hope they also offer a place where thoughts and emotions, in the face of this eco-tragedy, are heard and acknowledged.

Wholistic Assessment of Disease and Discontent

When it comes to healing, the word *wholistic* is generally understood to refer to the connections between a person's body, mind, emotions, and spirit and how each contributes to human health.[21] This framing, however, requires some expansion when considering the ecologizing perspective, since human health cannot be separated from community, environmental, and planetary health. This link goes both ways: humans are affected by the health of the air, water, and soil around them and the plants and animals they ingest; likewise, the air, water, soil, flora, and fauna are affected by the health of humans, that is, by the individual and cultural health of human bodies, emotions, ideas, ontologies, epistemologies, and cultural norms. Just as our environment cannot be healed by attending to only one river, one species, or one mining site at a time, so too our mental and physical well-being cannot be fully addressed by focusing on one mental health diagnosis, cognitive "disorder," or social issue at a time. Indeed, cancer and river pollution may be linked, as might schizophrenia and air quality as well as systemic racism and diabetes.

From an ecologizing perspective, healing means shifting focus from individual humans to our relationships with each other and all-our-relations and also to the cultural practices, assumptions, and beliefs impacting these relationships. This healing is embedded in personal and cultural ways of being and knowing and in daily habits. While rivers, grasslands, whales, and others need healing, the source of global environmental destruction is not located in them. The source of most ecological ill health—and much contemporary human illness—is located in contemporary, techno-industrial human culture and the way it is absorbed and enacted by individuals and societies upon all bodies. That is why, in this chapter, when we talk about healing, we mostly focus on what needs to heal in humans—more specifically, in particular human cultures—in order to right the relationships between humans and coral reefs, old-growth forests, endangered frogs, and so on. Further to this, we recognize that reefs and forests tend to self-heal when they avoid particular kinds of human attention.[22] Our aim is not to begin with human healing and then move to environmental healing, but rather to recognize the two as indelibly linked.

These kinds of healings can be difficult because they require actively swimming against the tide of mainstream culture. For some, that journey means an unsettling exploration into unchartered social, emotional, cognitive, and ecological territory. For others, this journey feels like a returning—regaining the right to "come home" to one's traditional culture, family culture, or childhood understanding of the world. Regardless of one's personal path, it's helpful to recognize the systemic barriers to such healing and the ways we may have internalized them. By pushing against these barriers—these values, assumptions, and practices of mainstream culture—we create enough distance to see broader connections. In so doing, we might begin to heal the beliefs and values that put our own beings and the other beings of the earth at so much risk.

The standard medical model looks at a person's ailments in isolation.[23] Seen from an ecologizing perspective, however, a person's ailments—just like the ailments of the Western Pine, the Chicago River, and those resulting from the COVID virus—must be understood within the broader context of relationships and environmental contexts. With rates of anxiety and other mood disorders rapidly rising across much of the world,[24] tremendous effort has been spent examining potential flaws in human biochemistry. In contrast, remarkably little effort has been spent considering the ways dramatic environmental changes—such as pesticide accumulations,[25] a thinning stratosphere,[26] a 30 percent increase in ocean acidification,[27] and never-before-experienced levels of cellular and electromagnetic radiation[28]—might impact human biochemistry. And almost no one is asking what it might be about the culture itself that is causing such a rise in suffering.[29]

Some might point a finger at environmental movements and suggest that the stress of hearing about these ecological crises raises stress hormones and contributes to unwellness. But that claim assumes humans are not connected to the world around them and have no mechanisms for detecting stress in our environments. It also returns us to the troubling happiness narrative and an assumption that "not knowing" is somehow natural and psychologically sound. Human physiology is a delicate thing. It is hard to believe that massive planetary changes would *not* influence human well-being. Imagining that humans are utterly immune might seem "logical" from a stoutly individualistic worldview. But as we have seen, humans are not detached self-supporting entities, and the notion that we are must be completely rejected. From our inherited and ingested microbes to our ability to care and create relationships to our dependence upon water, nutrients, and sunlight, our bodies are the very manifestations of interconnections and interdependencies.

Seen from this perspective, perhaps anxiety and depression are *not* mental illnesses rooted in individual biochemistry as we've been led to believe. By taking a broad view of mental health, other analysts have already concluded that the biochemical model for treating these disorders (1) is unsupported by the research,[30] (2) is largely not working,[31] and (3) makes little sense from a sociocultural perspective.[32] Perhaps anxiety and depression can be better understood as an alarm system rooted in relationship. Perhaps it's a built-in mechanism, part of our evolutionary design, intended to pull our species back from the brink of a shared disaster. What if the burgeoning crisis merely evidences a fracture in the profound primacy of our relationships—a flashing emergency light intended to remind us of how intimately connected we are to Mackerel, Ocean, and the tens of millions of other humans around the globe currently taking mood medication?

When we recognize the world as a deeply connected, entangled mesh of relationships, massive rates of mood disorders begin to resemble a symptom of a problem rather than the problem itself. That problem may well be disconnection, disruption, and shared trauma. A symptom, of course, is not a malfunction of the body, designed to bring random suffering. Rather, it is a warning of illness, a message that deeper healing is needed. Perhaps the message is that the cultural stance of isolated beings is dangerously unsustainable. The invitation presented is a shift back to relationship—to heal what is within *the relationship*, not within the isolated self. Set within the context of standard psychology and medical care, however, these messages most often go unheard. The "successful" patient is the one who realigns with the acceptable status quo and learns to tune out and deny the rest. Meanwhile, mood medication consumption increased 3,001 percent from 1991 to 2018 in the United States alone.[33] And only now are medical establishments beginning to consider the potentially far-reaching effects for humans, animals, and plants of mood medication runoff in our soils and waterways.[34]

Americans don't deal well with grief, as Laura van Dernoot Lipsky, the director of the Trauma Stewardship Institute in the United States, recently pointed out: "We don't talk about loss. By and large, it's all about consumption to help numb you out."[35] The earth is in a collective state of grief right now, as habitats are being destroyed and unprecedented numbers of species are becoming extinct. Is it too much of a stretch to imagine that some of the earth's humans can sense this aching loss, this feeling that something is "not quite right" or profoundly "off" about the health of the planet?

In other health matters, although it's not yet known where COVID originated, one theory posits that human encroachment on animal habitats has brought diseased animals into greater contact with humans.[36] And higher pollution rates, we now know, are linked to more severe outcomes for humans who contract the disease.[37] Meanwhile, whole books have been devoted to explaining robust and complex links between cancer and the environment.[38] In the documentary *The Wisdom of Trauma* renowned medical doctor Gabor Maté sums this discussion up: "In the United States, the richest society in history, fully half of the citizens have a chronic disorder, such as high blood pressure or diabetes. Anxiety amongst young people is growing rapidly. Asthma and autoimmune diseases are on the rise, as are addictions. Depression is rising. Youth suicide is rising. All is not well."[39] It seems the deterioration of the planet's health is running in tandem with human mental health. Ultimately, it may not be possible to have true human well-being without ecological well-being, and both are entwined with seemingly disparate issues, such as Indigenous reconciliation, racial justice, gender rights, and many others.

Your well-being and that of the world's children is important. When we are mentally unwell and physically ill—or, worse, are rushing from crisis to crisis—we lack the capacity to make the kinds of deep cultural changes needed at this time. When in survival mode, we are low on the mental, emotional, and physical resources needed to cope with complexities. The same may be true for those of us traumatized by standard schooling, systemic racism, or a host of other traumas linked to contemporary North American culture. Yet, due to an individualistic focus, the solutions offered by contemporary mainstream culture are too narrow in scope to truly engage with this substantive work.

Mainstream neoliberal culture separates us from the natural world and in so doing contributes to ill health. This alienation then leads to further destruction of the planet and deepening health challenges—and finally to the problematic, self-fulfilling move to blame these challenges on the isolated individual. Too great a burden is placed on individuals, who are expected to fix themselves, even when the culture itself is making them ill. As Maté articulates, "The very essence of the society we live in, then—organized around disconnection, individualism, and compromised authenticity—breeds trauma, and thus engenders ill health."[40]

We've been talking here about the subtle but pervasive ways that mainstream culture undermines emotional, cognitive, and physical well-being. Across the globe, however, droughts, floods, storms, heat waves, and wildfires are having a brutal, direct impact on human lives. An alliance of the American Psychological Association and Eco-America reports that, as homes, lives, livelihoods, and communities are lost due to climate change, "increases in trauma and shock, post-traumatic stress disorder (PTSD), compound stress, anxiety, substance abuse, and depression" are occurring.[41] Impacted communities experience elevated rates of violence and mental health emergencies, along with "loss of social identity and cohesion, hostility, violence, and interpersonal and intergroup aggression." The alliance notes that women, children, the poor, the disabled, the elderly, Indigenous communities, and some communities of color are particularly at risk. Most importantly, they assert that "climate solutions are available now, are widespread, and support psychological health."

Rather than gripping tightly to outdated ideologies, we would do well to look at what actually contributes to improved well-being—for us and for our fellow humans and more-than-human kin. If we come together to lean in and learn from all-our-relations, we may begin to understand our illnesses as having meaning that goes beyond ourselves. We are sick because the earth is unwell. And the earth's illnesses are, in part, a product of alienation, extending beyond just the physical to include the mental, emotional, and relational. Working from a sense of innate belonging, we can turn to the earth to heal through relationships—through living with, touching, breathing in, and protecting the wild places that live around, touch, breathe with, and protect us.

The Gift of Healing

When Anton, a neurodivergent boy, first arrived at the Maple Ridge Environmental School in grade 1, he had difficulty interacting with other children in socially appropriate ways. Consequently, he lived on the fringes of the group until, as resource teacher Jodi MacQuarrie put it, "he made inroads with one student."[42] At the environmental school, just like at his previous school, Anton's nervous system would often become either over- or understimulated by noise. Back at his conventional school, these nervous-system interferences were probably calmed with white-noise headsets, balls, fiddle toys, and a sensory room. At the ecologizing school, Anton has found other ways to cope with these challenges. He quickly gravitated to sticks and pinecones as fiddle toys. And the less-structured approach at the environmental school allows him to find places, micro-niches, that help him to self-regulate without interventions and in interesting ways. An open field or an ordered woodcut becomes a haven from overstimulation, and a riparian zone or ecotonal area filled with diversity becomes the location for counteracting understimulation. The freedom to move his body as needed allows these interactions with the space and place to occur in rich ways.

Anton's relationships with other children improved when he began to successfully manage his sensory load. Doing so required increasing self-awareness and complex negotiation of natural spaces. Through being attuned to self and by experimenting with locale, all of Anton's relationships improved. The diverse terrain and beings that Anton encountered in various locations healed through *relationship* to place. How different this was from the standard sensory room that neurodivergent students like Anton often experience. Anton came to know the trees, bushes, and birds that frequented these diverse spaces. Essentially, he learned to locate himself in the landscapes that were emotionally, mentally, and physically supportive of him. On top of this, as he developed this care for and interest in the place and its myriad denizens, he began to develop skills needed to be a good bird watcher (for Anton it was all about birds). Careful "fox steps" (slow movements), "owl eyes" (scanning vision), and "deer ears" (attentive listening)[43] became important skills for Anton, which also became helpful and transferrable skills in other settings. "The library is a good place to use our fox steps, Anton," teacher might remind.

Western science has only recently turned toward the idea that being in nature may confer cognitive, emotional, and physical benefits. Research in this field is relatively new, extremely promising, and likely to develop significantly over the next decade or so. It seems that every year new studies uncover yet another reason to celebrate walking in forests, swimming in natural bodies of water, and interacting with soil. In insidious and invisible ways, modern humanmade spaces sometimes undermine health, relationships, and the profound connection between them, but the benefits of natural spaces may be rendered similarly invisible due to cultural biases. While it is obvious that encounters with falling trees, cougars, and other natural dangers remind us of the need for responsible and informed outdoor experiences, the inherent boons of experiencing wilder green spaces have been largely overlooked by Western science until recently.

Where mainstream culture struggles to resolve burgeoning anxiety and other mental health disorders, nature exposure offers some perhaps surprising protections and remedies. Researchers studied almost a million Danish residents and discovered a link between the amount of green space children were exposed to and the likelihood of them developing a psychiatric disorder. Specifically, children who grew up around fewer forests, fields, and parks were 55 percent more likely to develop schizophrenia, depression, bipolar disorder, an eating disorder, and other psychiatric disorders by the teen years or young adulthood.[44] The study controlled for socioeconomic factors, family history of mental illness, and even urbanization. Elsewhere, ecopsychologists have been exploring the mental health advantages of open-water swimming and horticulture therapy.[45] Looking at studies from countries across the globe, Masashi Soga and colleagues concluded that regular gardening results in "a wide range of health outcomes, such as reductions in depression, anxiety, and body mass index, as well as increases in life satisfaction, quality of life, and sense of community."[46] The environmental scientist Ming Kuo concludes: "The range of specific health outcomes tied to nature is startling, including depression and anxiety disorder, diabetes mellitus, attention deficit/hyperactivity disorder (ADHD), various infectious diseases, cancer, healing from surgery, obesity, birth outcomes, cardiovascular disease, musculoskeletal complaints, migraines, respiratory disease, and others. . . . Finally, neighborhood greenness has been consistently tied to life expectancy and all-cause mortality."[47] Even with limited research, we're already seeing that nature exposure can benefit aspects of human cognition, behavior, physiology, and psychology in wide-reaching ways.

Kuo and others have tried to identify precisely *how* human health benefits from nature exposure.[48] Numerous theories have been posited. One suggests that the benefits of nature exposure are linked to human psychology. People tend to relax when they see the color green or hear the sound of ocean waves or trickling water. Kuo notes that health benefits could be a result of "deep relaxation, attention restoration, impulse control" along with better air quality, physical activity, social ties, and sleep.[49] On the other hand, perhaps the benefits are less about human psychology and more about the way the body processes sensory and somatic experiences. Fractals are geometric patterns of diminishing sizes commonly found in nature, such as the spiral of a snail shell or the narrowing of a fern frond. Providing both comfort and stimulation to humans, the mathematical design of fractals "evokes active interest" and "allow[s] for inward attention and restoration," according to Caroline Hagerhall and her team of researchers.[50] They also discovered that natural soundscapes, such as birdsong and ocean waves, induced a feeling of tranquility and may contribute to "stress recovery," while humanmade soundscapes of the same volume and quality were consistently perceived as more aggravating.[51]

It seems, though, that many of the health benefits of nature tend toward physiological pathways rather than sensory or psychological ones. Negative air ions, found in high concentrations near waterfalls and in forests, appear to reduce depression and improve cognitive function while offering a host of other potential benefits that are still being studied.[52] Inhaling phytoncides (microscopic organic compounds that drift off plant matter) increases natural killer cells, which help the immune system fight infections and cancer.[53] Exposure to dirt, particularly from wild soils as opposed to urban or monocropped soils, appears to increase beneficial gut microbes, which reduces the risk of food allergies, asthma, and other inflammatory diseases.[54] Winfried Blum and colleagues suggest that, in light of the increase in diseases associated with the human intestinal microbiome, "it may be useful to adopt a different perspective and to consider the human intestinal microbiome as well as the soil/root microbiome as 'superorganisms' which, by close contact, replenish each other with inoculants, genes and growth-sustaining molecules."[55] Kuo concludes that the nature-health dynamic can likely be best summed up by suggesting that nature simply "enhance[s] immune function."[56] This is just a brief overview of what constitutes a rapidly growing body of evidence about previously unknown (at least in the West) health impacts of living in and being regularly exposed to our natural habitats as a species.

Beyond the question of *how* nature benefits health is yet another question: *Why* does nature benefit human health? If our more-than-human neighbors predominantly experience humans as a blight upon the earth (more about this belief later), wouldn't they have collectively evolved to ward us off? Individual species of flora and fauna have done this or do this in moments as necessary. Poison Oak and its cousins leave an itchy and blistering "do not touch" message on human skin but are harmless to dogs, birds, and most other animals.[57] Yet even here, the situation is much more complex than it initially appears. Indigenous Americans used the cooked poison oak plant medicinally to treat dysentery and diarrhea, while the dried and powdered plant was used effectively to heal wounds.[58] In *The Botany of Desire,* Michael Pollan traces the mutuality of the relationship of humans and several plants—Apple, Tulip, Marijuana, Potato—suggesting, quite compellingly, that these beings are equally involved in the back and forth "manipulation" of humans for their own benefit.[59]

Ultimately, answering the *why does nature help us* question takes us into the realm of worldviews. Sheridan and Longboat remind us that, from a Haudenosaunee perspective, *all* imaginative solutions and creative ideas are gifted from our more-than-human relations and that this gifting is a fundamental design to life on earth.[60] In her book *Braiding Sweetgrass,* the plant ecologist Robin Wall Kimmerer explains: "We make a grave error if we try to separate individual well-being from the health of the whole. The gift of abundance from pecans is also a gift to themselves. By sating squirrels and people, the trees are ensuring their own survival."[61] Kimmerer explains a worldview wherein "random acts of kindness" from the land are freely available to the humble and open-eyed.[62] In the gift worldview, abundance, connection, respect, responsibility, and gratitude are key, while reciprocity is the central feature.[63] The gift worldview contradicts many aspects of human life that neoliberal capitalism pedals as fact: that nothing worthwhile is freely given, that everything can be purchased, that the world is fundamentally a place of competition, and that scarcity is the driving truth of our existence. In fact, many humans have been so conditioned by this "logic" that even when freely offered a gift—a compliment, a basket of strawberries, a paid day off work—their automatic response is either to refuse—*Oh, no, I'm not deserving. I haven't earned it*—or to be suspicious of the giver's motive—*What are the strings attached? What do you want from me?*

If we begin to see the world as a place of abundance, the yearning and urgency to participate in consumerism wane. Wildflowers offer rich stashes of Pollen to Butterfly. Maple offers diverse climbing experiences for children. Fresh water, clean air, firewood, basket-making materials, Blackberry, Thimbleberry, Fiddlehead, Stinging Nettle, Salmon, and Clam are a few of the gifts offered in our generous region of the world. All these gifts are operating in relation, in complex circles and cycles of reciprocity. Salmon offers self to Bear, Bear leaves parts of Salmon as gifts to Cedar (see the nitrogen cycle), Cedar provides shade and holds soil that keeps water cool and clear, which is the perfect home for wee Salmon.

Kimmerer clarifies, "In the gift economy, gifts are not free. The essence of the gift is that it creates a set of relationships."[64] Gifts entail responsibilities to respect the spaces and lives of these species, to respect them with gratitude, humility, and an eye toward our shared future. While not all ecosystems are the same, generosity and reciprocity are primary qualities of the majority of Earth's terrain. Kimmerer invites us to consider the "honorable harvest," where we respect nature's gifts, ask before taking, take only what's needed, and share the bounty.[65] When humans see the world as a place of complex supportive interactions, natural abundance, and gifts—rather than a place where they must "compete ferociously, even pitilessly, to maintain or improve [their] position"[66]—they tend to turn toward more generous, reciprocal, cooperative, and relational ways of being in the world. They accept nature's gift of healing.

Linear Time and the "White Man's Apocalypse"

Climate change and other anthropogenically caused environmental challenges are tragically impacting ecosystems and individual species, but are they causing increasing crisis, unrest, and health challenges in human lives? Your answer to that question depends, in part, on who you are. Over the past several centuries, white people (particularly men) and the wealthy have tended to live stable, prosperous lives where "progress" and comfort are linked to income. Many people in these groups have been shocked and galvanized as news of climate change has become a daily, no longer ignorable event. Activists working from this standpoint might call on fellow humans to mobilize and attend to the urgency—before all hell breaks loose.

However, many African Americans note that all hell broke loose a long way back. "Armageddon *been*-in-effect"[67] for hundreds of years, as the hip-hop group *Public Enemy* put it. African American individuals and communities have faced and continue to face uncertain, disrupted, environmentally degraded,[68] and dangerous conditions on a daily basis. Segregation, the "war on drugs,"[69] racialized incarceration, deaths at the hands of police officers, doubled rates of COVID-19 deaths,[70] and stress caused by systemic and chronic racism, which tends to wear down the body and reduces life spans,[71] are all affecting health and well-being. Additionally, African Americans tend to have to live in more environmentally problematic areas. These realities—often overlooked by white activists—caused one recent Afrocentrism conference attendee to comment that this climate change disaster is just "the white man's apocalypse" and that "the world has always been coming to an end for Black people."[72]

Similarly, genocide, repeated plagues, residential school systems, loss of land, and outlawed and suppressed cultures have prevented a sense of stability, security, health, and well-being for nations of Indigenous peoples. The turmoil of today's heightened natural disasters and COVID-19 epidemic are set within a wider context of disruptions. Stan Rushworth reports:

> Between 1848 and the late 1870s, there was a 90 percent population reduction of California Indians. That's what I would call a disruptive time for Indigenous people. . . . So, to me, these disruptive times are more of the same. When you have sixty million buffalo killed in sixty years, forty million killed in one twelve-year period, in order to starve the Plains people into submission in the 1800s, that's the same kind of thing. So, to the destruction people now are saying is "the end of life as we know it," I say, "well, talk to . . . an Indigenous person if you want to know what that's like."[73]

The phrase "the end of life as we know it" contains different shades of meaning depending on who is hearing it.

It's tempting to point out that for the more-than-humans of the earth, the stakes are higher than they've ever been. Although Bison, American Chestnut, Ohio River, Atlantic Cod populations, and a great many others have suffered ecocide, the scale of what's to come is unprecedented. The earth is in the sixth mass extinction.[74] Almost all our more-than-human brothers and sisters are at risk. Consequently, one might feel quite justified in shouting—for the sake of the earth: *We must stop the ecocide now! There's no more time to waste!*

Yet, according to some, it's precisely this attitude that has caused so much harm. As Rushworth responds, "There has never *been* time to waste." He believes that a major part of the problem lies with notions of linear time and with the fixation that *now* is independent of both past and future. When we conceive of time as a line aiming into an infinite future—where the present moment is a singular dot and the past extends "way back there"—we tend to see the past as irretrievable and the future as untouched. We are then accountable to neither.

Linearity is associated with ecologically problematic notions of efficiency and progress. And its focus tends to land on a small window of *now*, which leads to values that prioritize quick fixes over complex thinking, short-term gains over long-term impacts, and infrastructure development over preservation of wild spaces. Linear notions of time also make little room for the accounting of generational errors or suffering, for studying the cultural path that has led to looming ecological collapse, and for untangling the complexity of errors that link the two together. It also can lead us into solutions and responses that exacerbate the problems because the responses are arising within the same framework that caused the problems in the first place. *Humans know what is best. Science will pull us through. We now know enough to make the right decisions around conservation, stewardship, and the natural world.* For example, as Naomi Klein points out, many of the proposed eco-technicist solutions to climate change (for example, putting iron filings into the oceans and billions of mirrors into the atmosphere) are only likely to create further unanticipated problems.[75] Think of invasive species. Think of DDT as a pesticide. We usually think our interventions and manipulations of the environment are a good idea at the time.

Many Indigenous traditions view time in much less linear ways. In other words, what happened long ago may be close at hand and critical to the current moment and the future. The genocide of millions of Indigenous peoples is intricately woven with ongoing ecocide. Rushworth explains: "If everything is connected across time and space, then your sense of responsibility is to the entirety of time and space. If you see that everything you do through every day expands through all time and space, then there is no room for lack of responsibility."[76] Linearity, however, posits mainstream North American culture in a perpetual present, leaning toward the future. From that perspective, "history" becomes a "topic" to be studied and put away, like a textbook slipped back into a desk, rather than a literal living breathing reality of the present and the future. Bayo Akomolafe suggests that mainstream conceptions of time are degrading along with the environment and more ancient understandings are being revitalized and renewed:

> In fact, the Anthropocene does something queer and perverse to spacetime—upsetting its presumed linearity and unidirectionality, making the past contemporaneous with the present, and resituating the "future" with the present and the past in the thick "now." Time folds and melds in the Anthropocene the way taffy folds in on itself in the levers of a machine. My people, the Yoruba people, speak of circular time, slushy time, or time that collapses on itself. There are no arrows of time that fly forwards in Yoruba indigenous imagination; none of the incessant tick-tocking that has fuelled progress, that has become the soundtrack of our busy, delimited lives.[77]

Fueled by false beliefs in progress, North American settlers drained marshes, paved meadows, felled forests, and overused the planet to build schools and create a workforce to carry on the project of progress into an infinite and bright future.

Ecologizing education seeks to slow down this relentless forward momentum. When children study tree rings and geology, they begin to see that time is experienced in a variety of ways by our more-than-human relations and is far more complex than a line. Although we may not know for sure how our more-than-human relations operate, it seems that many plants and animals orient their lives around seasons, which are by definition cyclical, not linear. A river too may appear linear at first glance. But at any given point, it embodies the past—in the form of sediment, plant debris, salmon smolts, and the mineral memory of snow and ice. Carrying this recent and distant past, the river crashes on in a fleeting but perpetual present, as it rushes toward the future only to return to the headwaters as fresh rain in a month or a year's time. The future and past are made present again. In this way, a river's embodiment of time is innately entangled with past-present-future in a paradoxical knot of fluidity.

Nonlinear conceptions of time allow for deeper personal, community, and ecological healing. Some African American artists and scholars have turned to the philosophical and artistic movement of Afrofuturism (and retro-Afrofuturism) to locate hope, justice, and identity in the past-present-future. They see Afrofuturist novels, theatre productions, and music as opportunities to "critically review and repurpose lost avenues and buried horizons, as they reassess, reinvent and re-turn the past so as to unearth and infiltrate new futures into the present."[78] We sense that this hopeful move, toward recognizing one's rich roots, toward what some Canadian scholars are calling "resurgence," is a clear part of the path to cultural change and healing.

Afrofuturism's approach to time, as Tobias Van Veen explains, is aligned with *sankofa*, a Twi language word from Ghana, meaning "go back and get it."[79] The Black Student Union at the University of Illinois explains *sankofa* this way: "'Sankofa' teaches us that we must go back to our roots in order to move forward. That is, we should reach back and gather the best of what our past has to teach us, so that we can achieve our full potential as we move forward. Whatever we have lost, forgotten, forgone, or been stripped of can be reclaimed, revived, preserved, and perpetuated."[80] We highlight Afrofuturism, *sankofa*, as more spacious orientations to time to encourage individuals and communities to creatively respond to the questions of time and healing in ways that are personally, culturally, locally significant to them and to the places they inhabit.

An ecological approach to healing comes from honest recognition of uncomfortable emotions and a more wholistic understanding of time and our interconnectedness. We cannot heal alone. We need to heal together, with each other and with our more-than-human relations. Rushworth[81] believes that all of us—regardless of our cultural background—contain within us the memory of how to live well with the earth. It is time to "go back and get" what we lost, what we left behind or forgot, so more-than-humans and humans might heal together.

Healing the Wounds of Privilege and Power

Just as divergent emotions—say, joy and grief—may spring from the same source, so too might seemingly unconnected social issues. Indeed, many social issues are linked with ecologizing work. For example, eco-feminists have drawn attention to the parallels between men's treatment of nature and of women, suggesting that both nature and women are oppressed by the power dynamics inherent in patriarchal societies. The bodies of both have been subjected to violence, control, and domination. Val Plumwood maintains that the "backgrounding" and "instrumentalisation" of women and nature result from cultures being overly reliant on emotionally detached rationality.[82] Gilligan and Snider clarify that men also suffer under these systems because they are pressured to sever deep emotional attachments in order to conform to narrow parameters of socially accepted behavior.[83] They continue: "The sacrifice of love is the thumbprint of patriarchy. It clears the way for establishing and maintaining hierarchy. Patriarchy is an order of living that privileges some men over other men (straight over gay, rich over poor, white over black, fathers over sons, this religion over that religion, this caste over the others) and all men over women."[84] And all humans over nature.

While it's true that some men reap the benefits of patriarchy's narrowed expectations and power hierarchies, most men experience a mix of harms and privileges. Under patriarchal systems, many men, along with women and children and LGBTQ2+ individuals, can become disconnected from their emotions, pushed socially into voicelessness and inauthenticity in order to superficially belong. Because of this, they may not understand why or even that they feel frustration, rage, or pain. As a result, these men may take actions and make decisions that cause them and others harm without understanding their own motivations. These inner conflicts are often evidenced during the teen years. A teen boy may permanently sever his relationship to Creek and Maple with whom he spent his childhood in order to "fit in" and not seem like a "sissy" at school.[85] At these ecologizing schools, the teen boys who are afraid of their attachments to the more-than-humans around them and to each other may find themselves killing ants and trees or using homophobic slurs in order to "perform" maleness in a patriarchal, heteronormative, anti-environmental world.

Healing, in the ecologizing sense, means having the willingness to see the unhelpful ways we have internalized the structures of society. In reality, this can mean—for all of us, at some point—confronting both pain and guilt. In the section that follows, we examine a parallel situation: first the human story and then the more-than-human. In so doing, we follow the eco-feminist parallel between the female body and the body of the earth. In both cases, suffering has occurred and is largely hidden from view. By following the first to some depth, we find shared cause with the other. By extension, we can see that the resolution to one may also offer insights into working toward resolving the other. We don't highlight these tragedies to mire readers in discomfort. Rather, we understand that by acknowledging trauma and bravely examining the forces that compel it, we are better able to address it, protect against it, and heal from it. By seeing the complexity of threads knotting together culturally destructive ways, we are better able to untangle the whole mass. In seeking healing—or even a cure—it is helpful first to correctly identify the problem(s). Accurate diagnoses require a willingness to *see* the problem despite potential discomfort. In the healing process, discomfort is often the signal that something is shifting, changing, and even improving.

Students and teachers do not arrive to educational spaces as blank slates. Both may carry trauma. Sadly, within a span of several months, three promising, up-and-coming educators and one student separately confided in us that they are currently coping with the emotional fallout of a sexual assault. Like a sinister stone tossed in still water, sexual assault events ripple out across time and across communities, disrupting the individual's capacity to lead, learn, or connect. Since few individuals—quite understandably—feel safe publicly disclosing their experiences, these individual traumas are typically weighted with the burden of secrecy as well. By bearing witness to them here, we hope to overcome the silencing and assist in the healing.

Unbeknownst to each other and everyone else in the class, both the preteen student and her instructor struggle with invisible barriers as they try to focus on the lesson at hand. However, their wounds are slow to heal because the underlying cultural tendencies that caused their assaults haven't changed, so the threat of assault has not ended. It will not end until these toxic cultural patterns are redressed. In all but one of these cases, the perpetrator has neither been charged nor confronted due to the victim's sense of shame and the he-said-she-said nature of judicial trials. What hope is there for widespread healing and recovery amid that reality? Even if—despite the odds—these individuals are able to recover, other traumatized individuals will soon take their place because the root causes of these atrocities have not been addressed.

Likewise, the root causes of ongoing environmental degradation have not been addressed. Through tremendous effort, one community saves a river from toxic chemicals dumped by a local factory. Meanwhile, a similar factory has set up shop within the sacred landscapes of an Indigenous community. Eagle flourishes again, thanks to habitat restoration projects, while Salmon perishes in shallow, overheated rivers during a record-breaking heat wave. The teacher-in-training, who is now too frightened to walk alone, watches from her apartment window as the yellowed leaves of Birch fall two weeks too early. These troubles are not accidentally brushing up against each other; they share many roots: cultural norms that reward and prioritize destructive power, selfish individualism, and alienation.

Let's pursue the parallel situation further. Back to the human story for a minute. One of the assaults that took place in our recent circle exemplifies something that is distressingly common. In this case, both the victim and the perpetrator of the assault are known and loved by the community. People of any gender can be victims of assault, but in this instance, the victim is a teenage female. Even many months after the incident, the trauma she has experienced impacts her daily life. She disassociates regularly, is often queasy about being touched, now operates from a position of distrust and suspicion of men, and so on. The assailant is a teen male. He is not evil, inherently selfish, or even particularly unusual for a modern, Western man. In many moments, he acts kindly, putting others' needs ahead of his own.

The question arises: Why did the assault occur in the first place? That is, why did this particular person feel entitled to act as he did in that moment despite knowing (as he later admitted) that sexual intercourse was not wanted by the female? Broadly speaking, sexual assaults have long been explained as a desire for power and domination,[86] as motivated by the cultural objectification of women,[87] or as a "mating strategy" for highly selfish men.[88]

But in this particular case, the perpetrator himself has difficulty coming up with an answer to the question. He suggests that, in the moment, he wasn't thinking clearly and just didn't want to stop. He suggests that in the critical moment he just prioritized his own desires. This response evidences the psychic split in the relational self, where knowing (that the female didn't want sex) and not knowing (choosing not to see her distress) coexist. Here, the selfish male urge is prioritized, even culturally sanctioned, and the relational urge is repressed. Although he feels terrible, in private with other male friends he seeks to underplay his impact, to not know the pain he has caused, to minimize his responsibility by saying that other guys have committed "far worse" assaults. If he is like most perpetrators of assault, he has also significantly underestimated and didn't care enough to notice the impact his actions would have on the victim of his assault. While he may or may not have immediately registered some of the harm he caused, much of it, for cultural and psychological reasons, remained "invisible" to him. This invisibility too is a by-product of an individualistic orientation.

Educational spaces also may carry "invisible" or at least overlooked scars. The school building may sit where Beaver used to dam up Streams, where Waxwing used to rest and refuel during long migrations, where the local Indigenous population, prior to being forcibly pushed out by settler populations, engaged in age-old traditions of sustenance, ceremony, and social interaction. Just as the human perpetrator of sexual assault may not witness the vast fallout from his actions, descendants of colonizers and newer settlers are often in a state of "not knowing" the *ongoing* impact of these wrongs. This kind of "not knowing" is baked into the settler culture through educational omissions, systemic racism, human elitism, and an emphasis on individualistic values. And the excuses that sustain this detached knowing are present as well. In the meantime, the songbird population has plummeted. The local Indigenous population likely continues to experience the fallout of inherited trauma, loss of place-specific language and history, and a sense that their community's identity has been fractured by broken ties to their traditional lands.

In fact, once a person begins looking around at our North American lifestyle, it's easy to see the harms enacted upon our more-than-human neighbors. Cell phones, toxin-sprayed mattresses, fast fashion, exhaust-spewing oversized vehicles, and all those office supplies shipped from across the ocean are a few of the things we use daily that harm plants, animals, soil, water, air, and each other. The mind can easily boggle tallying up all the damage and confronting the ways that we, personally, are directly implicated in that damage. For some ecologically minded people, these realizations trickle in slowly over the course of years, eliciting a steady stream of emotional and lifestyle adjustments. For others, they crash through all at once, causing an existential crisis. Indeed, these realizations are often what lead people to pick up a book like this in the first place. Certainly, we have walked through our own canyons of guilt and despair, emotions that—along with love and gratitude for the natural world—have motivated this book and the work it seeks to further.

We live in a society where environmental harms are ongoing, pervasive, and nearly impossible to extricate oneself from. In fact, those who try often find themselves so far removed from society, they can no longer effect change within it. Because anti-ecological values underscore almost all aspects of North American culture, for most of us a gap persists between our ecological values and our actual ecological impacts. Even when we sense the gap, we can resist acknowledging it for complex psychological reasons, some of which we have pointed toward already. In part, we may simply have difficulty imagining another way to be in the world. (Part of the project of Maple Ridge was to offer an ongoing opportunity to imagine and experience a different way of teaching and learning and even being human.)

Further, though, as Gilligan and Snider clarify, "we can unconsciously absorb and reify a framework that we consciously and actively oppose."[89] To some extent, this may be a matter of not seeing the forest for the trees. Just as the young perpetrator of sexual assault may have great difficulty identifying and separating himself from the culture that objectifies women, fractures relationships, valorizes power, and encourages selfish individualism—North Americans may have difficulty identifying and extricating themselves from the culture that objectifies nature, fractures relationships with nature, valorizes power over nature, and encourages selfish anthropocentrism.

What can we do, then, to first recognize and then shift unresolved trauma and turn toward reconnection? In answering this question, some may find that, here too they have absorbed a framework misaligned with their ultimate goals and values. According to North American justice systems (and many religions), perpetrators should be punished, and the shame and threat of further punishment will supposedly prevent wrong actions from being repeated. As a primary mode of justice, this way of thinking sits firmly on the belief that the world is ultimately made up of separate entities who bump up against each other in conflict or relationship. Firstly, this system of justice focuses on individuals rather than on their contexts (it's not incidental that a great many maximum-security prisoners are also survivors of horrific childhoods and patently dysfunctional educational systems). By zeroing in on the individual, our justice system tends to treat the symptoms of dysfunction—the individual crime and criminal—rather than the cause—the familial, community, and cultural contexts. Secondly, while an ecosystem functions as a larger, shifting, dynamic balance of forces, the culture of punitive justice imagines that large swaths of the social ecosystem can simply be *disconnected* from the rest with no further impact.

Let's return to the story of assault for further exploration. What would the young male perpetrator of assault need to do to truly reconcile with the young woman he harmed and the community he impacted? In this instance, he has already taken the first steps in restorative justice and healing: he apologized, accepted blame, and told the wider community the truth to alleviate the burden of secrecy on the victim. Since issues of masculine power and privilege are so pervasive in our society, he needs help to identify that psychological patterning both in the wider culture and in himself. Here, he might examine deep-seated beliefs about the roles and rights of women and men, how those beliefs contradict his conscious values, and the excuses he makes to himself that allow him to act outside his professed values.

Bringing to light psychological patterning can be helpful in addressing ecological harms too. Shifting oneself away from the broader societal machinery of anti-ecologicalism is extremely difficult and an ongoing process, but the first step involves identifying the underlying beliefs and values of anti-ecologicalism and the way they condition our own thinking and actions. We may need deep and consistent immersion and engagement with the more-than-human world, but we also need criticality, to enable us to identify belief patterns previously obscured by status quo ways of being. We need to ask ourselves some difficult questions: How might an admission of truth begin an ecological reconciliation process? What specific harms have we caused? Who in the more-than-human realm has been harmed, directly or indirectly? How has the burden of secrecy been felt? In examining the reasons that we personally act outside our ecological values, perhaps we may find an echo of the sexual assaulter's justifications. We may find ourselves thinking: *The rights of the more-than-human were not as important to me in those moments. Everybody is doing these things. In fact, the actions of many others are far more heinous than mine. Besides, I really wanted to do x, y, and z. And I've been slow to or don't want to truly recognize the impact I've had.*

Perhaps too the dominant North American culture undermines environmental efforts not only by prioritizing opposing values (anthropocentrism, hyper-individualism, dominance over nature) but also by inadvertently instilling a sense of angst. Gabor Maté writes, "To be normal in this society is to conform to requirements that are profoundly abnormal in regard to human nature itself, contrary to it and thus harmful to human beings."[90] Frustration, powerlessness, and the grief of profound disconnection may, in part, motivate sexual assault, self-sabotaging ecocidal behavior, and a host of other toxic tendencies. For example, this particular young male perpetrator of assault may have been acting out of a deep-seated, unconscious or conscious sense of anger and inadequacy resulting from the emotional and psychic injuries of living in a culture of hyper-separation, competition, and trivial materialistic rewards.

Colonialization, racism, misogyny, and the destruction of nature's ecosystems are born out of a false sense of entitlement and superiority. Indeed, they are born out of a fallacious sense of the individual as better than and isolated from others. Economic collapse instigated by fraudulent bankers and toxic wastes left by mining companies stem from deep-seated beliefs about whose "needs" trump whose. The destruction of family units in the wake of domestic abuse and the razing of rainforests result from savage and shortsighted abuses of power.

There are many reasons to resist the personal process of reconciliation. It hurts. It's uncomfortable. It's incredibly complex. In many ways, it's uncharted territory. And once we begin to recognize one wrong—the active marginalization, oppression, and abuse through clearcuts and a concretized urbanscape, for example—we bear witness to other atrocities—the forced expulsion, violent abuse, and cultural conformity experienced by the Coast Salish Peoples. Rushworth frames this moment of healing helpfully: "Facing errors is part of the way of being human. We have all these emotions for a reason—guilt is one of them. These emotions are tools. Indigenous sustainability comes from remembering where we've made huge mistakes, so we don't make them again. Indigenous stories tell what mistakes have been made, so we can remember."[91] While the pain and grief are real, we can face them with courage and humility. And despite the messages of the cultural positivity mandate, difficult emotions can prompt deeply transformative work. The reconciliation process is not prescriptive. The decisions made about what concrete actions will be taken and which will be ceased depend on factors individual to all the beings involved. There are at least as many positive, enduring ways to relate to the earth as negative ones. Whichever path of reconciliation we might take, the goal is the same: healing, more relationship and connection, expanded humility and sense of gratitude, and a renewed and changed understanding of what it means to be a human.

At the same time, it's important to remember that this is not an exercise in self-flagellation. The goal is not to sit around marinating in self-blame. Doing so merely enacts other psychoses. When Harney and Moten talk about the need to dismantle white power structures in *The Undercommons*, they write that "no one will really be able to embrace the mission of tearing 'this shit down' until they realize that the structures they oppose are not only bad for some of us, they are bad for all of us."[92] When we apply this thinking to the ecologizing project, we can assess all the ways that competitive, consumerist, anthropocentric culture harms *all* humans.

Expanding Possibility by Reducing Self-Suppression

The process of deep healing means being open to new possibility. But how can we be open when some of us have been taught since early childhood to suppress and censor ourselves and our knowing? How can we heal while at the same time busily suppressing that which we are not supposed to know? In this case, we can actively break down barriers by first acknowledging them.

One of these barriers to deep relationship may involve opting for shallower relationships and damaging interactions in a desire to fit in with societal norms. We may feel guilty about knowing what is supposed to be unknown and may suffer for feeling what many don't feel or have suppressed. For example, one young adult, a recent survivor of standard education, reports that he felt "guilt and embarrassment" and "worry" about picking up on the private emotional worlds of his teachers. He recalls, "It was like accidentally reading someone's diary. I felt part of the reason I know these things is because I'm different from other kids—and that's a bad thing."[93] Importantly, actively shutting down ways of knowing and feeling requires energy that could have been used elsewhere. It requires emotional distancing that can become a permanent state. Here is a boy who might choose to play with rough and unkind boys instead of lingering by the tree where he feels a sense of mutual caring and affinity. Here is the student who pretends not to know what the tree tells him about its root system, because the teacher doesn't seem to know, and it doesn't seem right to be differently knowledgeable than an adult. Here is the student who dreamed the night before that Woodland Salamander was calling to him, but the teacher wants to explore something else.

The fear of being emotionally overwhelmed is another barrier we might be called upon to acknowledge. One ecologically concerned researcher recently opined, "I don't want to feel that much grief." In fact, for some particularly sensitive and relationally attuned children, a deliberate emotional-psychic shutting down is a fact of school as familiar as pencil and paper. And while walking around as a living sponge absorbing everything is likely unhelpful for anyone (except, maybe, sponges), so too is deliberate and chronic self-censorship. Many children have learned the hard way that living with deeply engaged relationships within conventional education ironically leads to loneliness and isolation in the human realm in our current culture.

On the other hand, deep relationships with more-than-humans are meaningful bonds. They can offer children and adults greater clarity about the organization of the world. These relationships offer guidance and protection at multiple levels—from sensing that the tree drawing needs more branches, to sensing the presence of Bear. Protectiveness goes the other way too because the boy who "listens" as the tree describes the breadth of its roots will work to protect those roots from harm. These deep relationships also allow children to belong, to be truly seen—their whole personhood acknowledged—and to be emplaced; likewise, the more-than-humans are truly seen—their whole beingness acknowledged. As Rasunah Marden notes, "'firsthand knowledge,' or *experience*, reveals that the essence of particular natures, or spirit, within all created beings can eventually be discovered and personally understood."[94]

These are intercultural relationships—where one party brings a human culture and the other party, a more-than-human culture. Diversity in these relationships, just like human cultural diversity in an ordinary classroom, leads to greater creativity and expands our possibilities regarding how we might *be* in the world.[95] These relationships can be a curative for loneliness and offer a sense of joined forces, even belonging, for the oppressed. Additionally, the kinds of intuitive knowledges made available by sharing within the context of these deep relational bonds are wide-ranging and can be transferred more quickly and more accurately since they aren't reliant on clumsy and limited human language.

Ultimately, ecological healing is about returning to the relational and recognizing the inherent gifts and obligations within relationships. As we make room to know differently, including listening to the relational self and listening—or re-listening—to all-our-relations, we may come to accept that more relational, shared knowing is not only *possible* but *likely* when we recognize and prioritize our deep connections—the betweenness—rather than seeing only individuals and objects precariously connected through thin and easily broken lines.

Ecological healing also means recognizing that the current culture unjustly awards power and privileges to some, leaving a disproportionate burden of linked social and environmental problems to others. Although the guilt, grief, and anger can be overwhelming at times, we can find ways to support each other through the journey, increasing equality and sidestepping the cultural snares of performed happiness and hyper-individualism. By healing the split psyche and returning to our whole selves, we can renew and celebrate fractured alliances with the more-than-human world.

When we fall ill, in mind or body, we might begin by asking: How might this illness evidence my link to the natural world and the conditions my more-than-human relations are suffering? When we identify illness in our more-than-human relations, we might begin by asking: How might my own actions have contributed to this and what actions are called for now? We can also mirror the wisdom of ecosystems by recognizing diversity in our own species as a sign of health.

All of these inquiries involve deep epistemological, ontological, axiological, cosmological, and psychological work. And it is to these five "ologies" that we turn our attention next. For some, ecological healing is inherently spiritual, a partaking in ancient renewals of hope, gratitude, and responsibility. And for all, this healing is also fundamentally a physical journey, as we step more often and more respectfully into wild places and spaces to sink our extremities into the sand, to stare up at the stars, to touch the ragged bark of our neighbors, to smell the Oregon Grape blooming in December, to immerse and encounter, and to feel gratitude for the love and abundance offered to us.

4

THEORIZING
Exploring the Five "Ologies" of Cultural Change

Giant Redwood Trees tower above tiny humans in Navarro River State Park in California. A dozen miles away in Van Damme State Park, however, a collection of Cypress and Pine stand barely inches taller than an average human. The trees in both areas may be one hundred years old or older, yet Redwood shoulders hundreds of feet into the sky while Cypress and Pine average less than an inch of growth per year. The trunks of the redwoods are so wide, it would take several people holding hands to circle their base. In contrast, a person could easily circle the trunks of the cypresses with thumb and forefinger.

What causes the difference between these trees? At first glance, one might conclude that tree variety is responsible for the discrepancy. After all, Redwoods are one of the largest tree varieties in the world. But Pine can grow over 200 feet and Cypress over 100 feet in some areas. The primary difference, in fact, lies in the soil. The soil's depth or shallowness, acidity or alkalinity, sandiness or clayeyness—as well as its nutrient values—account for these differences by offering the perfect terrain for redwoods in one location and making redwood life impossible in another. Where shallow soil in sections of Van Damme Park cancels Redwood life, it provides a unique—if harsh—space for the heartiest Cypress and Pine to eke out a pygmy forest.[1]

Theory is like soil—often overlooked yet essential in determining the direction, rate, and variety of growth. The underlying theory that drives one's teaching practice has implications for how one teaches and what is learned. Consider this classic example: Are humans by nature—that is, as they arrive in the world at birth—good, bad, or neither? If educators perceive humans as fundamentally

98

good, they might chafe at deficit-thinking models, seek to find the good in all their students, or be willing to give students lots of space and autonomy (because they are unlikely to get up to too much mischief). If bad, educators might tend to prefer clear systems of rules and consequences to maintain order, seek to control the "bad eggs" with positive strokes, and worry about a class left alone because chaos might erupt. If neither, educators might actively try to provide rewards for goodness, do what they can to push learners away from troublesome influences and "bad" crowds, and tentatively try group work with the right mix of students.

Taking any one of these approaches doesn't necessarily indicate a philosophical position. Yet, often, we teachers don't even consider our position or our implicit assumptions. But over time, the actions a teacher or a system takes (or the actions the system requires teachers to take) become a pretty good indicator of one's stance. And this seemingly innocuous theoretical position can have huge implications.

Just like soil, theory provides a critical hummus that allows for certain growth, development, and actions—and not others. Theory is particularly significant when the project aims to change current cultural norms. Culture rests on implicit substrates—theoretical frames that shape and sustain it and act as guidelines for maintaining or sometimes changing culture. Ecologizing education argues that the culture of education in much of North American schooling is environmentally problematic and unjust—and needs to change. Thus, a close examination of the theories that sustain it is warranted. The challenge is to find replacement theories—but not replacements in the sense of maintaining the culture as it currently stands, like putting a new muffler on a gas-guzzling car. Rather, this deeper change is more like designing urban centers so that the car disappears altogether and people can walk or take alternative energy–powered public transit. This ecologizing work is not about tinkering—it's about substantive change.

Philosophers of education, who assess the theoretical structures important in macro-philosophical work, tend to focus on three overlapping and interconnected areas of inquiry: epistemology, ontology, and axiology. These three, along with cosmology and psychology, are critical to the project of ecologizing education. Providing a comprehensive understanding of these five "ologies" as they currently exist, overlap, influence, and sustain public education—or ecologizing education—is too mammoth a task for this book. And even though the ecologizing project clearly resonates globally and transculturally, it is just beginning to bud. Our project here, then, will be to tackle these issues as they emerge, from the ground up, in conjunction with and within rich communities of diverse humans and more-than-humans.

Ecologizing Epistemology: On the Question of Knowledge

Any attempt to seriously rethink education must necessarily tussle with knowledge, what those in the philosophy of education biz call "epistemology." Epistemology is the study of knowledge, and epistemologists ask questions such as the following: What *is* knowledge? How does knowledge work and get transferred? How are meaning made and understanding arrived at? How does one display knowledge? How do we come to know what another knows? Importantly, how does knowledge differ between and among communities and cultures? What knowledge is prioritized? Who is positioned as "knowing"? What are the ethical issues around knowledge? These questions are consequential for anyone involved in education—and particularly for those in ecologizing education, since understandings of knowledge can be more or less ecological in nature.

Our understanding of *what knowledge is* and *how it works* has implications for how we teach. It also affects how the learner comes to make sense of the world or even what world it is they know. *Different knowledge systems create different worlds.* That idea may sound odd, but it underscores this entire chapter. Just as beliefs about people being born good, bad, or neither influence pedagogical practice, so too do beliefs about the world being made of completely separate, detached objects or as communities of interactions. Similarly, beliefs about the world as being divided between human and other, animate and not, subject and object, influence pedagogical practice.

Let's examine epistemology by looking at three different metaphors for how knowledge and meaning-making might be understood. These metaphors illustrate that there isn't a single universal concept of knowledge. The way one understands knowledge, which is likely driven by the metaphors they choose to employ, has implications for how they teach. Further, one's understanding of knowledge also has implications for how the natural world is involved in the educational process.

Metaphor 1: Knowledge Grows Like Building a House

The house-building metaphor might be the most prevalent way that knowledge is understood within public education in North America. As with any building project, blueprints, guides, and official plans provide a clear sense of the final goal and the pieces needed to "construct" a knowledgeable person. A group of people are involved in interpreting those blueprints, and some are better at it than others, better at making the imagined appear in actuality. In this situation, that group includes teachers, parents/caregivers, and administrators. The vision-ary/architect behind all this might include educational theorists, historical practices, and maybe even the culture. Another component of the building metaphor is that things are added in a particular order. The shingles can't go on without a roof; the floor joists need a foundation.

Metaphors having to do with buildings and their construction are a common part of educational language. Teachers talk about "laying a good foundation" and "foundational skills," "scaffolding" the learner, "constructing" lessons, and even, sometimes, thinking outside "the frame." The process of building is pretty gener-alizable, sometimes incredibly so. Consider some of the recent suburbs appearing around big cities: the foundations always look the same, and every house needs a garage. As educators, we get a plan, something generally applicable, and we have the sense that knowledge is built up through individual fragments—like LEGO blocks—which when assembled correctly bring us to the desired outcome.

The builder makes decisions about *what*, *when*, and *where* with regard to the growing house. Foundational knowledge, once laid properly, supports further knowledge, eventually leading to a complete structure: a knowing adult, an en-gaged citizen, even. This process also implies that some fragments are basically useless until their time comes. No point offering up the chimney cap before the fireplace exists. In fact, the whole structure has the potential to collapse if not assembled thoughtfully and in the right order. This particular conception of knowledge, then, puts a lot of pressure on and power with the teachers/build-ers. Before the constructing process begins, a student's knowledge is just a hole in the ground and an empty lot. This metaphor can be expanded, of course, to add the natural world and the student themselves into the role of builders. Some might imagine this to be more like constructing a neighborhood, but it's still a building metaphor. Its key points are (1) the fragmented and ordered nature of knowledge; (2) the pretty generalizable route to being knowledgeable; (3) the in-dividual nature of the result; (4) the progression from less, empty, simple, in-complete to more, full, complex, finished; and (5) the role of teacher as builder and interpreter of blueprints.

Metaphor 2: Knowledge Grows Like Traversing a Spiderweb

On a bright spring day, graduate students in education gather on the lush, well-cared-for grass of a local urban park. Into the middle of the circle, the professor introduces a single wool sock. It is a fairly indistinct example of the sock spe-cies, except that it is exceptionally dirty. Its filth is the result of a mountain wan-der in receding snows. The professor's request regarding this soiled relic of high meanderings is that these teacher-learners partner and discuss the creation of lesson plans around the sock itself.

At first, the uptake is slow. The high school math and history teachers appear completely stumped, whereas the grade 4 teachers discuss how literacy requirements could be met through writing stories from the perspective of the sock and producing various poems about it. "Ode to the Filthy Sock" is sure to draw interest from the average nine-year-old.

Then, suddenly, inspiration strikes, and the history teachers begin seeing connections. What is the sock made of? What is the history of wool in the world? What role have sheep played in economic, environmental, and colonial realities across the globe? Soon they are on to issues of global trade, of migration, of invasive species, and of domestication. But what of the math teacher? Drawn in by the weft and warp of the sock, she explores questions of threads per square inch, of the mathematics of the weave itself. Because of its crusted mud, the sock holds its shape, and she recognizes the entrée into mapping, geometry, and even calculus. In fact, soon teachers are seeing connections between the sock and the entire content of their subjects and grades across the year. One educator comments: "I am amazed at how interconnected everything is."

The preceding is an example of the knowledge-as-spiderweb metaphor in action. Here knowledge has an interconnected nature such that one can travel from one place on the web to another via multiple routes. The classic spiderweb radiates threads out and away from a central point. But what is positioned at the center? Theories of knowledge tend to posit two answers to this question. The first, like the preceding tale, positions an object or an event in the center. For example, teachers in programs such as Expeditionary Learning will posit something like "ancient China" as the starting place and then build a monthlong integrated unit, touching into all subjects and required learning outcomes.[2] This webby theory of knowledge allows more space for spontaneous and unexpected occurrences. The diverse pathways of learning allow for different encounters along the way. Likewise, when taking a trip from Seattle to Toronto, the sites and sights will vary depending on the route taken. In some situations, the teacher becomes a facilitator and responder to the journey rather than the guide for it. This role calls for more trust in one's ability to find connections, ask good questions, and provide the rich, sometimes dirty, impetus.

The web's center can also be the student themselves. This positioning suggests that the student has myriad directions they might go and that knowledge is something the learner is immersed in. Knowledge is understood as being all-available, and exploring the knowledge web doesn't require a singular path, as is implied in the house metaphor. The paths through it are infinite, but choices must be made—one cannot necessarily jump from one part of the web to another. As such, the conception of knowledge as a web fosters a sense of learning as gathering, exploring, flexible, and growing. In this style of education, we can hear echoes of child-centered pedagogy with the teacher along for the ride, offering mediations and interventions when the learner finds themselves hanging upside down on the web of knowledge or tangled up and glued to a single strand.

Metaphor 3: Knowledge Grows Like Rhizomes

On a late fall day on Canada's West Coast, the graduate class wanders along the bank of a small stream. On this *sound walk*, the students are focused on listening. Recent rains have raised the water level, and initially most of the walkers sense just a singular roaring sound. However, as the class wends its way along and the teacher draws attention to careful listening, all begin to notice subtle differences. Sound rises and falls, wave-like, as they move closer and farther away. The underlying burbles and murmurs become more distinct and recognizable. The banks, log jams, and stones themselves shape, reflect, and influence the tenor and robustness of the sound. After about twenty minutes of this silent parade, the group gathers to reflect and respond to the experience.

Voices emerge slowly out of the shared sanctity of human silence. Some noticed the scratchings and twitterings of the variegated Thrushes gathering for the long flight south. Some wondered at the bass tones of big trucks passing on the highway below. Several noticed a plane passing high above. Still others noted the subtle changes of their own passing footsteps over the terrain. Many are struck by how much they *didn't* hear outside their own focus on the liquid symphony.

Each thread of discovery leads in a multiplicity of directions, which begin to emerge as the teacher searches for implications beyond the registered sounds. Some voices head in the direction of noise pollution, and a debate commences about felt differences between the natural and not-so-natural. Other voices are intrigued by the musicality of it all: where music comes from, what defines it, and whether some of these sounds could be produced on a sampler, a pulsing loop for a watery hip-hop. Still others begin to gather ideas around the physics of sound and the dynamics of water; some testing of theories ensues. One voice quietly suggests something important about the inner sounds, the times we lose connection to hearing the outside because we are contemplating something else. This strand leads to further discussions about attention, anxiety, and the challenges of being present.

Finally, a last voice wonders aloud how rocks, plants, stones, and birds feel about all this noise. Are some noises good and some painful? How does each individual find their own preferred situation in this soundscape? Eventually American Dipper pops into view at the edge of the wild water, drawing attention back to the musicality of stream and place. We move on to a more planned lesson with each student finding a natural noisemaker. Soon the glade is awash with sticks breaking, rocks banging, garbage crinkling, and voices howling. The stream seems to slide, surprisingly quietly, into the background.

This description of a learning experience rests on more recent theoretical work in philosophy and educational theory, work that critiques linearity and the compartmentalizable model of knowledge as well as the vision of the singular detached learner. Here the metaphor, drawn from the work of Deleuze and Guattari,[3] is the rhizome—those tiny, threadlike stem structures in some ferns, bamboos, and irises that spread out underground and fill the soils of the planet. In some places, thousands of miles of these beings weave through a cubic meter of dirt. Rhizomes have a remarkable capacity to press into any place and rise up through any crack with near-teleporting agility. A rhizome may follow a particular trajectory for a while but then stop, and suddenly another appears ten feet away, heading in a different direction. Then that one backtracks and joins with another that has been lying dormant for the last year.

The spontaneous, organic, surprising development that is characteristic of the rhizome parallels the diversity of responses from the sound walkers. During the sound walk, the student is immersed in knowledge and can be charging off, popping up, and resting in myriad locations all at the same time. Their sound observations lack an obvious linearity or directedness. This metaphor gains strength when one considers the soil and all its component beings to be knowledge, with the rhizomes as efflorescences of discovery. The teacher becomes, metaphorically, part of the soil, an aspect of the learning that is encountered, helps build richness, and is left behind—all at the same time. Given the more linear and "builderly" kind of training most educators have had, they are often challenged to imagine how this might work in practice. Yet thinking about knowledge in this way might help expand educational practices in important ecologizing ways.

Ultimately, finding metaphors that support one's theory and experience of knowledge is important. Metaphors can be generative, explanatory, and supportive, but they also shape and direct pedagogical imagination and implementation. Significantly different educational encounters for learners will be created by each of the various approaches to knowledge, that is, whether one is, metaphorically, building a house, traversing a spiderweb, or developing rhizomatically. Unsurprisingly, ecologizing education tends toward more natural metaphors, where knowledge is understood as being relational, diffuse, interconnectable, fluid, and shared. However, in any particular teaching moment, either the seemingly totally spontaneous or the linear blueprint approach could make more sense. Given that public education tends to prioritize a Western orientation to knowledge—fragmented, compartmentalizable, hyper-rational, and scientific—the educators at NEST and

Maple Ridge are working at finding ways to reduce the house-building approach and increase the web and the rhizomatic approaches. This idea of expanding the range of knowledges involved in education—shifting across the three metaphors or including nature and its denizens as co-teachers—has implications for practice and the ways educators might close off particular ways of knowing, often accidentally.

Here is a relatively common and seemingly innocuous situation. A six-year-old approaches their human teacher with a complex and intriguing question: "Why is Sky different shades of blue?" or "How come Leaf used to be green and is now mostly red?" or "If Lichen is actually a relationship between two or more beings, how do they come together in the first place?" Drawing from their own knowledge, the teacher responds by talking about the scattering of light rays, something related to sugar levels and how that interacts with various kinds of photosynthesizing cells, or maybe a mumbled comment about bumping into each other on a bare rock face.

These answers aren't wrong, although they are incomplete. What is important, though, is that each of these responses imposes epistemological assumptions on the questioner. In fact, any answer the teacher gives is necessarily incomplete, since answers to these questions are still growing, changing, and expanding. Yet offering an answer without a caveat—for instance, "there is much more to this, but this is what I know"—can suggest that the response *is* complete. This then reifies a series of assumptions: *Complete answers exist for most— even all—questions somewhere out there. There are experts who know these things. The process of acquiring knowledge is really about asking the right questions—to the right people—and then gathering the responses and building your own warehouse of knowledge. Humans, usually adults, are the sources of this knowledge, along with human tools like books or the internet. There is a potential totality in the process of knowledge-building, so we could eventually know it all. And in this way, we "make progress" and "perfect" our knowledge as we become older.* Of course, this is not really how knowledge works in an ecologizing education setting. Thus, the decision to answer the question without acknowledging its incompleteness deceives the questioner as to what knowledge is, where it is found, and how it might be held.

So, then, how do assumptions about knowledge shift with a different kind of answer? Consider these varied responses the teacher might give: "Interesting question—here is what I know about that subject, but it is definitely not the end of the story" or "Interesting question—what do you know about this?" or "Interesting question—let's get the group together and see what everyone thinks, and maybe then we could ask Google and your parents too" or "Interesting question—let's keep playing with it, but I think maybe we should ask this

Tree, and those Clouds, and spend more time with that Lichen, since they have some important insights." In short, the particular way a question is answered reveals how the speaker thinks knowledge works, where it is located, and how meaning is made. For ecologizing education, Lichen is a co-teacher, and as such, we might well ask whether Lichen has knowings to offer to our human understanding. In fact, some knowings aren't possible unless human learner and Lichen are co-present. Lichen might even care how they come to be known—most humans do, after all. Consequently, knowledge-building becomes a much more distributed, shared, and relational endeavor.

By conceptualizing and enacting knowledge in this way, ecologizing education also pushes back on some troublesome tropes explored throughout this book. The first trope is anthropocentrism and the notion that the human teacher is the gatekeeper to or has all the answers. In ecologizing education, we recognize the distribution and diffusion of knowing. We are moving the human from the center, from a position as "the being that knows" to a position as just one of many contributors in the process of coming to know. This not only decenters the human teacher but, interestingly, also undercuts the hierarchy between adult and child, expert and nonexpert. If the human teacher is but one source of knowledge, learners and their peers are also knowers who have something to offer.

A second trope addressed by this epistemological move away from the all-knowing human teacher is the idea of Truth with a capital T and the belief that any person can come to *completely* know anything. Here, in ecologizing education, knowledge is always incomplete, and even if we were to chase it forever, some things would still escape us, slide through our fingers—which has further varied and deeper implications. First, this image of knowledge escaping suggests that knowledge is no longer *in bondage*, no longer a *possession* of the human individual. Second, this incompleteness and slipperiness of knowing allow for the necessary and ongoing attitude of wonder. One can always ask more questions, hear more understandings, do more wonder wandering. And third, in ecologizing education, it is possible for knowledge to belong to a group/community such that each individual only ever holds a part thereof and the learning project expands beyond "I" to "we."

The third trope that ecologizing educations pushes back against is the prioritizing of a particular form of "reason"—where the subject and object of the "knowing" are detached and are in opposition to one another. This approach to reason and knowledge tends to ignore and even denigrate myriad other forms of knowing. For example, it often sidelines and dismisses Indigenous ways of knowing, where ceremony, the land, the ancestors are all involved;[4] or the experiential, physical, artistic knowing of craftspersons or labourers or nurturers;

or the knowing of Robin when Cooper's Hawk appears (and all other knowing that exists between, among, and throughout the natural world).

In sum, our conception of knowledge makes a difference, both in what can be learned and in our approach to teaching. Some metaphors of knowledge don't require humans to be the center, the all-knowing, the sole designer. And those metaphors better map onto our desire to decenter the human and bring the natural world into the educational process. How, then, can teachers evaluate their practices? How might they determine, for example, whether any particular lesson is ecologizing—or not? How might they make the necessary changes? For that, we need a bit of axiological talk.

Ecologizing Axiology: On the Question of Values

All cultures have value systems, ways deemed good or bad, actions that are praised or punished, and concepts of lives well lived. These ideas are often so deeply embedded in cultural norms that members thereof speak of "common sense" and "conscience," as if systems for knowing right from wrong were so obvious as to be undeniable, even immutable, laws written on the universe. But being "good" ecologically is often different from what public education thinks is good. The question then becomes one of seeking to understand how a culture comes to create, commit to, and change its values.

Axiology is, in part, the study of values—what is important to a community, how these things are determined, and what behaviors are prioritized as a result. This field of study is in a great deal of flux right now, as historically accepted values are being undone, critiqued, and rightfully redrawn and redrafted. To see these important discussions—and, hopefully, changes—happening around the patriarchy, systemic racism, ableism, ageism, and so on is both enlivening and enlightening for those seeking ecojustice. The ecologizing educator is stepping into a time of change and possibility as they examine the values of their culture and begin to create and live into—alongside their students and the natural world—their desired culture.

Formulating an ecologizing ethic for a more eco-socially just culture is well beyond the project of this book, but we can make a start. Let's begin with an idea and an aim. Following Albert Camus's *The Rebel*,[5] we posit the idea—the rebel teacher—and, in the spirit of deep ecology and the eco-feminists, we propose the aim—mutually beneficial flourishing.

Idea: The Rebel Teacher

Education is often overlooked, both as practice and as scholarly activity, when academics turn their attention to changing culture. Social theorists, political scientists, philosophers, and historians all advocate for and theorize about change. Yet these theories often gain little traction in the world. Perhaps that is because these theorists have ignored what educators and educational scholars might contribute to the process of cultural change. Indeed, we believe that contributions from the field of education are, in fact, desperately needed in the neoliberal modern West if we are going to survive as a species and maybe even thrive alongside all our twittering, swimming, and photosynthesizing kith and kin.

Shifting a community from its current beliefs, priorities, foundational stories, systems of governance, and ways of interacting to something different is not, of course, a spontaneous event. A culture doesn't go to bed on Tuesday, read a theory about how to be different—say, more environmentally and socially just—and then wake up changed on Wednesday morning. People, systems, and institutions have deeply embedded habits and structures that *resist* change. New tools, stories, voices, and ways of being must be heard, crafted and learned, created and taught. Power must shift, values must be reconsidered, and priorities must change. All of this involves education, since people, systems, and institutions have to *learn* how to *be* differently. Cultural change is, therefore, at its core, an educational endeavor. But education doesn't necessarily support change. It can, in fact, in some forms, if not carefully and critically considered, do the exact opposite and maintain the problematic status quo. This means that ecologizing educators are going to have to "get their rebel on."

In 1957, Camus was awarded the Nobel Prize for Literature for his essay *The Rebel*. In his acceptance speech for the award, he clarified that this work is not "in the service of those who make history" but "at the service of those who suffer it." He then posited that the nobility of the writer—and we suggest the same for educators—is always rooted in two commitments: one is "the refusal to lie about what one knows" and the other is "the resistance to oppression."[6] Thus, we see ecologizing educators as acting in service of those suffering because of modernity. They bear witness to the current environmental and social challenges while naming the lie(s) that modern Western culture tells about the environment. We see this role as resisting oppression while supporting those, human and beyond, who are suffering it. Let's look more closely at the ideas explored in *The Rebel* and how the rebel educator can play an important role in establishing an ecologizing ethic that will move the culture toward justice.

In *The Rebel*, Camus questions the orchestrators and theorizers of revolutions, suggesting that they often miss some integral pieces that must be present if change is to actually happen. For Camus, revolutions tend to start well because people recognize a clear and immediate challenge and rally together to respond to, say, a set of ecological challenges and social injustices. They have an idea, an image, of a potential future, one that is better in myriad ways.

The trouble, Camus explains, happens *in between* the overcoming of the immediate problem and the arriving at the posited goal. The process for change often fails to account for the effort and incentives that are needed in order for real people who are immersed in a real culture surrounded by real institutions and real structures to move to a significantly different place. The new place is just an idea, after all, evident only in scholarly books or issuing from the frothing lips of a revolutionary. Only after the revolt has begun, Camus says, do the revolutionaries begin to cast around for tools, systems, and ways of being that might help them become these different people in a potentially better culture. But often they come up empty. They fall back on using the tools of the culture they are familiar with and immersed in. As a result, they end up recapitulating and returning to the status quo.

The problem Camus identifies is essentially a gap in education. Real cultural change requires us to understand the world differently, positioning care and placing significance in new ways. But this is not a simple, straightforward process. We see the idea, the image of the future, and we take a step toward it. With each move, evaluation occurs. We compare the aim with the results thus far and then take the next step as needed. These are slow, careful, albeit uncertain, steps along a meandering path in a very long journey. This messy work cannot be circumvented if we are to find success in our project of moving from an unjust environmentally destructive anthropocentric way of being toward something better. Happily, though, each step offers a new view, allows us to live differently, tosses up new challenges, and adds solidity to the aim. Each step is a learning process that involves, by definition, education. Thus, this project of cultural change must involve thoughtful educators who accompany learners through all the steps. By extension, educators also accompany the culture at large through the dynamic twists and turns of cultural change. We must acknowledge, though, that this puts an immense responsibility onto the shoulders of educators and educational theorists. Hence, the rebel teacher.

Camus was interested not only in rebellion but also in the rebels themselves—people with a sense of the vision and larger goal, who are anchored in the reality of the here and now and are willing to name some of the problems; to resist the structures, ideas, and languages that further the problem; and to support the oppressed. This is our rebel teacher: the educator who is ecologizing their practices, engaging with the voices of their places and communities (including the marginalized humans and the natural world), advocating for a more eco-socially just world, resisting problematic cultural norms, and feeling energized about the rich possibilities for change.

Being a rebel may excite some educators and concern others—and rightly so. Change of the kind we are interested in with this ecologizing education project is a challenge that is complex, layered, and ongoing. Our rebel teacher will have to be up to such a challenge. Next, we briefly offer what we believe are three traits of the rebel ecologizing educator.

Courageous: This first trait relates to bearing witness to the problem—that the natural world, our kith and kin, is in trouble—and courageously speaking the simple truth of this, both out loud and, when necessary, to power.

Persevering: The second trait involves developing the ability to lean in and do the difficult work even when the project seems hopeless. These efforts might include giving care and solace to those immediately present while also seeking to contain and limit the expansion of said problem. They might also include creating an infrastructure of allies bringing their own gifts and abilities to bear on the work. In Camus's novel *The Plague*, which was written in parallel to *The Rebel*, many of those allies were drawn from the ranks of the ignored, isolated, and marginalized, those who understood the problems, experienced the suffering, and were willing to do the work of change.

Committed: The final trait of the rebel ecologizing educator brings us back, full circle, to Camus's ideas around commitment. Medical doctors take the Hippocratic oath, which is quite a clear values statement that serves as a framework and impetus for response and behavior in light of illness and working with the sick. A pledge of sorts might apply to ecologizing educators too.

Key to the Hippocratic oath is the end point: that of health/well-being, even flourishing, and the mitigation of pain. Let's turn now to the similar end point/aim we have proposed for the rebel teacher and our ecologizing education project: mutually beneficial flourishing.

Aim: Mutually Beneficial Flourishing

We have proposed that the rebel teacher's aim, distant though it might be, is to teach toward *mutually beneficial flourishing*. It is important to note that this goal extends beyond the meager and odd concept of *sustainability*—what is it we are trying to sustain, anyway?—toward the more inclusive, more ecologically and socially just idea of *flourishing*.

The language of flourishing is drawn from eco-philosophy, particularly deep ecology and eco-feminism. Eco-philosophy posits that all beings across the globe have agency and inherent value and therefore have a right to enact, in their own ways, what they desire to become. All beings—Bear, Flea, Anton, Spruce—should have the opportunity to become their best selves, without being limited by the needs of a privileged few.

Consider, for example, lone Black Spruce stuck in a concrete planter on a busy Vancouver intersection. On whose terms does this tree exist? After all, Spruce is a community-based plant, and this one has been transported thousands of miles from its home in Canada's north—the land that shaped, supported, and knows Spruce. What happens to flourishing when humans are making the choices? Or when one is compelled to serve another's purposes? The concept of flourishing nudges us to answer questions—whose choice? whose purpose? and on whose terms?—and compels us to somehow involve the individual in question. What did Black Spruce want in all this? What would Black Spruce like to become, and what are the elements that best make this possible?

Despite what some humans believe, the freedom to flourish is not simply about individuals doing whatever they want. Along with freedom comes a responsibility to one's community to not destroy or revoke the freedom of others. The freedom to flourish, then, includes restraints—not taking too much, not impinging on the rights and freedoms of others, and doing least harm. In fact, freedom in this sense mirrors quite powerfully the way a rich, robust, diverse, and functioning ecosystem works. Everything in the system is of worth because all have a necessary role to play if the entire system is to function at its best. The worms and fungi are just as important as the plants and birds. The contributions of the apex carnivores are no more important or significant than those of that same carnivore's gut flora or the sun-eating capacities of Strawberry, Licorice Fern, and Dandelion. Outbreaks of disease, mass die-offs, and the predominance of any particular species are indicators that the dynamic equilibrium of the healthy ecosystem has been compromised.

COVID-19 is one of those indicators, a deadly example of an unbalanced system. As a species, we can respond to the massive threat of this new virus, but we should also respond to the imbalance that made COVID-19 and its spread so possible. In today's Anthropocene, the species most responsible for throwing off that balance—by undermining the freedoms of others and by failing to live up to its ecological responsibilities—is the modern, industrialized, rapacious, imperialistic human.

We have added a modifying phrase—*mutually beneficial*—to our aim as a reminder that our own individual flourishing is not the goal. The natural world exists and needs to be heard and considered. Individual flourishing must be seen within a larger context, community, and culture. Thus, flourishing is also about limiting oneself, mitigating one's own freedom, recognizing the importance of balance and diversity for healthy ecosystems, and acknowledging the significant roles other beings play in our own well-being. Mutually beneficial flourishing involves recognizing the ties that bind one's flourishing to that of others. *I can-not be fully human (or even fully myself) unless all humans are also afforded that possibility, and the same proves true for all-our-relations.* Just as the most diverse, successful, resilient, and richest ecosystems honor and involve all their members, big or small, so it is with the well-being of humans and human communities: our fullest range of possibilities and becomings is tied to the world despite our efforts to convince ourselves otherwise. We will rise only on a shared tide.

Ecologizing Ontology: On the Question of Being and Being Human

Picture this: Dusk is approaching, and you and five friends have just found a campsite for the evening. After a dry and dusty day of bike-packing, everyone is tired and thirsty. You volunteer to fetch water from a marshy lake nearby. In your rush, you fail to notice and then trample on some of the hundreds of Western Toadlings just beginning their exodus from pond to land. Tinged with sadness because you know some have died through this moment of carelessness, you wait. Many of us have been in similar situations and have had to recognize and feel the consequences of our action.

A particular way of being human in the world—the Westernized, self-absorbed, colonial way—has been and continues to be detrimental, not only to small toads and the natural world but also to other cultures. The Western way is privileged; it assumes that humans have priority over others, and it crashes down to the water or paves over all of Marsh with total disregard for what the locals are doing. It rests in a sense of itself as "better than," and it fails to notice its effects. *Humans are thirsty or need work or want a swimming pool.* The Western way also has a habit of creating confirming systems, theories, and blind spots, a self-fulfilling deception. *Humans are better. We think, we feel, we have opposable thumbs and bigger brains. We even know that we exist. Surely toads, trees, wetlands are somewhat inferior. Besides, they feel no pain, they don't do anything for us, they mass-produce for exactly this reason, and they should know to get out of the way.*

Sadly, this sense of privilege that infuses the Western way is often transferred to children through public education. Certain things are prioritized, listened to, ignored: all influence how learners come to understand their humanness, their significance, and how their community exists in the larger world. Although we don't often think in these terms, this is the realm of ontology, the study of *being.* Ontology's big questions are as fundamental as they come: What exists? What is reality? What does it mean to *be*? But there are other, more particular, more personal questions too: How is the being of Mosquito, Mollusc, Mango, and Monica the same or different? What does it mean to be human or to be a teacher? And what does it mean to be *me*?

We've selected three ontological issues to explore here, which we see as particularly applicable to our ecologizing education project: becoming embodied, undoing alienation, undoing the nature/culture divide.

Becoming Embodied

It's early September, and you have just returned to Boston after a summer in the backcountry. "Reentry" is always challenging. Strangely, though, this time the first assault comes from an unexpected quarter. As you turn your bike onto the quiet path along River, you are overwhelmed by the stench. The smell of garbage and sewage, exhaust fumes, and overly coiffed humans is overpowering. Tiny tears leak from your eyes, as if you have just cut into an onion. You cannot believe that people tolerate this revolting odor. Yet there they are—exercising, chasing puppies and children, and having lazy picnics along River, all under this repulsive fragrance.

After four months on trail, your sense of smell has been recalibrated to appreciate a world of subtlety and nuance, recognizing the flavor of incoming rain on the wind, the sweet crackle of pine resin, or the deep musk of Woodland Caribou. In a world where scents are subtle, you've expanded your olfactory range and improved your sensory potential.

Here, next to the assaulting miasma of urban stink on this first day back in the city, your nose, brain, and body can't handle the incoming load. You are forced to restrict, limit, numb, dampen, detach from sensitivities to survive without being permanently nauseous. And, yes, your body does begin to adjust, adapting to a situation you cannot change. You start to "not smell" that which you know exists. And so, five days later, you ride next to the river without even a hint of the malodorous. You know the stench has not disappeared—no miracle cleanup has occurred. You also know and regret that you have been forced to separate yourself from the larger, natural world around you, to *desensitize* in order to survive this built-over space.

One might reasonably ask how the dulling of senses fits into a discussion about how to be human in the world. The response is twofold. First, the loss of one's sense of smell works as a parallel to how our sense of being part of the world, our relationality, is shut down. Clearly, part of the shutting down is about protecting oneself from being overwhelmed physically, but there is a psychological side to this as well: the smell and what it indicates (in this case, human waste production and lack of care) come to be *not known*, not smelled. The expression "out of sight, out of mind" applies to other senses too and demonstrates the clear connection between what is sensed and what is thought about. No bad smell, no thinking about the human role in its creation, and, therefore, no need to respond.

Second, our senses are gifts the world has given us. Our senses provide the means for us to gather information, to learn, and to "make sense of" the world and our position in it. Our senses provide pathways into beauty and meaning. Having evolved over generations, these tools assist in our becoming human. To not use them, to not embody ourselves in the world, is to reject the offerings of the earth and our ancestors, whose experiences and encounters with the more-than-human shaped them. It means potentially reducing our range of possibilities for enacting our humanness. Full uptake of our senses is a way to honor those gifts, exercise our skills, encounter nuance, and situate ourselves in the world while not solely relying on the culture to frame how to be human in this world.

To smell rain or garbage is to be *embodied in place* and usually requires a response: take shelter or stop fouling. To really hear the symphony of spring birds, see the loss of insects and the disappearance of their companion flowers, and taste the pesticide on the air is to acknowledge our kinship, our relations, to feel our way back home. But experiencing the world like this also means recognizing a different way of being human. Perspectives, worldviews, experiences, and responsibilities change if we sense ourselves as being part of a larger gathering or even understand ourselves to be incomplete without our sensory range. Those who choose not see, hear, or smell the world and the suffering within it occupy, in fact, a privileged position—one absent of *sense*.

The senses have long been a key pedagogical entry point into building relationship with the natural world. Encountering and then admiring the artistic palette of riotous color, listening to the orchestral workings of natural beings, and immersing one's fingers in fecund soil all tend to deepen connection with and care for one's neighbors and relations. For the ecologizing educator, developing a sense of care for the world involves building relationship, which requires encountering, coming to know, overcoming ignorance. Regrettably, many of us live in places that never give our senses a chance.

Outdoor educators have noted that many humans hardly notice the natural world around them. Children can recognize hundreds of corporate brands (think the golden arches or the swoop) while struggling to identify five local bird species. Adults know the names of Pine, Oak, and Tulip from reading without being able to recognize an individual from those species. Since the Enlightenment, the philosopher Michel Serres[7] notes, the modern West has been taught that we humans are independent from the world around us. Even as that belief has become increasingly unsustainable, particular political and economic forces seek to ignore or minimize our interconnections to the places we live. They strive to have us *not* see, *not* smell, *not* feel our world. And, frankly, we think that stinks!

Environmental education has long focused on what each of us can do to respond to the myriad ecological crises we face. We are encouraged to build our own relationships with our local places and work toward reducing, reusing, recycling. Responding to our environmental challenges has been framed as a process of taking individual responsibility, working at the local level, and changing one's behavior such that each of us does their share and the planet benefits. While none of this is problematic in itself, this approach inevitably fails, crucially because it ignores the systemic problem—the politics and privileges of furthering human alienation.

Ecologizing educators acknowledge the slowness of change and the politics of privilege and conclude that the challenge cannot be addressed solely at the individual level. In fact, downloading community and cultural problems onto individuals has long been a tool of the colonial mindset. If the project is one of cultural change and not simply individual change, we need to ecologize at the ontological level. This is a question of challenging what it means to be human in the world. As such, a key concern is to undo the Enlightenment notion of the modern human as separate, in mind and body, from—and better than—the rest of the world.

Undoing Alienation

What does it mean to be human? How does the human being exist in the world? Two significantly different positions exist for these ontological questions: one proposes that the human is a separate, independent being, while the other contends that the human is a relational, dialogical being. As we have already noted previously, the positioning of the human as a being separate from the natural world has been taught in Western culture for centuries. As it has been lived out in the modern West (through, for instance, colonization, overuse of resources, extractive forms of knowledge creation, absence of rights and voice for all-our-relations), this philosophical stance not only has contributed significantly to the various environmental crises we now face but also is woefully inadequate to address, forestall, or remedy those crises.

Ecologizing education adopts the other position—that humans are relational, dialogical beings—and seeks to undo the alienation that underpins the dominant culture in the West. Fundamental to this "undoing" project and informed by how pedagogy plays out in practice is the belief that the learner is not simply an individual being bounded by skin (or a brain bounded by skull) but that consideration must also be given to their communities, their stories and histories, the classroom ecosystem, their bodies, and the bodies that surround and inter-act with them. And if we listen to and learn from our more-than-human rela-tions (as ecologizing education seeks to do), we might discover that even at the level of the human body (bounded by skin) we are not individuals. Let's con-sider, for a moment, Lichen.

For the mycologist Merlin Sheldrake, the lichen is far more complex than the easy formula—one Fungi and one Algae coming together—that many of us learned in high school biology.[8] Lichen is an amalgam of different beings—yes, Fungi and Algae, but also Bacterium and other microorganisms. Its symbi-otic relationships are not fixed, as partners come and go. This is a community, a symbiosis, and a functioning democracy. In describing Lichen, Sheldrake—recognizing the limits of the English language and its underlying ontological assumptions about individuality—suggests that Lichen is like a living orches-tration, a poly-vocal song, with parts being carried by the various members. There are no solo performances, no independent cello or quiet alto. Lichen only works as ensemble, just as the organs of the human body or a group of learners only work as a *togetherness*.

To be clear, Sheldrake is not suggesting a magical all-is-good-all-the-time gathering. In his description of Lichen, he invokes the family, something that exists as a coming together but can be anything from wonderful to toxic, de-pending on balance. No doubt, Lichen has much to teach us about ourselves and the unseen, often unacknowledged, connections we have to the world around—and within—us.

For ecologizing education, the ontological point is not to find ways to com-pletely undo the individual human, placing us in a soup of total oneness. Rather, ecologizing education tries to overcome this positioning of human as completely separate from, solely individual, and better than and to move instead toward rec-ognizing the "both/and" nature of our being in the world, recognizing humans as fluid individuals *and* dynamic communities.

Undoing the Nature/Culture Divide

In many critical fields (gender, race, sexuality, ability), simple binaries such as man/woman, civilized/primitive, culture/nature, being/nonbeing, able/disabled are considered problematic for several reasons. First, such binaries ignore the wondrous range that exists between, around, and beyond each of these two imagined poles. In doing so, they force beings—and this is often detrimental to those beings—into one of two fairly restrictive positions. Second, these simple binaries lead to hierarchies and dangerous assumptions about which is "better than"—which then leads to privileging one side of the binary and to justifications not only for the marginalization and silencing of the other but also for violence toward it. For these reasons, environmental theorists and educators have pushed back on the hierarchical binary of culture versus nature, which places humans at the top of the pile called "all living things." Claims that "we are all nature" and writings stressing entanglements of "natureculture" abound.[9] This idea isn't wrong per se, but we think it's worth exercising some caution before we celebrate too much the return of humans to the natural fold.

First, we believe it is important to recognize the distinction between theory and practice, between the "idea" and the way things are actually enacted. Claiming that there is no nature/culture divide does not change the fact that, in practice, all of us continue to operate in a world where there explicitly is. In the classroom, human students are still prioritized over all others. Metaphors and language still paint the other as "lesser than." For example, lessons might impart the belief that humans are more advanced rationally and linguistically. Time spent outside might include the experience of trees being pushed over in search of salamanders, worms being crushed in loving hands after being pulled from their homes, or birds being stressed away from their nests for the sake of a math lesson under a tree. We still live in a cultural milieu that gains umpteen privileges from the unpaid and unrecognized labor of other beings—clean air and water, dairy, meat, vegetables—and we blithely assume that this is our right. Saying "there is no difference between humans and nature" is easy, but if we don't do the hard work to actualize that reality, the phrase is merely the vacuous claim of the privileged.

This ontological shift—from humans as separate and better to "we are all nature"—parallels similar efforts in other critical discourses. Some gender theorists (usually cisgendered males) or race theorists (usually white) have made claims of a gender-free or colorblind world. The response from feminist and critical race scholars is that they still live in a world where they are unheard, ignored, and subjected to unwanted advances and myriad violences. At best, the theory is a postulated goal; it is certainly not a reality. Furthermore, it is not up to the oppressor classes to make this determination. We suggest that the same problem exists in the nature/culture binary. Ultimately, it is not the prerogative of the self-proclaimed "top" of the binary hierarchy, whether it be male, white, hetero, or human, to declare that the binary has been overcome and is no longer applicable. One wonders what Orca, Salmon, and Cedar have to say on the matter.

We would also do well to reflect on the political implications and potential manipulations of a statement such as "we are all nature." Some might want to interpret that statement in this way: if humans are synonymous with nature, then all the products and results of human action are "natural." We can see that such a position makes judging actions almost impossible. Dolphins drowning in seining nets are simply part of how nature works. Marshes being filled in for high-rise developments is the natural way of the world. Interpreted in this way, "we are all nature" does nothing for the cause of ecojustice.

Ultimately, the aim of "bringing humans back to nature," or flattening the ontological hierarchy, is worth striving toward. This cannot be done, however, through the stroke of a pen or by theoretical intention alone, no matter how true the statement "humans are nature too" might be. Active work, educational energy, and political struggle are required to change what it means to be a modern human in the world. In particular, work against this nature/culture binary will need to involve, even foreground, those who are not "privileged," whose voices are too often not heard.

Ecologizing Cosmology: On the Question of Foundational Stories

Where did the world come from? How was it created? The stories we tell to answer these questions form our cosmology. Literally "the study of the cosmos," cosmology is often framed in scientific terms, with a focus on the nature of the universe, its structure and evolution, and the laws of space and time. Essentially, though, cosmology is about how our planet Earth and all its beings came to be. It is about origins and existence.

The metaphysical, rather than the physical, components of cosmology are particularly important to ecologizing education because it is through foundational stories that culture comes into being and operationalizes itself in the world. Our origin stories might prioritize the human or glorify competition or embrace time as circular and ever-present—whatever the case, they have rippling implications because these stories not only explain where we come from but also sustain and shape the culture. Additionally, these stories shape schooling, no matter the culture, for they are the grist for what can and can't happen, for what is and isn't prioritized, and for who does and doesn't belong.

Stories have always been used to educate. Cultures based in an oral tradition use stories to help community members learn how to live, position themselves in the world, discover the goods and the bads (from edible to ethical), understand how to feel about things, and encounter shared joys, losses, possibilities, and histories. Stories play a similar, though somewhat understated, role in today's writing-based cultures and public education systems. Yet one has only to open a book and begin reading out loud in a kindergarten classroom to see the power of story: ears tune in, heads turn, bodies slow, sound drops, as imaginations join the storyteller on the journey. After thousands of years of orality, humans seem wired to tune into and learn from stories. The Russian psychologist Lev Vygotsky called stories a cultural tool. Indeed, educators often discuss and argue about what, where, when, and how stories should be told.[10]

For instance, Waldorf teachers feel quite strongly that, when working with younger children, picture books should not be used to tell a story. Instead, the teacher memorizes the story and shares it orally—as exactly as possible, since four-year-old memories are quick to learn a tale. Waldorf teachers want to activate children's imaginations, unrestricted by an artist's renditions. Thus, every story told has a classroom of children doing their own imaginative work. Waldorf theory suggests that being able to imagine one's own talking Bear or flying Horse exercises muscles that might allow for more divergent and expansive creativity in the future.

In his lecture series (and book) *The Truth about Stories,* the Indigenous poet, writer, and historian Thomas King positions two creation stories in relation to each other: the Christian one and an Indigenous one.[11] He examines how differences in the stories produce, influence, and reflect the resulting cultures. Creation stories shape and are shaped by the norms, values, and ways of being in the world for a particular culture. Subsequently, they influence the range of possibilities available to the culture and its members. For example, King suggests that Christian and Indigenous creation stories illustrate differences in human positioning vis-à-vis other humans and the more-than-human, along with differences in where power is located and distributed. These differences are illustrated in part, for instance, by the contrast between the perfect but detached creator of the Christian origin story and the communal, multispecies creation effort in the Indigenous origin story. King also points out that many ecological and equity challenges we face today are built into the foundational Christian tales.

Similarly, the French feminist philosopher Luce Irigaray and the American Australian anthropologist Deborah Bird Rose have analyzed foundational Judeo-Christian stories, suggesting that these tales reify and sustain problematic cultural values. Irigaray highlights troublesome tropes related to gender, parenting, familial violence, and trauma in the biblical tale of Abraham, Sarah, Isaac, Hagar, and Ishmael.[12] She asserts that this tale forms part of the bedrock of modern Western cultural assumptions regarding how to be in the world.

Bird Rose's work responds to King and Irigaray by using components of these foundational stories to create a different narrative, with the intent of enabling different ways of being in the world.[13] For example, through careful research, Bird Rose postulates a second Adam story, wherein Adam is much more clearly of and from the earth, more place-based, more equal to the rest of the earthy beings, more ecological. To be clear, Bird Rose is not inventing this earthy Adam out of whole cloth. She is changing the emphases, translations, and interpretations in order to bring forward that which is currently backgrounded. For her, earthy Adam is already present. It is just a matter of telling the story differently, changing the emphasis. For both Bird Rose and King, different origin stories allow for different ways of being in the world. With this in mind, ecologizing educators should tread gently when their practices rest in or reify detached, patriarchal, anthropocentric cosmologies.

Stories are profound sociocultural tools that shape us in all kinds of implicit and explicit ways. They help us fit into the world but also hinder us because we are shaped in particular, often limiting, ways. If cultural stories point in unjust and unecological directions, they need scrutiny.

Being gathered into and shaped by a particular culture and its stories has both beneficial and detrimental repercussions. On the positive side, the infant or child immersed in story starts to integrate into culturally created and normed ways of being in the world. They start to make sense of the people, language, rules, priorities, and natural world around them, giving the child a sense of belonging and community. Thus, a child grows into a community of others who understand the world in the same way and who grow from the stories. However, on the negative side, no matter what culture one is dropped into, other stories are inherently or even actively excluded. Thus, every child is also limited by the tools that shape them—and this shaping is not explicit. In other words, children—and adults for that matter—do not know they are being shut out of certain ways of being, living, thinking. For them, the habits, beliefs, and ideas shaping their existence are the only option—even the Truth.

Foundational stories not only shape the individual but also extend throughout the culture, undergirding and sustaining the entire cultural edifice. Institutions, ethical systems, politics, the arts, relations to other cultures and communities, relations to the more-than-human, and especially and explicitly *education*—all are created and sustained through truths and beliefs communicated through stories. Thus, as the environmental thinker Paul Kingsnorth suggests, the environmental crisis is not a crisis of economics, politics, or technology—although these are problematic too—it is a crisis of story.[14] Unless we can find new, different, flexible stories that allow for different, more relational, less anthropocentric possibilities to be produced, we are oddly stuck.

What does the ecologizing educator do, then, in light of this seemingly mammoth challenge to rewrite/retell/replace the foundational stories of Western culture? The difficulty is not just in deciding what specific stories to tell in the classroom. We must determine how to tell these stories and how to teach students to hear, understand, and make sense of the stories they encounter. Additionally, in literacy-based cultures, like that of the North American school system, students often don't learn how to listen to and interpret stories particularly well. Students might not be experiencing enough orality, not learning how to *listen* to stories before they are pushed into the silent, individualized act of reading. It is also important for teachers to adopt an ongoing critical stance toward the stories that form the fabric of the school system. What tale of success is being told? Who is shaping and controlling the message? What cultural frame is being reenforced? Where can we find justice, equity, and the natural world in these stories? And what stories might need to be told in order to shift influence, effect change, and possibly start something new—or, at the very least, give learners a wider range of possibilities for who they might become in the world?

In part, the role of the ecologizing educator is to find ways to make significant and important stories from myriad cultures available to learners. If Vygotsky is right, this ensures that learners are encountering and being shaped by a wider range of sense-making tools from beyond their particular cultural positionalities. Finding those stories and storytellers whose origins and roots are deeply embedded in the local place is of great importance. Local Indigenous communities speak in the voices of the place and its many beings. Both the stories and the languages in which those stories are told are the result of extended interactions with the place itself. As students hear and take in these stories, possibilities will arise for different and more meaningful kinds of relationships to blossom within those places.

Ecologizing Psychology: On the Question of Human Development

Psychology, the study of the psyche, is a wide-ranging field. Psychologists analyze why an individual responds in a particular way; chart the development stages of the "normal," healthy person; and study the behavioral "whys," moral "whats," and the challenging "hows" of being a functioning adult in the larger culture. These considerations are critical in an educational context. From moment to moment, teachers are assessing the whys of behaviors while simultaneously trying to determine where learners are developmentally, what the roadblocks to development might be, and what activities, encounters, and learning possibilities will further their intellectual, psychological, and axiological development toward adulthood. These tasks are often further complicated by the need to respond well to the impacts of trauma and support the mental health needs of diverse students.

In recent years, many educators have pushed back hard against some of the more "traditional" psychological frameworks. They are actively questioning deficit-model thinking and a system that locates the problem in the individual student, often to the detriment of their self-esteem. Social-emotional skills have become more emphasized, helping learners to better understand their own emotional landscapes and how these affect and influence their relationships with others. Growing theoretical criticisms have identified that many of the psychological frameworks being employed are biased with regard to gender, race, socioeconomic status, and diverse cultural ways of being. Lastly, a growing conversation has emerged about the presence of trauma in the lives of many learners and the need to teach in trauma-informed ways—so that, at the very least, the educational experience is one that does not inflict *more* suffering.

These psychological dimensions of education have become important in ecologizing education conversations. In our research, we have seen eco-relational children struggle as the larger culture pushes them into particular ways of being human. We have watched them abandon their love for and relationships with the natural world in order to remain part of their larger peer group. We have also heard from many parents. They tell us that the traditional system was traumatic both for their children and for themselves, with learners being unheard, pigeonholed as problematic, set upon by peers and educators, and forced to hide their authentic selves for various reasons: sexual orientation, unconventional interests, emotional range, fear of violence, and love of/care for the natural world. These challenges warrant a more concrete exploration and ecologizing of educational psychology.

A Question of Bullying

On a blustery, sunny day, kindergarten and grade 1 children are spread out, playing individually and in small groups along the oceanfront. The tide is low, and the wind whips up small waves. Above, Gull circles, waiting for tasty bits to fall out of people's lunches. The students tend to be drawn to things much smaller than sky and sea.

Several have set up stores using stones and driftwood and are now "selling" stones and other paraphernalia to their friends. In this caring space and due to an incredible abundance, no one goes without, and no sale is ever rejected. Something deeply social seems to exist within this economy, since sellers are willing to accept almost anything in exchange. One child simply picks up another rock from the ground in front of the store, and the deal is quickly closed. Neither hoarding nor profit motive is seen. A curious onlooker might wonder how long it will take before those environmentally problematic norms take hold.

Other children are busy exploring the tidal area. One group is currently absorbed in watching the sand above a known Clam bed, enjoying the surprising squirts of water and wondering about how deep into the sand these bivalves are.

In the distance, at the edge of the tidal area and the small grassy sward next to the sidewalk, Sunil has found a very active ant colony.[15] A budding entomologist, Sunil is extraordinarily patient, and he has settled in to watch the activity. Another boy, slightly older and substantially bigger, introduces himself into this scene. Billy has been having a bit of trouble connecting with the other students lately. He tends to whirl around the outdoor spaces, entering and exiting the play of others. He is a loud, happy, extroverted type—in marked contrast to Sunil. Billy also tends to seek attention, to want to be noticed, to be the center of the action. With this in mind, one of the human teachers notices as Billy enters Sunil's world and shortly thereafter begins to step on Ants as they move between their burrow and a piece of apple Sunil had placed nearby. In response to this, Sunil becomes quickly agitated, trying to push Billy away to protect the many more Ants who are now being drawn to the scene of the crushings, since Ants tend to defend their own. The teacher quickly approaches and . . . does what?

Take a moment to think through this relatively common scenario. What would *you* do in this situation? What is a thoughtful, meaningful, but *ecologizing* way to engage and deal with this? There is clearly an aggressor. Do you remove Billy, as you would a bully, in order to protect Sunil? Do you pull the two of them together into a conversation about feelings, about space, about caring for each other, and about right actions? Would an apology be the goal? Who needs to be apologized to? How do the Ants figure into all of this? Are they collateral damage to a human learning moment, or might their deaths be given more significance? Also, what is happening here for Sunil, and what is up with Billy's behavior? How do we deal with violence in our ecologizing classrooms when it also involves natural kin?

Dealing with the questions and challenges of violence and troubling interstudent relations are part of every classroom, but in ecologizing settings, classic "disciplinary" responses might not work. In this situation, the killing of Ant struck Sunil so deeply, he was willing to fight for them, taking action that was clearly out of character for him. A human teacher might have had a similar response as a result of Billy's actions, but they also might be immersed in a cultural reality where Ant is seen as lesser beings, even a resource.

In this actual case, the teacher chose to bring the human participants together, a short distance from the still-disturbed and quite panicked anthill. This step allowed a distraught Sunil to settle down a bit before the facilitated discussion began: *What happened? Why? How did it make you feel? Billy, are you hearing what Sunil is saying?* Eventually Billy was able to apologize, and some sense of closure ensued between humans. But here the human teacher, at Sunil's insistence, returned to the potentially more aggrieved members of this encounter— the ant colony. After the teacher framed the project as a kind of offering of apology and restitution, it was decided that together Billy and Sunil would build a kind of protective wall around the anthill, make a sign warning other humans of its presence, and offer some crumbled food from their lunches (just a bit because they didn't want Ant to become dependent on this surprise food source). The result was an extended and potentially rich play encounter between Sunil and Billy and a rather elaborate compound, including play and workout structures, for Ant. We offer this story not as an example of the perfect response to this situation but to explore how changing commitments—to each other and to the more-than-humans around us—brings about changes in priorities and, thus, in the responses of the players.

After all, if we want to move kith and kin into roles of significance, then our responses need to reflect that. Walking away from dead ants risks reenforcing cultural norms of their insignificance. Another component that might have been ignored in this scenario is how all of this lands psychologically for Sunil. What happens when something one cares about, even if others don't, is wantonly destroyed? For many students in the schools we have worked with, for many of our adult researchers and educators, and for many more people than are willing to admit it, their connection to the natural world goes beyond a utilitarian admiration of beauty. Sunil suffered alongside the crushed and panicking ants, and that psychic pain is often unseen and, consequently, repressed.

But the story doesn't end here. Episodes similar to both the previous and the upcoming Sunil/Billy story have happened multiple times during our research, in various settings. In fact, when presenting our findings at various academic and practitioner conferences, we have heard many audience members offer similar stories. Clearly, the pain runs deep. This makes these encounters important to consider in the work of ecologizing education, and as we'll see, they lead us more directly into the psyche of an unecological culture.

Consider the story of Sunil again, but from another angle. At the edge of a grassy sward next to the sidewalk, Sunil, a cisgendered male—for that is how he currently identifies—has found a very active ant colony. His curiosity piqued, this bug lover and slightly eccentric character settles in to watch the goings-on. Over the next ten minutes, he notes the regular travel routes, follows a single ant to the edge of its range, and places a small slice of Apple within reach in order to determine how long it takes for the morsel to be discovered and the message of "food" relayed to all and sundry. Ant begins to carve small chunks off the apple piece. Sunil can contain his excitement no longer and calls loudly to a cisgendered female researcher who is watching Clam spit water into the air nearby.

For more than a year, Zinta has been with this class for at least one day a week. She has a great relationship with everyone. She is also well known for her rich knowledge of all things natural-worldly, for her deep curiosity, and for her profound care for the more-than-human. She is an ideal partner for Sunil's interests, and the two of them settle in to watch, ponder, and discuss. The questions are rich, and the hypotheses are eclectic. Meanwhile, more ants are arriving at Apple.

It is into this tableau that cisgendered male Billy—who might be thought of as a boyish boy—introduces himself. As mentioned, he is a rambunctious and active kid, outgoing and gregarious, who likes the crashes and bangs of media and childhood more than the quiet contemplative elements. He has also of late been having trouble catching on with a particular group of friends. This difficulty does not arise out of malice—although he has begun to experiment with power through physicality and size—but because he has an elevated level of enthusiasm and a need for dominance. Other children find it challenging to play with Billy for long.

From a distance, Billy spies Sunil and Zinta absorbed in Ant. He approaches slowly, mulling over an idea. Then he inserts himself by carefully stepping on the ants one by one, assertively crushing them. This agitates Sunil more and more with each killing such that he, quite angry and flustered at this point, begins to push the much larger Billy away. Zinta, upset by all of this, moves to intervene and begins to start some of the restorative work already described.

There is yet another aspect of this situation that is important and troubling. With each Ant killed, Billy does not look at Sunil or Ant, other than to locate the next victim. In fact, it would appear that Sunil and the Ants—and their feelings—are completely unimportant to Billy. His focus is on Zinta. It seems that Billy is trying to gauge, understand, confirm a hypothesis about how his killing actions affect Zinta. Perhaps he is looking to determine the range of his power over this adult woman.

A myriad of complex, important, and disturbing issues are evident in this second version of the situation.[16] However, our goal here is to simply point in the direction of psychology as both problem and possibility. Of note—and we shall extend these ideas in the following section—is the role that violence and the threat thereof plays in limiting human possibility. Next, in light of ecologizing education, we want to consider three things: ways in which the vision of the psychologically mature adult might be understood differently, a mechanism or two for protecting those who love nature and, most importantly, the psychic needs of some learners.

Violence, Eco-Double Consciousness, and the Splitting of the Psyche

Stories shared with us over the years suggest that there are a lot of Sunils out there. Many people feel deep spiritual, mental, emotional, and physical connections to the natural world, and they suffer when reading about or witnessing its destruction, disappearance, or marginalization. Often in these stories, violence and its threat are activated at multiple levels but usually for the purpose of restraining behavior, limiting voice, and expressing power over. Violence was perpetrated on Ant by Billy, but the intention was to see how it landed on Zinta and to educate Sunil about the ways that the world, power, and patriarchy work.

Violence, and the threat thereof, is a common experience for those outside the narrow masculine, white, hetero, able-bodied, settler norm. Violence toward those outside the human realm is often less acknowledged. In response, many people dull, stunt, and/or conceal their emotions and care for the natural world (as we saw in the story of the cyclist in Boston whose olfactory senses adjusted in order to survive the urban reality). Many find that this is the only way they can function in a culture where, at the interpersonal level, such attachments are frowned upon and seen as weird or flaky and where, at the personal level, there is so much violence and ongoing destruction that caring means opening oneself up to continuous pain. At a global level, the degree of destruction and pain is simply staggering.

Sufferers also tend to develop the psychological skills needed to hide connections, grief, and "weaknesses." They do this, in part, because the culture, often represented and reenforced by the Billys of the world, "teaches" them that something is wrong with their way of being in the world. Sunil is "learning" how to be a cisgendered boy in this world and learning what might happen if he doesn't go along with this plan. In our research and observations, this process of enculturation through "separation from" and "denial of" appears active and ongoing.

Many students we have encountered are explicit about needing to negotiate who they are, what they say, and how to be in different settings. They actively move to protect themselves in certain situations, particularly around new people or those with whom they have had previous problematic experiences. They have learned, often through bitter and painful experience, that in some places and with some people, it is truly unsafe to be green. These moves to self-protect include hiding oneself, not exposing their ecological selves, avoiding "dangerous" topics, adopting non-green language, performing "normally," and working hard to read the threat level of the other. They adopt these techniques because they have experience with shaming, violence, and ostracism, a lesson five-year-old Sunil is in the process of learning. These threats are real, violence happens, limits are imposed, and cultural expectations are explicitly taught.

This use of violence and ostracism to force individuals to conform exists, often even more explicitly, in other diversity contexts as well (that is, in the context of gender, race, sexuality, ability, ethnicity) and often in combination (for example, Billy is "norming" both human and gender), as the eco-feminists point out. After all, the patriarchal, colonial gaze and power-over mechanisms are transferable and operate toward gendered bodies and onto more-than-human bodies in much same way. For example, the threat of violence, human male violence, acts to restrict the independent other—say, a cisgendered female—from seeking solace in, connection to, and well-being from Forest nearby. At the same time, the culture explicitly suggests that the desire to be in relationship, sitting under Cedar, talking to Dipper, or immersing one's hands in Creek is itself an odd idea. The combination of these strictures ultimately makes such a relationship potentially impossible, even if these outdoor wilder spaces might be safer than a woman's home and more welcoming than a nonbinary child's school.

For some of these students, a painful psychic-splitting process occurs, where they are forced to position a green self and a "real world" self against each other. These independent ways of being in and relating to the world are often, as W. E. B. DuBois explains in his work on double consciousness, at odds with each other.[17] For DuBois, a more authentic Black consciousness exists inside the "souls of black folks," but it is often on the defensive against a culturally accepted, white consciousness that has been foisted on them by the colonial structures. DuBois writes that not only does he encounter racism, white supremacy, and violence toward his authentic Black self from the institutions and people he engages with every day—he also encounters some of that orientation within his own psyche. He is, in a way, critiquing himself with this racist lens. The same kind of psychic splitting and double consciousness appears to exist for many environmentally interested people, and it may be part of the developmental process of public schooling. That is, it may be part of the psychological makeup of the modern person.

Loss and Stewarding the World's Sunils

For the Sunils of the world, developing psychological self-protection skills is often a response to the pain of loss—the loss of relationship, connection, to a living, gifting, caring, sharing, embracing other—as cultural norms undermine their experiences of connection to the more-than-human and as they witness ongoing violence toward the natural world. After all, to stay open to relationship, to continue to care about living beings and ecosystems, is to leave oneself open to an ongoing world of hurt. Consequently, people often move to protect themselves from further pain.

Sunil might even be told, "It is just a couple of ants," and this might be said either out of kindness (to help him get over his distress) or in a spirit of derision. In either case, Sunil might begin to adopt this language of "just a couple" as a means of self-preservation. People may start to "not know that which they know" about the agency, vibrancy, wild-freedom, and moral significance of their flying, buzzing, greening, sun-eating relations—this, in order to simply survive in a culture that fails to acknowledge those beings and to mitigate the psychic pain, loss, and trauma such a culture induces.

In fact, all of us are impacted by loss, this separation from the natural world, this shutting down of relationship. We are also impacted by the limitations this puts on who we might become in the world. Many, like Sunil, feel helpless to respond in the face of it all. These are the individuals who wonder how Grass feels about being cut all the time, who bring Snail or Frog home in their pockets, who constantly stop to look and wonder at stuff even when everyone else is busy getting somewhere, who argue with city works people about the cutting down of the neighborhood Cherry and then hold a ceremony around either its loss or survival, who talk constantly about lessening our impact on the planet and getting outside, and who argue against filling in Marsh for yet another golf course, housing project, or mini-mall. They are also those who fill with joy and catch their breath when Damselfly lands on their fingertip, who stop in the road to watch the first flock of Trumpeter Swans headed north, who stop to greet each and every dog they encounter, who know an amazing amount about Fern, and who often have Dirt stuffed under their fingernails. As judged by the larger culture, they appear to be a little tree-huggy, weirdly emotional about Owl and Stickleback, and a touch "woolly headed," too emotional or lacking objectivity when expounding on the gifts of nature. They feel better about themselves, healthier and happier, when in connection with the natural world and with others who are like-minded. And for the ecologizing educator, they are living members of our student groups. They are also in danger of being hurt psychologically if their connections and cares are ignored and denigrated.

The Cultural Problematics of Educating toward the Independent, Autonomous, Human Citizen

Ecologizing educators often find this psychological conversation daunting. Indeed, very little of the psychological theory connected to public education in North America involves the natural world at all. In fact, much of it appears to aim toward separation, autonomy, and a good dollop of superiority. It is deemed healthy developmentally to give up one's "dependent relationships" with caregivers, imaginary friends, and natural beings as one "grows up." Adult psychological health is synonymous with independence, personal strength, and autonomy. As a result, we don't really know what a healthy, ecologically connected, relationally interdependent psyche might look like within the auspices of Western modernity. Even at these eco-schools, where relationship is prioritized, honored, and given credence, the research reveals a cultural push toward individualization, anthropocentrism, and species elitism. Still, we believe that more ecological pathways for human psychological development are possible.

First, in acknowledging that particular psychological theories may be flawed, we open ourselves up to other possibilities as they appear in feminist psychology, in eco-psychology, and in various cross-cultural psychological movements. Second, being aware that Sunils and Zintas exist and are present in our classrooms and staff rooms challenges us to be inclusive and careful with our language, our advice, and our pedagogies so as not to further their separation from the natural world. We can find ways to honor and appreciate the gifts they bring to learning and to recognize how powerful those skills of deep connection-building and that sense of belonging can be for some, even all, learners. Third, we can find ways to create spaces where those green gifts, ways of knowing, and kinds of care are possible, allowable, encouraged, even honored. Comprehending the world as complex, interdependent, vibrant, filled with agency, and deeply communicative is not wrong. It is different, and those differences reveal new questions, unexpected categories of understanding, and novel ways of being.

This concludes our very short wander through some of the theorizing involved with ecologizing education. Cultural change work in education is complex, as Camus pointed out, as it involves not only good theorizing—or maybe *un-* and *re-*theorizing—but also action. It means doing things that align with all this theory-building—and undoing those that don't.

PRACTICING
Ecologizing Curriculum and Pedagogy

At the Maple Ridge school, River warbles over palm-sized, brown, beige, and gray stones. The symmetry of branches spirals into blue sky. Tiny staircases of luminescent white fungi ascend fallen logs. A lean banana slug rests on wet earth, while a fat one curls over a twig. The footprint of a young black Bear slowly fills with rainwater. Raven cocks its head to watch the theater of children parading below Tree. These children learn within cathedrals of moss-covered trees, banked with rows of Ferns. Only the rarest of standard classrooms could be called beautiful. But the environmental school, while often muddy and cold, is, as a whole, beautiful, compelling, fascinating, and, in moments, breathtaking.

Although many people struggle to imagine how learning occurs at a school with no building and no walls, in fact, here at the environmental school potential lessons all across the curriculum abound, as the alert, curious, open teacher readily observes. Indeed, one of the biggest challenges for teachers is learning how to be a teacher amid all this possibility. Of course, there are the forms, the getting permission, the hounding of parents/caregivers to get things signed and to send appropriate clothing, and the soliciting of extras for those students who might not have enough. Then too there is the need for adult volunteers, for emergency action plans, and for reconnaissance trips to the places all this occurs. And on top of all that, there is the weather. But these initial challenges are usually quickly overcome with some creativity and determination, and they soon pale in comparison to the deeper worries and uncertainties. How do you teach in places where the unexpected might occur, where you are not the expert (for who really can know all two thousand species of fungi in a temperate rainforest), and, perhaps most importantly, where you, the human teacher, are not in control? Oh, yes, and you are also being tasked with the challenge to change the culture.

A teacher and a group of twenty students have gathered on a forested slope looking down at a hard-used boggy area through which a confused Creek is again trying to make its way. Footprints abound, the ground has been turned to mud, the shape of the space has been radically altered, and even the usually clear water is turbid and fetid. The ground-dwelling Moss and Lichens have been churned out of existence, and the bigger shrubs and Skunk Cabbages bear signs of hard usage. Some are damaged beyond survival. It is time for the class to create a new plan, a different way of being in this sensitive low-lying place.

Together, they decide that more information is needed. At the very least, though, the place should be left alone until further notice. After all, not enough is understood by the group in terms of who lives here and what their needs and rights are, in terms of how much disruption can be sustained and how humans should be in this place, or even in terms of this area's importance to the larger ecosystem. Through it all, we notice the teacher facilitating: carefully drawing students out and, at times, back to the place and the voices of the place; asking good questions that move the discussion forward; and also addressing anthropocentric tendencies by seeking to listen to all involved and to notice the diverse range of possibilities being offered.

This practice of teaching outdoors in a more eco-socially just way requires change: it means undoing previous ways of doing things and seeking out new ways. It means *being teacher* differently. For example, if we want to listen to the more-than-human world, we must go where they are, decenter ourselves and our voices, and be attentive to their many and varied voices.

Many teachers in standard indoor schools know this. They are well aware of the irony of teaching environmental awareness from a largely indoor setting. They may sense that the indoor classroom, the standard curriculum—even when tweaked to a more earth-centered approach—contains the tangled, knotted, and damaged roots of human-centerism, of destructive cultural tendencies. Some educators, though, might not actually recognize how deep these knots go, what a tangled problem this really is, and how so much of what they take for granted as good teaching—stuff that has served them well in a rich career—might be problematic when raising up the eco-lens for a closer look. But how does one come to see the problems when they are, as they say, the water in which our schools swim?

For most of us, when we think about education, we are often thinking of *stuff.* The *what* of the learning experience. What do the lessons look like? What equipment, supplies, or handouts are needed? What skills will be learned? What knowledge created? What will the learning outcomes be? What assessments and evaluations will be employed? This is what we call the *curriculum*.[1]

For the educational theorist, though, looking at educational practice also means dealing with the *how* of education: how the lessons are arranged, how the teacher uses their time, how ideas are presented and accessed, how relations are built and supported between and among teachers, learners, subject matters. Just as importantly, educational practice involves the *who* of the human teacher: teacher as facilitator, teacher as community-builder, teacher as ally and activist and more. This combination of "how and by whom" we call the *pedagogy*, an area that requires further discussion with regard to the ecologizing process. But first, let's consider a brief, nonenvironmental story to get us into the swing of pedagogy.

Recently, a guest speaker was invited to a small gathering of the Centre for Dialogue at Simon Fraser University. The guest was an acknowledged global expert in the area of participatory democracy and spent several days giving talks, meeting people, and attending gatherings. In short, he worked hard for the time he was here.

One get-together was billed as a dialogue about future questions pertinent in participatory democracy. As the process unfolded, though, little attention was paid to how people might learn to be active citizens. Many crucial questions were not even considered. For instance, how does one develop the skills to actually "participate" in democracy? How does one become a contributing and valuable member of society? And how does one develop the ability to critically engage in the ways of governance and to learn that they can be an agent of change?

Apparently, such questions run up against the reality that North American public education is deeply undemocratic, not only at the student/teacher level but also at the teacher/principal and principal/superintendent levels as well. We know that students have little say in their daily lives. They are certainly not allowed to voice their disagreement about many of the most foundational components of the educational process, nor are they allowed to choose something different for themselves if what is currently happening is not important or is damaging to them. They do not vote for their teachers or for anything more important than the homecoming queen, nor are they able to strike, sit in, walk out, or demand better wages and study conditions. There have been moments when students have tried to do some of this work, often with the support of a more radical teacher, but these efforts are inevitably and summarily shut down. Knuckles are rapped all around, and the school newsletter returns to telling fluff pieces about the yearbook and pumping school spirit. Such realities made the guest speaker's talk on participatory democracy all the more relevant and crucial. If not in school, then where might this kind of participatory, action-oriented, democratic citizenship be learned—as it clearly isn't an innate property of all humans?

When the attendees at our gathering posed some of these crucial questions, the distinguished guest responded by citing some research done at the high school level, where a civics course was added to the curriculum. Note the focus on the *what* and not the *how* or *by whom*. Students were tested with regard to their community engagement and sense of empowerment before and after the course. Turns out, the change was negligible. One might have had more success taking the kids on a march or showing a movie about Rosa Parks. Consequently, education as a place to learn participatory democracy was swiftly dismissed by the expert in our midst.

Unfortunately, our guest speaker had made the classic mistake of believing that education is all about the content, the *what*. The assumption is that one can tell the class about participatory democracy, or brain surgery for that matter, and students will translate that into becoming active citizens or capable doctors.

Let's imagine for a moment the likely scenario for this aforementioned civics course. Given that this was a course outside the usual subject areas, the person teaching it probably wasn't an expert in anything related to governance or participatory democracy. Odds are pretty good they happened to draw the short straw on this one. If, in addition, the course was offered on, say, a Friday afternoon or after lunch for about forty minutes, one could suppose that engaging and inspiring students would have been an uphill battle.

We can be pretty sure, as well, that the course wasn't taught as a participatory democracy. The students weren't involved in deciding what the content would be or in developing the assessment process. They didn't have the option to remove the teacher and engage different educators who better met their needs. They didn't learn the skills of dialogue, nor did they identify a community issue that was of concern and engage with it at a serious level where they could actually effect change beyond the school walls. They also likely weren't being taught by an educator who was intentionally decentering themselves as leader, knowledge-holder, driver of learning, and evaluator of learning outcomes.

In short, the students weren't immersed in a participatory democracy, so they never had the chance to learn what it is from the inside out or see what it means to be part of one. The *how* and *by whom* of the teaching practice, the pedagogy, didn't align with the *what* of the content, the curriculum. As such, the course content focused on one thing, but the practice illuminated and oddly reaffirmed the opposite.

Pedagogy is important, then, because most of us don't change what we do, who we are, or often what we know just by *hearing* about something else. Indeed, this fact is one of the big challenges facing the educator in the ecologizing process. After all, what does a pedagogy that is relational, interdependent, nonanthropocentric, and cooperative look like? What are the skills, the ways of being "teacher" that are most supportive of ecologizing education? Sadly, there are times when really good content is lost because of pedagogical choices that are, often implicitly, made—such as, for example, when participatory democracy is taught in a top-down manner. The same pitfalls await the ecologizing educator. Consider, for instance, the irony of teaching how important relationships are, how the natural world is mutually supportive, how we should work together for the mutual benefit of all—and then testing students individually in a competitive environment. One wonders which message actually lands.

With that challenge in mind, then, we want to frame this chapter on the important topic of pedagogy by offering one caution and by asking one question. First, the caution: ecologizing education is complex, challenging, and ever-changing work. It extends beyond just adding fields trips, messing with plants in science class, and telling kids they should care. And *delivery* is crucial: by whom and how and resting on what superstructure of theories, ideas, and commitments. Second, the question: How does one align the commitments of ecologizing education—such as relationality, the agency and rights of more-than-humans, and decentering the human—with the art and practices of teaching?

The rest of this chapter will be our attempt, at this moment in time (in this ever-changing work), to best answer that framing question, while bearing in mind the caution. Of course, our "answers" are not intended to be prescriptive, for that would be antithetical to the whole premise here. As a reminder of this, we offer up the metaphor of the cairn, a pile of rocks left for walkers, which indicates where they are and where they might go next in a landscape.[2] What follows here, then, is a series of six cairns. The first three are directed toward the question of *how* the natural world can be involved—nature as co-teacher, nature as possibility, nature as imaginative gifter—while the remaining three point toward the question *by whom*, with a focus on who the human teacher might become—teacher as activist, teacher as identity worker, teacher as cultural change worker. These ideas shape a potential orientation toward pedagogy. They are sets of concepts and ways of being teacher drawn from our research and experience. Like cairns encountered on a walk in an unfamiliar landscape, we imagine them rising hopefully from the surrounding mists in the little-trodden, under-mapped terrain of a more ecologizing education.

Cairn 1: Nature as Co-Teacher, Human Teacher Stepping Back

Recently, a graduate student in our Place- and Nature-Based Experiential Learning program shared a story with the rest of the class, which set off an interesting chain reaction of stories about similar experiences. The original story involved

Wasp, also known as "Frank" (for so the children had named Wasp). Frank had likely entered through the open window. This is not surprising, since the more one tries to ecologize education, the more one opens windows and takes note of the outdoors. Of course, typically, a wasp in the classroom leads to an eruption among the students—screams, wild handwaving, and shouts to "kill it!" The response involves the teacher coming to grips with the situation and deciding what should be done with this "dangerous" interloper.

Here, in this classroom, though, the tale deviates from the norm. The human teacher does not follow the regular, the expected, or the shouted-for trajectory. As a result of a growing relationship with the natural world and an interest in having nature as a co-teacher, the human teacher decides against the easy kill or removal of Wasp and instead focuses on the teaching moment that Wasp has presented. The itinerant being is gently captured.

Once captured, Frank becomes the centerpiece of discussions around wasp species, their likes and dislikes, and the whys, wheres, and hows of their living arrangements. Soon Frank is calmly returned to what may or may not be a more hospitable environment outside the classroom. Now there is an opportunity to track Wasp's movements upon release, to imagine, to think into, and to write about this winged mystery that appeared in the classroom. Next, the human teacher, excited personally and by the students' engagement, spends the evening researching Frank and making a plan for the following day that will continue the questions and learnings that happened in response to an event created—even facilitated—by Frank. The next day, it is apparent that many of the students had made similar inquiries about Wasp after they got home from school.

After hearing this story, many of the other teachers in the graduate class related similar experiences of rich learning that had resulted from unplanned intrusions by Wasp, Spider, Ant, and Fly. They also observed how children operated differently when given permission to notice and care for Wasp or Spider. We educators ought to pay close attention to this. Our response to the natural world greatly influences how our students come to make sense of the natural world as well. To simply squash and discard a living other is to affirm a particular hierarchy—and that lands painfully for many.

For these teachers, this moment of allowing Frank to be noticed and encountered also created an opening toward changing the *how* of teaching. Recognizing nature as co-teacher means changing one's perspective, being invited into a different relationship, and taking up new obligations. When the human teacher in this story took one small step in this new way of teaching, it set off an interesting cascade of events. First, the students' hysterical and seemingly threatened responses changed to expressions of interest and even care. This, in turn, challenged the human teacher (and inspired some of the students) to follow this interest further. The result was that space was opened for further learning, discussion, and possibility. And for a while at least, the class escaped from the more controlled, human-centered, fully structured, carefully planned, learning outcome–directed lesson on the agenda. For who doesn't want to learn more about the mystery of Frank?

Just as more-than-human denizens participated in the cocreation of the Maple Ridge Environmental School, an important part of ecologizing education involves actively trying to recognize teaching as a shared endeavor. On a human level, this kind of thinking is already quite common in education, with teachers committed to lifelong learning and many noting that they learn from their students. In ecologizing education, though, the goal is to take this idea of co-teaching much further. After all, the lessons that teachers receive from their students are often "accidental." They are certainly not intentionally solicited. The student is not preparing a lesson, being positioned as the teacher, and/or given space to enact their chosen pedagogy. And, as the previous participatory democracy example revealed, to democratically participate in the education at hand, co-teachers (children and more-than-human) need to be recognized as equals and thus be able to cocreate the educational practices. The ecologizing teacher's reaction to Frank illustrates how we might begin to recognize and respect the natural world as co-teacher and ultimately come to understand that the myriad denizens of the natural world have something to share with our learners and ourselves and are deserving of the respect and space in which to offer it.

Many human teachers consider this notion odd and perhaps a bit scary. Acknowledging the natural world as teacher means going outside on a consistent basis and leaving space for the natural world to appear. That means not planning everything down to the second. It means finding ways to step back and honor what comes—*and* the way it comes, for the natural world often employs very different pedagogies. It means being willing to follow a co-teacher's lead, whether that co-teacher is a parade of insects, the shade cast by a tree, or owl pellets filled with mice bones. Intriguingly, it also means trusting the learners to come into the process and find things, ideas, curiosities that draw them in. The further implication of this, of course, is that the human teacher gives up a bit of control so that co-teachers and learners have the freedom to teach and learn what fits for them at this specific moment.

Let's return to Frank's story for a moment: notice that the human teacher relinquished some of their control, worked to decenter themselves, and adapted in response to Frank's interactions with the students. Notice too that the students were also taking a risk in not doing what the system expected of them. Recognizing and naming this has been important for our graduate students, for it has become apparent how much we police and limit ourselves in light of how we think we are supposed to teach and be teachers. For many, this can be a difficult process. Whispers are heard down school hallways as parents and caregivers wonder where the "real learning" is. The oppression of scarce linear time coupled with the desire to "do a good job" make changing one's practice a risky endeavor. Yet, in releasing a little bit of control, in honoring their own desire for richer relationships with the natural world, and in decentering themselves as the sole expert, many teachers we have worked with have found a wealth of unexpected learning.

Importantly, recognizing nature as a co-teacher involves trusting the natural world to "come through," though not in an anthropocentric way, as if Bottlefly, Spruce, and Basalt are just waiting to offer small humans lessons. Cultivating this attitude of trust is no easy feat, though. Some human teachers think, "If I do this nature-as-co-teacher thing and nothing happens, won't I just be wasting everyone's time?" These worries are often accompanied by anxiety about being considered "out there" and being accused of always playing outside and not teaching anything. However, experience suggests that, although those feelings are very real, especially in the beginning, the natural world *always* offers something. It is filled with endless possibilities, affordances, and wonders. (And, if nothing seems to be working, the teacher can always go back to the ever-popular and readily available topic: poo.)

It's also important to think about what we mean when we say that we trust the natural world to "come through." In our experience, teachers who are just beginning this journey are often tempted to focus solely on "mega-events," like Bald Eagle fighting Grizzly Bear or Meadow Vole giving birth to four tiny pups. If this is the expectation, then much disappointment is inevitable, and cultivating the attitude of trust will be difficult indeed. We have found, however, that if teachers work to develop careful, humble, and deeply receptive attentivity to both the natural world and their students, some kind of learning experience is always happening—and trust follows.

We'll end with two brief points—consider them to be two small rocks added to the top of Cairn 1. First, *how we respond* to Wasp or Spider actively shows what we prioritize—that is, is the natural world important to us, as human teacher, or not? Our answer to this question makes a difference for all our learners, but in particular for those prone to deep caring about other living things. When we respond by ignoring Fern or killing Ant, we shut down particular ways of being in the world. But when we respond by engaging with and prioritizing the more-than-human, this serves as a model for learning—showing how one goes from an interesting, curiosity-sparking surprise to substantive, engaged knowing. It is important that human teachers not only model the process, but also share whatever tools are needed.

The second small rock we want to add to the top of Cairn 1 is to point out that changing one's teaching practice might not be the Herculean task it initially seems to be. The teachers and graduate students we have worked with are talented, capable, and imaginative, but not out-of-this-world extraordinary (though that's not what we tell them). They simply saw that the need to change, or just acknowledge, their relationship to the natural world presented opportunities to further discover and flex their practices. A small move, to recognize Frank as a co-teacher, led to a full day outside—which is Frank's home, after all. It included a partially decentered human teacher and a move away from total control (where the teacher possesses all the knowledge, designs all the activities, and predetermines all learning outcomes). It also flipped their practice, from one driven solely by learning outcomes to one where wonder, interest, and the place itself become the starting point. The expected learning outcomes—plus a surprising abundance of unexpected others—appear as a result.

Cairn 2: Nature as Possibility, Teacher as Curriculum Messer

Think about the process of designing a lesson. Some readers went through teacher's college, where lesson planning was drummed in from the get-go. For other readers, the task may not seem quite so easy, yet anyone who has had education done to them for many years can imagine their way into it. Usually, what appears in our imaginary lesson-planning process is some version of the Tylerian rationale. Ralph Tyler was a professor at University of Chicago in the mid-twentieth century and had a large influence on the areas of evaluation and assessment in education. In response to questions about his own teaching, he wrote a book that outlined a linear—*very* linear but much copied—process for curriculum design.[3]

Tyler's process of lesson design goes like this: First, the human teacher selects the objectives. (Here, in British Columbia, the term "learning outcomes" is used, but the idea is the same.) Second, the teacher decides on the learning experiences to be offered, usually those they consider most likely to lead to the desired outcomes. Third, the teacher organizes, implements, and "puts on" the learning experiences. Fourth, the whole process is evaluated, or at least the learners are, to see if the objectives have landed and the aimed-for learning has been achieved. Finally, repeat with either new learning objectives or the same ones if the process failed.

Admittedly, much critique of Tyler has occurred,[4] and you can find many examples of lesson planning strategies that are more creative and less linear, yet oddly, even in these less linear approaches, the skeletal structure of Tyler's process often still remains because in many ways it is quite successful. But it is not the approach we want to use in ecologizing education, and we'll briefly outline the reasons for this here, before moving on to our suggestions for more appropriate approaches to lesson design and curriculum development.

One obvious trouble spot in Tyler's method is the central role of the single knower, teacher, planner, controller, human. This means that co-teachers of whatever stripe—and some do have stripes—are left out. Further, in its singular focus on particular outcomes, this method actively limits the range of learning that can happen. Perhaps the reader can hear the particular epistemological assumptions of the building metaphor we discussed previously in chapter 4. By extension, Tyler's structure necessarily implies a sameness for all learners. The assumption is that everyone needs the same knowledge and that this knowledge is built and arrived at in the same way for everyone. Thus, diversity of learning styles, of learner experience, of cultural difference, of context, of situation, of outcomes, of ways of knowing all tend to disappear. Quite worryingly, this homogenizing of the learning experience also means that more marginalized and richly diverse populations are underserved, for they may be culturally, experientially, socially, or imaginatively not of the "norm" from which most teachers, and Tyler for that matter, come.

Another troubling outcome of Tyler's linear approach is that learners come to recognize this structure and begin to orient around "figuring out what the teacher wants"—and this certainly does not fit the purposes of ecologizing education. After all, if today's learners are going to find ways to cope with, respond to, and find possibilities within our massively changing world, they need to be able to think outside of teacher expectations, step outside the normal, and be creative and critical.

How, then, might ecologizing educators come to "mess with" curriculum while still keeping their jobs and changing the system? What skills might be involved? Let's explore two approaches that we think can offer fertile possibilities for ecologizing education: the curriculum of the dirty sock (yes, we are returning to the dirty sock) and the inverted curriculum, also known as "letting the learning outcomes just come falling out."

Back to the Curriculum of the Dirty Sock

At the Maple Ridge Environmental School, teachers wrestled with the challenge of shifting their practices—moving from lessons that could be carefully preplanned with controlled outcomes toward more ecologizing ones. Specifically, they were seeking practices that were more spontaneous, emergent, and responsive to nature as co-teacher as well as to the emotional realities and interests of the students. Furthermore, they needed practices that recognized and worked well with the affordances of place. As they moved in these directions, it became apparent that a previously underrecognized pedagogical ability was called for—one that allows the human teacher to accompany the learners along a web of interconnected knowledge or into a rhizomatic entanglement of spontaneous discovery. The skill itself came to be called "lateral thinking," and it rests upon at least two key ingredients: an unconstrained curiosity and a flexibility of mind.

The reader will remember the challenge—to find learning pathways for any subject matter starting from a dirty sock—or, to be more precise, starting from the experience of encountering such an unclean item of clothing. To do this, our group of teachers had to find connections between the sock and said content, which necessarily involved asking good questions: *Where did it come from? What is it made of? How is it made? What is the story behind the dirt?* This initial curiosity is just the beginning, though. The trick is to identify and follow the curiosities that expand the encounter and these initial questions into prescribed content. After all, cotton leads us into history—explore the cotton trade and slavery. Wool and sheep-farming take us into politics—discuss immigration and the rights of animals (Dolly was a sheep after all). The weave, shape, and design of the dirty sock open the door into the arts and mathematics—learn about weaving and spinning and determine the tensile strength of individual strands. And so it continues. This ability to think laterally, to see connections between and amongst the seemingly disconnected, we refer to as flexibility of mind.

When our response to an encounter is driven by rich, maybe even untamed, curiosities, we naturally ask good questions—which lead not only to interesting answers but also to the skills needed to answer them. Coupling such curiosity with a flexibility of mind leads to further questions that can line up with mandated curricular expectations. Inevitably, a spiderweb of interconnections appears and learning radiates down chosen strands, while spontaneous unexpected growth erupts like a mushroom through the forest floor. The point here is that, as lateral thinking is developed and teachers become adept at recognizing moments of fecund possibility and asking the kinds of questions that lead to curricular connections, learning can start almost anywhere. If a dirty sock can inspire and advance curriculum and its proposed learning outcomes, then meeting curricular obligations starting from a giant old-growth Western Red Cedar, a sudden hatch of Mayflies, or a tiny pile of sand left by an unknown underground digger should be possible too.[5] Lateral thinking, wild curiosity, and mental flexibility are part and parcel of a way of thinking that understands knowledge and meaning-making as fluid, complex, interconnected, shared, and deep. But to make this work, teachers do need to have a good handle on the learning outcomes that are sought by the systems that employ them.

The Inverted Curriculum: "The Learning Outcomes Just Come Falling Out"

We have seen that the ecologizing educator must become adept at asking good questions, at helping to find interesting answers, at making generative and imaginative connections, and at responding to moments rich in possibility that co-teachers might be providing. But doesn't the curriculum of the dirty sock potentially lead learners down all kinds of rabbit holes that aren't part of the mandated curriculum? The answer is, yes, it can. That reality, in and of itself, can have some good results. But if we take seriously our ecologizing education project, then we will likely need other ways to "cover the curriculum" for those in a centralized public system. This is where we meet that lateral-thinking-good-questioning-wildly-curious ecologizing educator who also really knows the governmental curricular documents well.

During the third semester of a two-year program in Place- and Nature-Based Experiential Learning, the students have gathered to share the results of "community-based" lessons. They have worked hard on ideas such as nature as co-teacher, and they recognize that change only happens when risk is taken and something new is tried. Sasha opens the proceedings, and she is bursting with excitement. She took her class across the street to a local park and did some of the Aldo Leopold–inspired work we had been exploring together.[6] "What has happened here?" "What is happening here?" and "What should happen here?" These were her framing questions for her class. Students were given the opportunity to spend some time exploring the place and finding or maybe being offered some answers. As the class debriefed in a small glen by Creek, Sasha's attention was drawn to how rich and diverse the students' answers were and also how easy it was for her to track the learning outcomes. She could hear descriptions and discussions that "covered" not only social studies content but also content in the areas of social awareness, group understanding, self-discovery, politics, justice, and the environment. When she shares this story with us, she can't hide her obvious delight as she points out that she could never have pre-planned a lesson that covered so much content.

The point here is that the ecologizing educator with deep knowledge of the curricular guidelines can flip Tyler's structure right over, such that the objectives no longer drive the lesson. Instead, they are allowed to materialize in more meaningful ways. We have started to call this "inverting the curriculum." Rather than driving the learning experience, the outcomes seem to "just fall out" when the encounter happens within this environment of vibrant curiosity and rich questioning. Yet this is also not a move to full child-centeredness since there are outcomes being watched and there are many teachers and learners involved. The educator's job, then, is to gather and record these outcomes as they appear. In Sasha's case, this was a first attempt, and, successful as it was, she could also see clearly that she had missed many opportunities to step in and ask a question that might have pushed the learning further or in a different direction while helping it align with outcomes she must report on. Of course, every experience of the ecologizing educator will further hone their skills in this "inverting the curriculum" approach.

Cairn 3: Nature as Imaginative Gifter, Teacher as Critical Thinker

One of the unsettling experiences from our work with Maple Ridge has been how often we came across our own blind spots. We repeatedly confronted our own assumptions about who teacher is, faced reminders of our colonial views and deeply held anthropocentrisms, and realized the narrowness of our understandings when it comes to how learners make sense of and engage with everything around them. For example, when we meet a childlike Raven (from chapter 2), who talks to natural beings, we are thrust into having to rethink troublesomely rigid concepts, such as *What is language? How does communication work?* and *How do humans and Cattail, Squirrel, or Hummingbird relate?* At another moment, a parent names their trauma in relation to public schooling and the ongoing destruction of the natural world, and so we are pushed to consider holding space for pain, loss, and transformation while also "eco-street smarting" our green charges as they come into contact with the non-ecological world beyond the fringes of their school. Inevitably, the day comes when a school district requires "results," and we are confronted with systems of evaluation and assessment that are hierarchical, competitive, compartmentalized, profoundly individualized, and weirdly unecological. For us, doing this work has required a willingness to be open and critical, humble and strong, all at the same time.

With all of this in mind, we want to turn to a very recent challenge to our work that unexpectedly appeared. We don't yet and may never have a complete answer to it. It all started with this quote from the work of Joe Sheridan and Roronhiakewen "He Clears the Sky" Dan Longboat: "Imagination is understood to be a quality of mind in settler culture. In Haudenosaunee/ Mohawk tradition, the same quality is understood to be animal and spiritual helpers manifesting their presence in one's life. . . . [The settler conception of] imagination dominates where fear of the unknown, uncertainty of memory, and placelessness thrive."[7] (Readers may remember that this work of Sheridan and Longboat also informed our discussion on "old-growthing" in chapter 1.) It's one thing to appreciate theory, though, and quite another to enact it within our practices. We were unsettled—literally and metaphorically—by the implications and potentials of this quote for teaching practice.

We realized that, despite our emphasis on enacting pedagogies that honored the intrinsic worth of the natural world, that tried to leave space for and foreground the diversity of teachers around us, and that worked to move toward more relational conceptions and enactments of knowledge, we were still isolating a particular part of the educational process: the individual human mind. Comments such as "What are you thinking, Ahmed?" or "Great idea, Louise!" or "Awesome, your group has come up with such a creative idea!" were implicitly and normatively reifying the point Sheridan and Longboat are making: in settler culture, ideas, thoughts, and the imagination are uncritically assumed to belong to a single human or group of humans. To seriously consider this challenge—that the mind is a shared space and that ideas and imaginings are not the "product" of one's own brilliance but a gift from the world around us— we had to puzzle over our assumptions and practices again. We had to wrestle with the uncomfortable possibility that our assumptions not only were continuing to separate us from the world around us but also were sustaining a colonial fear-based way of being with, in, and upon this land now called Canada.

Notice what happens when you consider the mind to be a shared place—a relational space where gifts are offered and where dialogue, in whatever language, allows for the more-than-human world more broadly to speak and be heard. Now those comments have a markedly different flavor: "Wow, Ahmed, where do you think all those gifts are coming from?" "Nice, Louise, I hear River spilling through!" "Great work, group, don't forget to cite all your helpers." The ramifications are interesting and important. As we noted in chapter 1, for Sheridan and Longboat the individual imagination is actually just an early developmental step toward becoming a mature adult with an emplaced, "old-growth" mind. The language here is lovely and worth noting, but it is also *not* metaphoric for those of us interested in ecologizing education. In a way, Sheridan and Longboat are pointing toward a developmental model where the aim is not an autonomous, "self-reliant" individual but rather a sophisticated, embedded, place-thinking,[8] relational being. As such, the current goal for public education appears to be a quite-limited early step toward a land-based, even autochthonous, growing-out-of-place citizenship.

Sheridan and Longboat also make a direct connection between their understanding of the imagination and the need for changed relations between and amongst humans and the world. This different quality of mind, they propose, is "modernity's guide to recovering the necessary relationship between healthy ecologies of land and human minds."[9] Part of the educational project, then, becomes one of helping students start to grow out of the land they inhabit, whether they are Indigenous, are Indigenous to another place, or are part of a culture that requires them to be nonrelational.

This project of autochthony—to grow out of place—is, in fact, that "old-growthing of the mind" we discussed previously. So, in concert with Basso's assertion that wisdom sits in places,[10] this suggests that the deepest wisdom sits in the oldest places, with the oldest beings. It suggests the importance of allowing the geography of place and the gifts offered by animal and spirit helpers to be part of the shaping—the old-growthing—of human students' minds. This, in turn, involves providing space for those beings and the land to be heard, in the way they would wish to be heard. Gifts need to be offered and also thoughtfully, even reverentially, received, for as this imagination is developed, the human actually gains access to "a sentient landscape," as Longboat and Sheridan articulate.[11]

Even as ecologizing educators come to accept the sentience and wisdom of place, the spatial and shared nature of the imagination, and the importance of context, they are urged to slow down and listen yet again. There is more to do. They can make room to actively recognize the gifts being offered; to find ways to better "place" their work in order to allow the landscape to validate nascent learners like Raven as they encounter this wisdom; and to allow place to breathe, to speak, to teach, and eventually to thrive.

All of this may sound a little overwhelming for your average public school teacher. Frankly, it's a little overwhelming for us, too. And yet, can we really afford to keep replicating the status quo? Besides, overwhelming as it may be, this idea of old-growthing is where hope and possibility can be found—first, because it provides a frame for a more relational model of human development (which, while still a little foggy, if not completely invisible); and second, because there are already many examples of relationships being built, of lives changing, and of communities doing and being differently. Some of them are at Maple Ridge, examples that we have been documenting even before we knew what we were looking for.

Recall how Raven talked of "little words" curling into her mind, particularly when she isn't thinking.[12] We see this as an extraordinary description of how the world is gifting ideas; after all, there is no indication that Raven is leading this process. Here, the space of the mind is shared—ideas and imaginings curl into it, with Raven patently and patiently honoring the sentience of the living landscape. The reader must remember here that this is a nine-year-old child, enunciating, as best she can despite the limitations of the English language, what we think Sheridan and Longboat are pointing toward. Given the space to immerse herself in the outdoors, build relationships, and be heard—even though she is saying things that settler culture might denigrate or position as fantastical—Raven has the capacity to think *with place*. This gives us hope—not because Raven is unusual but because Raven is *quite usual*. The ecological imagination is part of all of us. Only when it is tamped down and consciously restricted, as it is in settler culture, do we fail to hear and know its presence. Only then do we miss out on its offerings of gifts.

Raven's story offers something further for us to reckon with. As she grew older, Raven became more aware of the responses of the larger world, that is, those from outside her family and the school. Often, those responses were unkind. At times, Raven would check in with her mother to confirm whether a particular place was "safe" for her to be her relational self. We know, in fact, that Raven's situation is not uncommon. Indeed, we have heard epithets and hateful comments directed toward some of our deeply relational young people. Some feel forced to choose between acknowledging and honoring their interconnected, relational true selves and their desire to be a part of more superficial but culturally sanctioned relationships. Too many times we have seen deeply connected students turn away from the natural world in order to remain part of the human group. Somehow, the ecologizing educator must find the wherewithal not only to respond to these experiences of deep loss, but also to be forthright about their own connections and diligent in preparing learners for this reality. This is a kind of eco-street smarting.

We'll end here by touching on one exciting but at the same time frustrating aspect of doing the questioning that is essential to ecologizing education: as we educators ask those important questions, we are, in a way, turning over cultural rocks and starting to dig around underneath—inevitably, though, this leads us to see other rocks that need flipping . . . or maybe this isn't the right metaphor. Let's try another one. We are examining a single tree, say, a Douglas Fir in a functioning ecosystem. We soon discover, though, that this tree is dialed into other trees, which in turn are connected to still further trees, which are themselves connected to rhizomes, to water sources, and on to spiders and woodpeckers. Exciting, yes, but challenging in its complexity and never-ending-ness. Just as there is no single being to examine here, there is no easy "remove and replace" if you want to change the culture.

Indeed, to consider nature as a co-teacher is to change how we think about knowledge, which has implications for assessment if educators follow *that* rhizomic thread in one direction. By following the thread in another direction, though, we come to realize that the very definition of *human* is in doubt. Yes, it can be somewhat unnerving, but we are not in this alone. Support and possibility are offered by all-our-relations, and our job might be to just quieten ourselves a bit and let them "curl" into us and our students. It is intriguing work. Thankfully, over time, we seem to have become better at sitting with the sense of not knowing. When we discover a tangle of threads, we can feel wonder and curiosity rather than the urge to compulsively untangle them. We are getting used to encountering our own failings over and over. We are getting used to listening to the wider more-than-human and accepting the gifts being offered. We are getting used to constant rock flipping. Sometimes these questions and challenges appear on cue, as expected, such as the challenges that will inevitably arise if you advocate for including the natural world in an authentic and active way in every PTA meeting.

Let's move on now to consider how teachers might practice and be teacher differently in order to support this project of decentering the human, building relationships, and healing. Here, the territory we are traversing becomes even foggier. It is hard to see the entire landscape of ecologizing education, but perhaps we will find that the cairns along the way offer some comfort that we are in the rightish place.

Cairn 4: Teacher as Activist, Moving toward Ally

It has happened again. One of us has just finished a public talk about ecologizing education, describing the challenges, positioning things as a cultural problem, naming the natural world as both co-teacher and colonized. Someone in the audience has queried—thankfully quite calmly this time because these are often very aggressive confrontations (red in face and tongue, as it were)—our "move to propagandize" learners. As they understand it, the act of foregrounding the natural world moves away from the "neutral," secular position of public education and into some form of green manipulation of young minds. These kinds of questions challenge us—and, by extension, anyone who seeks to ecologize education—to find ways to respond because propaganda and manipulation of any kind, even if aiming in a good direction, is problematic indeed. Who gets to decide what learners are exposed to? Who is included and excluded in any educational process? Whose notion of "good" do we rely on? What is prioritized in one's classroom? These important questions help frame our layered responses, which aim not only at individual educators and classrooms but also at the institutional and cultural structures in which those classrooms are situated.

The first response, aimed at the individual level, is to remind the questioner that everything is political. Perhaps this isn't immensely helpful as a comment, except it *does* challenge educators to remember that they are making public life decisions constantly. They are advocating for and in fact helping to construct a particular vision of society, no matter what they do. Those decisions—and non-decisions, of course—are indicators of what they, as educators, prioritize and how they believe learners might or should be in the world. Every decision point could go myriad ways, and each one positions us with regard to our politics. Students are called on to compete or cooperate. Resources, rights, responsibilities, and ideals are decided on and distributed. These are all political acts. Being political is not something we educators can avoid, no matter how much we might like to. Thus, the second, and related, response is to posit that we, as educators (and parents/caregivers for that matter), are *being asked* to be political actors, making decisions each and every day, maybe not at the global or national level but definitely at the particular, local, face-to-face interactional and public level. We constantly ask ourselves: What shall we do now, how are we expected to behave, and where might this all be leading for a small group of learners?

As the philosopher Martin Buber suggests in *Between Man and Man*, educators are bringing a world to the students.[13] The political nature of this process is implicit here, for it is not *the* world that is being offered but *a* world, suggesting that it is impossible to bring everything. Rather, the educator must make selections, impose limitations, and determine emphases—which means that, in making these choices and bringing this world to their students, the educator is also accepting a profound responsibility.

Even if our vision of this world is of one that is more equitable and participatory, that is, one where students and all-our-relations are treated with mutual respect, given the opportunity to flourish in their own ways, and work with the teacher to create this best world together (the world that we strive for in ecologizing education)—even in this scenario, the educator is still making political decisions about what needs to be discussed, challenged, problematized, and disrupted and about what could be added, extended, created, and embraced. This process still includes naming a vision and putting forward a plan for how the world works. It still demands particular ways of teaching, of talking about the natural world, of engaging with students and communities, of doing a lot of things that this book is proposing. The result is that actions, decisions, and curricular offerings all become part of this world being offered.

Ultimately, then, ecologizing education, like *all* teaching, is an ongoing series of political acts. Part of what we are doing is supporting and suggesting a vision of a world to learners. In choosing to use that vision as a lens through which to make decisions, we must acknowledge that there is a kind of propagandizing and manipulation going on. The audience member who asked that challenging question is correct, to that extent. The problem, however, is the questioner's assumption that there exists a form of education that is apolitical—neutral and propaganda-free. In

fact, a "neutral" position does not exist. Every teacher in every classroom continually makes decisions that enable learners to understand the world *in particular
ways*. That is, no teacher brings *the* world to their students; rather, every teacher
brings *a* world.

Let's step out of the individual classroom for a moment now and consider the
larger picture. After all, teachers are not autonomous beings operating in some
kind of utopian free-to-be-and-do wonderland. There are rules, of course: explicit and implicit centralized curricula and "accepted" pedagogies and structures, both physical (classrooms, timetables, Christmas concerts, exams, and
learning outcomes) and cultural (hierarchies, concepts of knowledge and knowing, ideas of success, various and intersecting forms of privilege, and so on),
that are often outside a teacher's control and even knowing.

We want to name those structures as being part of the "invisible" cultural
assumptions and social values that imbue mainstream education. These are the
often-unseen political values that resist change and tend to turn the innovations
of the most inspired teachers back to the status quo. They are embedded, unacknowledged propaganda. The system has deemed them important and necessary as part of the world that is being brought to the students. Because they are
in the center, in the mainstream, these norms, truths, politics being offered can
be positioned as neutral, common sense, and secular, by virtue of the assumption that most people agree with or have been immersed in them. Anyone doubting this fact might find a recent Muslim immigrant, transgender youth, or
Indigenous child and ask them whether the public education they encounter in
North America is propaganda-free with respect to Christian ideas or gender binaries or Caucasian epistemologies. Those on the margins inevitably recognize
the implicit and explicit propaganda of the center far better than the center does.

So where does this leave us in response to the question of ecologizing education
as a propagandizing machine? Given that *all* educators—ecologizing and mainstream and all the others—are always engaged in propagandizing and manipulat-
ing, then perhaps what is needed is to reframe the question. Let's ask instead:
Which forms of propagandizing and manipulation are we, as educators, willing to
be a part of? How aware and critical are we of the politics embedded in our practices and places of teaching? What kind of world do we want to bring to our students? And, if that is different from the one that the central structures are pushing,
what might we do in response? We believe that questions like these open the door
for the teacher to become advocate and activist, and to work toward allyship.

After all, if we accept the propagandizing argument and take seriously this
idea of bringing a world to students, then teachers are, by definition, advocating
for the world they choose to bring. The philosopher Jean-Paul Sartre argued this
exact point in suggesting that moral beliefs in the world are evidenced in one's

actions. Everything we do is a positing of value, whether this is thoughtfully done or not, and, for Sartre, intention is not as important as action. For example, the intention to recycle does not outweigh the fact of *not* recycling. For ecologizing educators working toward eco-social justice in critical response to anti-environmental culture and institutional systems that are anti-environmental, the move toward advocacy and activism has, we think, already been made.

While advocacy flows quite naturally from the choices a teacher makes in bringing a world to their students, the move to *activism* is slightly more difficult to make or even acknowledge. This is particularly true for teachers who, through their histories and their training, see themselves as needing to be "neutral," to present "balanced" accounts of everything, and to honor the diversity that appears in their classrooms. Unhelpfully, our vision of activism often involves marching, tipping cars, and going to jail. This vision is itself a particular kind of framing. But there isn't just one way to be an activist. In fact, large-scale change has never happened without a multilayered approach. Some people are shouting and fighting to get the message out, while others are involved in working with groups, putting change into action, and educating.

Let's return, then, to our idea of the rebel ecologizing teacher from the previous chapter, refining our definition of this rebel teacher now as *advocate* and *activist*. Their activism is tied directly to their offering of a different vision for the world. This vision includes mutually beneficial flourishing, which means resisting components of the educative process that are anti-ecological and unjust, and supporting students and all-our-relations to be heard in their authentic voices. As advocate, the rebel teacher leaves space for students to exercise their rights, to express dissent, and to expand the range of how to be student in the classroom and human in the world. Examples of activism, that is, moving toward something different from the status quo, include teaching about politics, political engagement, and the history of change; building students' capacity to be critical; and enacting these other ways of being in the classroom.

Remember too that this work also involves more than just talking. (Recall, for example, the failure of the participatory democracy course to inspire students to be more engaged and empowered as community members.) None of this discussion is likely to land if our practices don't embrace the ideas we are trying to communicate and if students don't get to name and experience the politics of the classroom or encounter a world where many more voices are involved in the decision-making processes. Activism is also about standing up and speaking against practices in schools, classrooms, and the system that are contrary to the vision of a more eco-socially just world. Another important part of the work is holding space for students and the group as a whole to live into their vision and to practice and become acclimatized to different ways of being.

Activism as pedagogy, within the frame of ecologizing education, includes not only teaching students the tools of criticality but also building alliances beyond one's classroom. For us, as ecologizing educators, moving toward allyship likely will include building deep relationships with diverse communities, particularly those that are marginalized within mainstream culture, including the natural world. Becoming an ally (which is an honor bestowed and not self-adopted) involves seeking out ways to listen to, to learn from, and to honor the diversity of the other. Ecologizing education and changing culture can only happen through listening, through building relationships (throughout the more-than-human), through decentering the singular educator and the human, and through having a chance to practice the more eco-socially just world we envision.

Cairn 5: Teacher as Identity Worker

Before the Maple Ridge Environmental School opened, we work hard to build community, find allies, share the vision, and then communicate that vision far and wide. This also involved much work with the school district itself. At one of the earliest meetings with the superintendent, we had, as mentioned before, a few requests: (1) no building; (2) a recognition that we wouldn't have all the answers up front (for example, we didn't really know how families would figure out the weather thing, but we knew they would—and they did, really quickly!); and (3) the opportunity to work intensively with the teachers assigned to the school—designing curriculum, undoing troublesome habits, and getting to know their places and co-teachers—for up to a year before opening.

As it turned out, we didn't get our third request—the certificate program was a workaround, and none of the assigned teachers were part of it—but we want to reiterate here the importance of having time for human teachers to work on their ecologizing pedagogies. Our request for that year of preparation was mostly about supporting teachers into a more outdoor, experiential, and imaginative pedagogy. The idea was to help them prepare lessons, get to know the outdoor locations, and start laying down new teacherly pathways that were different from some of their tried-and-true habits of indoor teaching. That year was also going to be about assessing risk-management and developing local operating procedures and protocols that are part and parcel of overall safety and learning outdoors. Ultimately, we were right about this. There was a noticeable difference at the beginning between NEST, where teachers did get some paid planning time and a whole summer to prepare, and Maple Ridge, where one teacher was hired the day before the school opened. However, even we failed to fully appreciate one aspect of this important preparatory process we had requested: the rethinking of teacher identity. That is, what does it mean to be a teacher? How do individuals in those roles—and the communities they engage with—make sense of and position the idea of "teacher"?

This rethinking of teacher identity is necessary because ecologizing education asks us, as human educators, to *change* our identity as teacher. For one thing, it asks us to undo our own centrality and spread the role around: as an ecologizing educator, we must accept nature as co-teacher, parents/caregivers as teaching partners, and so on. It also asks us to rethink where knowledge resides, reconsider how and with whom planning is done, reevaluate the status we render to the position itself, and reconceptualize other deep structures implicit to being teacher. In most North American education, teacher is expert, teacher is center, teacher is in control.

At the beginning of Maple Ridge, we didn't fully realize how deeply these ideas are entrenched and how much time it takes to unearth them and select and then learn different ways of being teacher. This process includes *everything* about being a teacher, some of which is really hard to change. Take, for example, teacher intuition, that deep-rooted, long-developed responsiveness that we grow and nurture over time and that we rely on to guide us when we are in the heart and heat of the teaching and learning process with twenty-five excited students circling. For the ecologizing educator, even one's intuition can be suspect (remember the response to "why are these leaves red?"). This is true at least until much work has been done to overlay those older, and identified as troublesome, ways with new, more eco-socially just, cultural change-y ones. This work takes time and, for those of us who are impatient for change, a certain amount of gentleness with oneself. One tool we used quite a bit in this difficult task—in support of both reflection and implementation—comes out of the work of the French philosopher Michel Foucault.

Foucault proposed that the way to make explicit this challenge to change, the way to actively resist the pull toward the status quo, was to assume an attitude of what we are translating as "hyperactive pessimism."[14] The hyperactive component of this attitude refers to an assumed orientation in the world. Think about prey animals in a particularly risky moment. Mouse on top of Snow heading for its home, Fawn waiting for its mother's return—both are always on the alert. In the case of the ecologizing educator, constant vigilance is required to recognize, name, and interpret ecologically and socially problematic habits, behaviors, teacher intuitions, and beliefs, many of which are unknown to us. They can sneak up and surprise, just like Owl on Mouse. Many readers likely already know this feeling a little bit: we find ourselves treading carefully to make sure that what we are saying and thinking is not degrading or offensive; we are continually aware that the expected ways of doing are no longer acceptable. Teachers in mainstream classrooms and elsewhere are already needing to examine and re-examine habits, behaviors, ways of speech, responses to students, observations, and priorities.

This hyperactive component is also about locating, creating, choosing, and then implementing new habits, behaviors, and responses to students. It's about implementing new beliefs, for without something to replace the troublesome ones, we are bound to be stuck. The goal is that these replacements are better aligned with who one wants to be in the world and how one seeks to have humans be in the world—although there is no guarantee. Thus, the hyperactive aspect of "hyperactive pessimism" recognizes the constant work and the need for continuing vigilance throughout the change process until such time as the new habits and behaviors are confirmed as being the ones desired and have replaced the old as the "automatic" ways of being. As we noted previously, this work parallels the kind being done in exploring questions of privilege.

For Foucault, the pessimism part of "hyperactive pessimism" relates to his assumption that if the challenges we are dealing with are built into the culture, then many of the "normal," "habitual," "common sense," and "instinctual" ways of doing and being are likely to be problematic, for they rest on the assumptions of the problematic culture. Consider, for example, some of the current justice movements, such as MeToo, Idle No More, Black Lives Matter, and the student climate strikes. Activists in these movements are coming up against the fact that the challenges being named—gendered violence and the patriarchy, racism, and environmental denialism—are deeply embedded in the culture. These causes are not railing against a few "bad apples" acting inappropriately. They are identifying a corrupt milieu. This is the "systemic" in systemic racism, after all. Thus, our assumed ways of being are thrown under the microscope of suspicion, and for Foucault, being pessimistic about those assumed ways of being is an important start toward changing them.

For us, the idea of "hyperactive pessimism" is a reminder of the continuing incompleteness of the work and that we ought not to become too comfortable or complacent. Given that it has taken multiple generations to create the kind of anti-environmental, alienated culture that currently exists, it is unlikely we will quickly reach an ecologized version. Perhaps the best one can do is to begin to push the project in what seems to be the most promising direction and help the next generations continue the work in new and changing ways. Indeed, it is quite likely that much of the work we have done in good faith will have to be undone. Fortunately, hyperactive pessimism also helps us to maintain an attitude of humbleness, keeping in perspective our contribution to the ongoing work. After all, we are all on a journey, both individually and communally, and there are no totally right answers, no Truths, or, to push against educational language, no "best practices" at this point. There are just people doing things to the best of their abilities with integrity, who bring an attitude of active questioning of the status quo and a willingness to change, rethink, and undo as needed.

Some, though not enough unfortunately, are beginning to do the difficult work of constantly examining their actions and learning to check and then change themselves and their explicit and implicit assumptions, sexisms, and racisms. The same hard work is no doubt required regarding our relationships with the natural world. For instance, in the ecologizing education conversation, we have argued that modern Western culture is, in fact, *anti*-environmental in its orientations, habits, politics, and assumptions—thus, it is likely that every habit, belief, behavior, and sanctioned way of being is anti-environmental too. Consequently, unless we have carefully and deliberately thought through our behavior in any given situation using some version of a critical eco-lens, and unless we have then done the work to develop new ecologizing habits, it is likely that everything we are doing is potentially problematic. The "pessimism" of hyperactive pessimism does not imply that change can't happen, though. Rather, it assumes that the problematics run deep in the culture and, as such, the work to change will be difficult and slow and will require the utmost of attention and care.

Let's step now beyond teacher identity and how that might be changed and consider the larger identities of ourselves and our students. In fact, some elements of this conversation have been around in environmental education for a long time. For instance, an old environmental educational practice involves switching a student's environment. This gives them the possibility to try out being someone different, to change their identity. Often this has been done for—and to—students who are struggling. Sometimes it entails sending them outdoors to wilderness camps and other programs, because if someone really does want to change—and that part is important—it helps change not only schools and social groups but the entire context of learning, if possible. After all, context shapes us and, at the same time, positions and restricts us.

As an example, think back to those first return trips to your parental home after heading into the world and becoming an adult. Perhaps, upon stepping through the door, you were rapidly thrust back into your brooding, angry, lonely, goofy, or immature self despite best intentions. This is at least partially because your parents and family had not yet caught up with the changes you were going through, and so they remembered—and were responding to—a former version of you. No doubt, though, it was also partially a result of the house, the furniture, the neighborhood, and the community—the contexts in which you developed habits for how to be you. In some ways, the context itself didn't know the new you, and so it directed you back into the old ways it had known you.

Detaching from context and community, though, is not just about getting *away* from things. It is also about going *to* things. When you are in a new context, when those around you don't really know you, you have more freedom to "experiment" with yourself. You encounter fewer people who have pre-formed assumptions about you which might channel you into certain behaviors and ways of being. Also, different contexts offer different possibilities. For example, the natural world tends to have a larger diversity of "tools" to enable *being* in the world than most contexts in the North American mainstream, particularly if all-our-relations are understood as potential exemplars. It might seem to be a bit of a joke to ask, "What animal would you be?" but when taken a touch more seriously, this can be a source of possibility and even direction for growing identities. The answer to "What would nature do?" becomes a source of information. As we come to know the perseverance of Salmon or the transformability of Caterpillar or the community awareness of Cedar or the interconnectedness of Wolf and Caribou, these all become sources of inspiration and potential material for self-creation. Thus, part of being an ecologizing educator is about holding the space for these encounters to happen and be considered—and then allowing the time for reflection and practice such that possibilities can be sintered into one's transforming identity. In fact, this might also include transforming the very concept of identity.

For much of public education in North America, identity is seen as a fairly static thing. For those in the mainstream, identity seems to be quite easily adopted and there is little need for self-evaluation and soul-searching. For many outside the "norms," though, identity tends to be a constant struggle between authenticity and the colonizing power of those same norms. In fact, though, all of us establish, wrestle with, and change our identity over time, particularly through schooling and childhood. Hopefully, by adulthood, we have located and "settled into" a clearly established identity. Even then, however, we may find that identity shifts and changes.

Of course, often others are more than willing to reify our identities for us, to violently stuff our round selves into square holes. Sometimes we are pushed into an identity netherworld, where we are seen as other, less-than, and not belonging. Interestingly, part of the reason some people react angrily and violently at the notion of queer, fluid, binary, and trans ways of being is because admitting that this diversity exists also means critiquing the assumption of a solid and easily adopted identity. It means having to accept queerness as part of one's own possibility.

Work in queer ecology has compellingly shown how the natural world is drawn into these discussions in quite troublesome ways as well.[15] Cisgendered scientists, for example, appear to inscribe gender binaries (and patriarchies and heteronormativities) onto the natural world in their "scientific" work.[16] And then the culture uses the language of "natural" as an aggressive, even violent, tool against humans who do not fit these implied norms, even though ample evidence exists that the natural world is much more fluid (in sexuality, gender, and identity) than given credit for. We see the world through our cultural lenses, do not allow its diverse voices to come through, and then use our "findings" against the posited other. Sound familiar?

Three intertwined but different layers of identity relate to the work of the ecologizing educator. The first is at the conceptual level, that is, how we conceive of identity itself. Our sense is that identity is not as static, or essentialized, as traditionally posited. It is potentially much more fluid. This notion of identity as static is likely connected to the desire to control, to resolve into definiteness, and to create and affirm hierarchies. If we are correct, though, in seeing identity as more fluid, this means that more possibilities to teach "old dogs new tricks" exist and that these possibilities might be all around us if only we deign to dive under our assumptions and truly take in our surroundings. The natural world is much more fluid and dynamic than we often realize. See, for example, Slug, Earthworm, Bonobo, and Alligator to name just a few. This dynamism suggests, then, that we be very careful of the lenses we bring with us as we engage our more-than-human kin. Indeed, the careful attender might discover diverse possibilities, fluid examples, and imaginative ideas all around both the concept of identity and with regard to one's own particular identity choices.

The second layer of identity that relates to work of the ecologizing educator is at the level of the individual, the "who we be" and "who we become" in the world, that is, as Estella or Sean or teacher. Again, we want first to suggest that identity at this level is more fluid—a process, a verb even, rather than a noun. As such, we are Seaning, Estellaing, teachering. Second, our identities are actually never complete. We are complex, varied, flexible becomings (incomplete and fluid), and that diversity can change "who we are" and "who we be" depending on context, desire, and so on. Thus, we might find belonging in myriad locations, each sustaining and supporting our identity range. This fluidity also means that those who believe they know for sure who they are, no matter the situation, are likely wrong, either in terms of their range of self-awareness or in terms of their responsiveness to diverse situations. And finally, all of this suggests that part of being a human educator is not so much about helping the individual find their particular self, but rather about providing the space and, we think, the diversity of possibilities so that students can be continually finding, flexing, and reimagining themselves.

The third layer of this identity discussion relates to the identity of being human, writ large. This aspect of identity is not about the particular individual, but about the cultural concept of what it means to be human. Historically, change educators have most often focused on the individual without actually addressing the possibility of change for the larger concept of human. We sense that this oversight has left the work incomplete. As should be clear by now, part of ecologizing education is finding ways to critique, to challenge, and to change the modern West's concept of human and, further, to change the culture out of which that concept arises. This involves a complete renegotiation, in dialogue with the diversity of human cultures (the range of possibility expressed through what Wade Davis calls the ethnosphere[17]) and with the planet's biodiversity so that there is a better chance of the mutually beneficial flourishing we are all hopefully advocating for. So it seems that we have now stepped into the landscape of cultural change. And there, in the foggy distance, is one final cairn.

Cairn 6: Teacher as Cultural Change Worker

When we began this project of ecologizing education with Maple Ridge Environmental School, we understood the change challenge to be cultural, at its depth. We knew that the historical environmental education tradition, which focuses on changing the behavior of individuals, did not go far enough. That tradition was based on the idea that if enough people change their behaviors and care more actively for the natural world, the world will change. Unfortunately, though, fifty years of significant environmental education and activism effort had brought little change on a larger scale. Thus, we sought to change culture: we chose to work with the smallest semi-independent cultural unit of the educational system—the school—to see if we could make "changes all the way down."[18] Even at the beginning, we knew that things would arise that hadn't been planned for, that our understandings would change over time, and that we were going to have to be hyperactively pessimistic. Still, one of the biggest surprises was how underprepared we were for the actual work of cultural change.

One of the long-standing pedagogical ideas in environmental, outdoor, eco-change education work, which we advocate for throughout this book, has been to get students outside. Extending this, David Sobel has done wonderful work around the importance of children having spaces away from the prying eyes of adults, where they can be themselves, play at being adults, feel safe, and develop relationships.[19] Sobel has long advocated for setting aside pedagogical time when students get to build "forts" (more on that in a second), dens, bush-huts, hidey-holes, whatever. He even claims that this kind of play is almost universal across cultures. As a result, Maple Ridge decided to build in about forty-five minutes per day of mostly independent time for students to do just this. In fact, ours may have been one of the more comprehensive, long-term research endeavors looking at Sobel's work in action.

Over time, the students' play grew in sophistication. Many imaginative paths and projects were being pursued at the same time. Some of the projects were more all-encompassing and involved almost all the children, while others were very localized, involving just a few. The village itself—for that is what it became—eventually consisted of many structures. Eventually, some became two- and even three-story buildings, illustrating marvelous displays of lashing that were a testament to the students' visions and fine motor skills.

However, early on, teachers and researchers felt compelled to intervene on a couple of issues. The first involved the overuse of "resources" and the denuding of life in particular areas. The second related to the term "forts," for it became apparent that using that language and imagery was problematic as we considered and worked with our Indigenous partners and students. This led to adopting the term "village" and also to a much more considered and caring approach in selecting what might be appropriate for building. Overall, though, interventions by adults were kept to a minimum. This decision, at least partially, rested in the assumption that with independent time, immersion in nature, and opportunities for imaginative play, students will be automatically influenced in a "good" way by the world around them. But this was not our experience.

We wanted to give this independent play time a fair chance for success, but after about six months, we had to conclude that the influence of culture—that is, the mainstream eco-problematic culture—was stronger than the influence of nature. Our first hint should perhaps have been the denuding of areas and lack of care for the living denizens (Moss, Huckleberry, Salamander) as the students focused on acquiring "resources" needed for building. Soon, some students were complaining about not being allowed to play, about being left out of things, about not having access to some of the buildings and materials. In fact, the village had become a childlike and worrisome version of a police state. A single, self-appointed autocratic leader (an older boy) ruled. His power and position were reenforced by a posse (yes, that was the language) of enforcers (mostly the other older boys). Resources were centrally controlled—in particular, rope, building materials, and access to the buildings themselves. Pieces of wood had become currency, and violators of this single, centralized story were actually incarcerated in one of the three jails that now existed in this ninety-person village.

In essence, the children had recapitulated the mainstream culture, as they understood it, using it as imaginative building blocks. Consequently, all the social and ecological problematics the school itself was trying to undo were entering into and being exhibited and reenforced by the children's play. Because, as a group, we hadn't purposefully imagined our way into other options, the children were left with only the tools available, those of the mainstream culture, to build their own world.

It was now clear that, in order to address this challenge, educators needed to play a role in this time of free play by offering the students other tools, potential cultural scaffolds even, to avoid this reaffirmation of the troublesome culture. So we began to involve teachers more actively in the village. We also met and discussed together as educators and researchers to better understand what was happening and to consider what we might introduce. We were challenged to imagine into different cultural ways of being and to find tools and offerings for the students that might support the process of cultural change.

One of the changes we chose was to facilitate was to develop a more consensus-based, almost socio-cratic, decision-making process for the students. The entry point for this was quite apparent, given how disgruntled and even aggrieved many of the students felt about the centralized domination of the current form of governance. In fact, a lot of ideas for this were generated from the students themselves. Many of the quieter, perhaps more eco-connected, students didn't like the village play as it was enacted and just needed support, recognition, and minor interventions for their voices to be heard. A governance group was set up, facilitated by one of the educators, and representatives were chosen. Almost immediately, an expanded range of activities and play began happening in the village. More joy was evident, and two of the jails were quickly repurposed.

The second big change the educators involved themselves in, after politics and governance, might be understood as economic in nature. In the village, a very centralized, competitive, capitalistic ethos had appeared, as it does in mainstream culture, around the idea of scarcity. This seeming lack of the particular resources for the dominant activity in the village (that is, rope and wooden building materials for creating structures) meant that those who were "powerful" could collect, horde, restrict access to, and overinflate the values of these resources. It also meant that many were left out and marginalized from the play and community altogether, both because they had no access to resources and because they weren't interested in and didn't fit into the dominant narrative of competition and scarcity. This reality was named, and together students and teachers worked out a more equitable system of distribution, found an outside source of materials, and increased rope volume. More importantly, undoing the central dominant narrative allowed other play narratives to flourish, In fact, because many of these had no need for those particular resources, they began producing them as "extraneous" materials—and an eco-economic system was born.

The result was the disappearance of the dominant narrative of scarcity, a diversifying of how students could be, play, and imagine in the village and a quite obvious shift in the energy and even happiness of the culture therein. Ultimately, we wonder if this imaginary village in the woods might have something to teach us all about cultural change.

Given this village experience, we suggest that one of the starting points of ecologizing education as cultural change lies in the *not knowing*. That is, ecologizing education requires the fundamental *unlearning* of cultural habits, assumptions, expectations, and norms—both those that can readily be seen and, more challengingly, those that sit in cultural blind spots. It requires the willingness to "not know" but to try anyway. We like to think of it as *hum*ming softly with the *hum*ility of being *hum*an while joining with the more-than-*hum*ans in a new venture of experience-learning.

To the Question of Change

The project of cultural change and identity development is upon us—and upon you as well. If we are right, it means that a lot of the things that currently seem like common sense, that are everyday and obvious, become problematic once seen through the ecologizing lens. Consider, for instance, these assumptions: that humans come first no matter what; that new political and economic structures can be found without involving many diverse beings; that the natural world doesn't feel or do anything (or matter, for that matter). In ecologizing education, such challenges to our habitual, common-sense ways of thinking are played out at all levels of pedagogy, from the larger theoretical constructs—such as the concepts of politics and economics that are available for imaginative play and the framing of the classroom—right down to the immediate, decision-making level of the teacher in action in the playground or when responding to student questions and behaviors.

Imagine you are on yard duty today, and you notice two students running around a meadow, pretending to shoot each other with sticks. Your school has a no-shooting-games policy, so you call the children over to discuss this and to put a stop to the game. Then you notice that the sticks they are using were very recently alive. In fact, a few green leaves are still attached. When you question this, the students admit that they pulled up Willow from the edge of Stream to make their guns. The three of you head to Stream and you engage the students in a discussion about life, about interconnection between Willow/Stream/Water, and about Trout spawning. Proper reparations are discussed, and restorative actions are taken.

Notice that for the nonecological school this story would have ended after the second sentence—when the game is stopped. The priority is the no-gunplay rule, and where the sticks came from is background noise. Within the frame of ecological and cultural change, however, the priorities and emphases are different. Yes, no gunplay still stands, but ripping up Willow is the main focus of the discussion and the main determinant of consequences. The focus on the death of Willow is an acknowledgment of the changing ecological emphasis and the importance of care for neighbors, while the acts of restoration and reparation suggest cultural change with regard to ideas of power and justice. The work of change that ecologizing education is pointing toward—this careful and critical awareness to detail and an ongoing willingness to reflect, to lean in, and to recreate beliefs and habits that sustain ourselves, our school systems, and our culture—is challenging indeed.

Part of the challenge, as our village example so clearly shows, is that people don't come to systemic change unaffected by the systems in which they live. Both educators and children are immersed in cultures, in our ways of being, in our habits and beliefs, with our cultural tools—and many of these are invisible to us. They are simply our "natural" ways of doing things. Change, then, requires identifying these cultural problematics while at the same time offering options for how to *be* differently at both the individual and cultural levels. And all of this must happen while we are immersed in a larger frame that is continually pushing us to return to the status quo.[20] Thus, the individual and cultural change process becomes a mutually reenforcing project, and the ecologizing educator who responds to gunplay and autocratic governance is having to think and work at the level of immediacy and the individual, while also enacting—creating even—processes and tools that align better with the larger cultural project.

The education system tends to be where we learn the rules of culture and how it works, but it can also be where we learn to deconstruct, challenge, and critique those norms and even change and live into new, vibrant, and rich ways of being human in the world. These root metaphors and cultural assumptions have shaped our identities as individuals and as humans, writ large.[21] They are the structures through which "normal" is first created and then enforced and evaluated on an ongoing basis.

And yet we believe these norms *can* be changed: we do not have to walk alone through the same landscape over and over again. There are options. Others have been here before us, and more—including all-our-relations—are interested in coming with us. The world in which we exist changes when we change our paths therein, and we aren't alone even if we don't totally know where we are or where we are going. Let's explore and try new things and continue to add our own stony, storied offerings that add to the cairns along the way.

CULTIVATING POSSIBILITIES FOR A BETTER WORLD

Every new school year, the Maple Ridge Environmental School begins by meeting the children at the Alouette River site. But not this year. After record-breaking heat domes scorched the land all summer, a series of atmospheric rivers pounded the area with rainstorm after rainstorm throughout the fall. Because of the danger, Alouette River Park was closed to the public, and the children were not allowed to return for many weeks. When they did, they witnessed the catastrophic effects of flooding for themselves.

Teacher Jodi MacQuarrie reflects, "There were kids in tears. Some of them said it looked like a bomb went off. All the analogies that the kids provided were very warlike—it was that level of destruction."[1] Windfall and river debris were scattered everywhere. All the gravel on the side of the riverbed was gone. Gentle slopes where Bear could fish had been chewed away by turbulent waters. Now there were two-meter drops. These students, like increasing numbers of children around the world, are experiencing the lived realities of the ecological crisis. The world around them is changing, and they know it.

The Maple Ridge children understand the situation in more visceral, comprehensive ways than many. Jodi explains that when everyone else was talking about the flooding of the plains and the impact on people, her students were talking about Salmon. They know that in two to four years, Salmon numbers will be catastrophically low. The children are deeply bonded to Salmon. Salmon lives are important to them. The older Maple Ridge children have studied generations of Salmon returning up this river, have watched their offspring swimming downstream toward the ocean every year. The students have created art, performed science experiments, and heard local Indigenous histories about Salmon. They feel a sense of obligation and connection to Salmon, a responsibility to care for and protect them. For the students—in the words of one Elder—"Salmon are family."

Consequently, the loss of most of a generation of Salmon is devasting and emotional for the Maple Ridge students. But, as Jodi reminds them, this is also why they are here. They are not helpless bystanders witnessing catastrophe (even if in some moments it feels like that). They are here to learn a different and more ecologically responsible way to *be* in the world, a better way to relate to our kin, a changed way to enact humanness. Supporting students through this tragedy means giving the little ones extra love. It means giving all of them the opportunity to voice their feelings, stress, and concerns. Fired up from the tragedy, some of the older children write a letter to a local developer, articulating the problematic impacts of a proposed development on local habitat. Because conversations around sustainability and ecological practices are daily occurrences at this school, the children have some framework both for understanding what caused the flooding and for what they personally can do to make more responsible choices than those being made in the broader culture.

As winter comes on, water is reabsorbed into the soil. River's roar begins to settle a little. Scattered salmon carcasses are eaten by scavengers, decomposed by insects, and composted into the earth. While some lives have been lost, the land itself absorbs, adjusts, settles, and composts much of the tragedy. At Maple Ridge, Jodi notes, children are learning to think like an ecosystem and learn from ecosystems. As the land heals and adapts, so might the children to some extent. But the stress is *real*—and all of this occurs against a backdrop of year two of the COVID-19 pandemic. In nearly thirty years of teaching, Jodi has not experienced so many mental health concerns with students. Indeed, across the school district, at every kind of school, mental health issues have risen drastically.[2] Though the broader culture continually reinforces an individual ontology, the huge numbers of young people suffering anxiety and depression are evidence of a much more connected world, where humans and all-our-relations suffer together—and potentially can heal together.

Educators are feeling the strain on their own emotions too. Jodi and other educators at the eco-school have worked harder than ever to build community during the polarizing political climate of COVID-19. They have also worked hard to support each other emotionally, by gathering often to debrief and express thoughts. But for these ecologizing educators, some comfort, respite, and healing comes too from simply being outside. When asked about her own self-care, Jodi comments, "The kids have been drumming a lot lately, and it resonates through the trees. I spend a lot of time listening to that." She has also been gifted a song to help her heal, and she spends time singing it to herself.

Doing School Differently

Despite the incredibly hard work and valiant efforts of many educators and administrators, standard education generally fails to make the deep changes necessary to shift culture toward being a more caring, just, and ecologically responsible one. And because of that, it is failing a great many students whose relational awareness, creativity, diversity, and multiple ways of knowing are overlooked. It's failing parents who report feeling traumatized by their own schooling experiences. It's failing environmentally minded educators who cannot attend to their students or the more-than-human world in meaningful ways because institutionalized education sets up implicit and explicit obstacles every step of the way. And it is failing our more-than-human kin, whose suffering, losses, and destruction have resulted from careless, elitist, and anthropocentric cultural tendencies.

We see ecologizing education as moving toward a meaningful alternative, an opportunity to bring about change in Western cultural modes of being. Here, Hemlock, Salal, and Water Strider are honored as co-teachers, as they offer rich and sometimes spontaneous lessons that exceed the lesson plans human teachers alone could create. Truth and reconciliation processes are active and ongoing, as Indigenous educators who have developed long relationships with students, educators, and administers share histories, stories, and ceremonies with the school communities. Parents, caregivers, and other community members are respectfully invited to share their own wisdom and expertise with students, marking the recognition of a more equitable distribution of knowledge, as opposed to a vision of knowledge as necessarily professionalized and hierarchical. This collectiveness fosters a greater sense of belonging and inclusivity and offers a wider range of learning. In doing so, it honors somatic, intuitive, relational, and diverse other ways of knowing. Bringing children outdoors into an ecologizing frame to interact with soils, plants, and waters supports their health and well-being, even as many struggle with the relational anxiety of the present world. Here, at this school without walls, practices of isolation and individualism are being undone, while practices of community-building, cultural and individual change, and collective healing are being enacted.

Furthermore, we believe that the immersive, critical, philosophically robust, and hands-on experiences of ecologizing schools better prepare children for our ecologically uncertain future and for understanding and caring for their local and global ecosystems. The children are able to build community, to take risks, to engage with the natural world, to question the status quo, and to have discussions about adaptation, self-care, and community, all in the context of their rapidly changing world. Activism is a part of their world, beginning in kindergarten, and at a fundamental level, they are learning a different way of being human in the world. This deeply relational education causes them to think first about how their actions will impact the ecological world. One wonders how the world might look if the leaders of tomorrow hold such commitments.

Imagining Cultural Change

What might North American culture look like if, indeed, it were to radically change? Having been dragged through standard education and being fully surrounded by the dominant culture ourselves, we sometimes struggle to imagine it. Yet we catch heartening glimpses here and there.

Some of the small-scale local farms popping up in our area offer one glimpse. The microfarm might have a market stand next to the road where locals come for eggs, greens, in-season veggies, maybe even a few jams and jellies. In front, a pile of small brown envelopes are tossed into a shoebox. Scrawled in purple crayon on the open lid are the words "Heritage seeds, free for the taking to a home that will love and care for them as they deserve." All around are signs of the work being done and of further jobs that need doing as well as many things that appear to be held together by love, twine, and duct tape. The human components of this microfarm might appear regularly at the local farmer's market, selling the results of their care and earthy relationships. The children and adults involved in these gardens can be overheard mumbling about seed-saving, microclimates, and composting. Sometimes, they are just talking quietly to their more-than-human partners. On occasion, they might hold forth a little against monocultures, big agriculture and factory farms, disappearing genetic diversity, pesticides, and soil loss.

Chances are, our microfarmers feel themselves to be outside and different from mainstream culture. At the same time, they feel a bond between and among the humans and more-than-humans in this enterprise. In fact, they might even feel that this is a shared project—where success will involve all beings playing their part—that undoes any sense that the humans are "in charge." And these people are onto something with their knowledge of the lands, their commitment to place, their desire to live and let live, and the diversity of the beings and the diversity of soils they work with. They point in a promising direction with their lived experience of shared flourishing and the real challenges those entail. They model eco-ethics with their concern for human alienation from the natural world, for the damage caused by the colonial orientation of the culture, and for the effects of all of this on our health and well-being, as well as that of future generations.

Ecologizing education does not require that humans visit distant and "wild" ecosystems. Rather, it is about finding, supporting, and sustaining the place *right here*, where most of us live and work, where humans and all-our-relations can live together in a mutually beneficial, flourishing relationship. That includes the city school and neighborhood. As we have seen, without some thoughtful and purposeful mediation, the culture as it currently stands merely recapitulates itself. Without such mediation, what we have is centralized human domination, a loss of diversity and voice, and, in education, a troubling monoculturing. Of course, many teachers in mainstream schools do incredible work in their classrooms to respond to the diversity of humanity which they encounter every day. Yet we question whether the more massive, sometimes factorylike, form of design is ultimately just as problematic in our schools as it is in our agriculture.[3] Hence, the reason we see the microfarms as a glimpse of the changing culture we seek.

Who, then, might be able to enact similar microcosms of ecologizing effort? The qualities called for include community-building, activism, care, a willingness to take risks, and an orientation toward change. Importantly, this work cannot be done alone. No one can care for and grow well all the seeds themselves. Different beings have different aptitudes. All are needed and are welcome. Anyone who understands seed-saving will readily recognize this. One person may take the lead in tomatoes (or even just protecting fifty species of sauce tomato) and another in rare types of beans or squash, creeping out at night to hand-pollinate and ensure parentage and lineage. Accepting seeds from the roadside shoebox comes with a responsibility to care, come into relationship, and keep the line alive.

Seeds are the adults and Elders of the future, be they Human, Tomato, Duck, or Aphid, and it makes a difference into what soil they are placed. It matters what foods, environments, possibilities, and cultures they are offered. It matters how they are cared for, what room they are given to grow, and how that growth is shaped, directed, limited, and enhanced. Educators, like farmers, play a huge role in all of this, and the range of possibilities for how to be teacher/farmer is tremendous. From monocultured agri-farming to place-based microfarming, the "results" are diverse.

Throughout this book, we have been pushing for an educational process that takes the natural world seriously, that questions the colonial and unjust relationships toward planet and people, and that sees possibility in these ecologizing education school projects. Now, as we near the end, we would like to turn our gaze once more to the ecologizing educators themselves. We offer a frame we call the 4 C's (or maybe four seeds), which are community, critical, care, and change. The first three of these represent important aspects of the ecologizing educator, and while most teachers doing this ecologizing work will have a certain measure of each of these, we'll discuss them individually. But rather than thinking of each section—the community-focused ecologizing educator, the critically engaged ecologizing educator, and the care-based ecologizing educator—as being a description of a single ecologizing educator who brings one *particular* strength or capacity or fluency to their work. We recommend thinking about these as much more fluid than that. Sometimes care, for instance, might be the purview of a single individual, but it is more likely to flex and move between, among, and across members depending on the particular situation or the energy of those involved. The fourth C—change-embracing ecological education—takes us back to the farm, where we are reminded that change will require vision, timely action, risk-taking, creative energy, perseverance, and an enduring optimism.

The Community-Focused Ecologizing Educator[4]

Community is the soil of ecologizing education. Without it, not much happens. Yes, it's possible to produce food from marginal soil. However, that is largely a testament to plant resilience, and plants in such conditions are hardly flourishing. Unfortunately, in many educational situations, community is an underconsidered component of the work. Not so at NEST and Maple Ridge. We see community as an important factor in our mutually beneficial flourishing, so much of our work is about having, creating, retreating into, finding, and growing it. Just like creating good compost, creating community involves bringing many sources of energy and minerals together, monitoring them on an ongoing basis, turning the whole mix over, adding heat at times when things are not breaking down, and letting the detritivores and processes do their thing. For the ecologizing educator, community work involves careful consideration of place, all-our-relations, and all human members of the community, including those not immediately proximal to the work (for example, grandparents, neighbors, and educators from other schools).

This work also includes recognizing and at times facilitating the importance and range of diversity present, a conscious gathering of skills, an active engagement while building internal, authentic systems. In many cases—and perhaps this is little surprising—community-building also includes conscious acts of separation from the mainstream or neighboring but different communities. In our work, separation from "the outside" has helped create safety, mutual understanding, and the space to practice different ways of being and knowing in the world, away from larger cultural pressures. In gardening terms, this work might be like creating a micro-niche—an ideal growing space for plants (ways of being) that are usually not sustained by the larger ecosystem in which one finds oneself. Where we live, for example, soft body fruits can only be grown by changing the soil, by building reflective walls, and by protecting the plants from too much rain and insufficient heat.

At both schools, particular individuals understand their role as that of "gate-keeper." They act as translators for and protectors of the community, often, it should be noted, at a cost to their own well-being. For example, they might be responsible for communicating the school's mission to a new administrative body or translating the community's needs, ideas, and values into other lan-guages, that of funders, for instance. These individuals act as a kind of educator for those who might be interested in our project but only have a passing con-nection. This work is similar to the work of the farmer at the weekend market when someone asks about seed-saving or about growing such amazing pole beans. In the case of the eco-school, the work might involve helping superin-tendents understand in empirical and individualized terms the weird language of a more relational and qualitative assessment process. It might involve shar-ing with colleagues, through professional development, for instance, some of the lessons and learnings that are working "down on the farm."

At other times, our gatekeepers prevent curious but ill-informed guests from casually visiting. Doing this work provides a layer of protection for the commu-nity to grow, take root, and create its own culture. This act of separating and protecting the ecologizing project from the mainstream is also a political recog-nition that often these nascent communities are under threat and aren't com-pletely viable as separate entities yet. They need time to build resistance, and they need beings willing to stand up for them. We have found that doing this work of protector and translator for developing extended community awareness miti-gates the extent to which the school and its more immediate community has had to deal with potential aggression, violence, and suspicions of the general culture.

The community-focused ecologizing educator also facilitates new traditions to signify and orient members toward different priorities. To make our change goal explicit, it is important that we consider how chosen traditions reify and glorify particular acts and ways of being. In other words, we must ask ourselves what traditions, ceremonies, and celebrations best align with who we as a com-munity are wanting to be and become? For example, graduating students have offered gifts of care and a plant to each incoming kindergartener. They have even started to transfer "friend-tree" relationships, such that the leaving student who has had a deep connection with a particular tree/microsite in the area invites an incoming student into that community.

Community-based forums have been created so that students can share their learnings with the larger community while also educating the community itself

about the education that is happening at these schools. Having students explain
the differences between raptors, accipiters, and strigiformes while standing beneath full-sized artistic models of these birds of prey makes the learnings at these
"different" schools concrete and explicit in important ways. Additionally, Elders
have been invited to lead ceremonies, helping establish and give significance to
new/old traditions that orient these communities toward Land and local beings
in different ways. These acts of cultural resurgence support ways of being and
knowing that have been backgrounded and disavowed by the mainstream. They
have also provided important epistemological and cosmological inspiration for
our schools as they seek to separate themselves from troublesome norms.

Our research suggests that alternative schools and communities that overlook these deeper, cultural implications of traditions sometimes struggle to
maintain their meaningful and hard-fought changes. Partly, this is because without these traditions they don't have something to lean on when the "perfectly
reasonable" mainstream—in the form of a superintendent, a concerned parent,
or even that little doubting voice in one's head—comes calling. When it comes
to durable, transformative change, keeping the status quo at bay can be an unending challenge. Deeper meaning, sustained by thoughtful traditions and celebrations, can assist a community through challenging times. But we offer one
final piece of advice: new traditions should be created with caution, for once offered, they can be difficult to undo. Do a thing twice, and it can become the
"way things are done."

Another part of the community educator's work involves including more diversity. On the farm, we might think of nutrients, minerals, and a full range of
detritivores and species in order to respond to disease. But we would also want
to consider genetics and the diversity of that "library of the possible." After all,
the more diverse the genes, the more options the garden has. In some ways, this
takes us back to idea of *old-growthing*, which is at the core of what we do. For
community educators, diversity is about involving and listening to different
voices and experiences within the membership—and not the merely human. Just
as one might expand the number of volumes in a library, this is about having
the widest range of ideas, imaginations, and possibilities included.

Of course, community is not a static end point. It is not some *thing* that can
be reached. "Community" is a process, a verb, rather than an entity, a noun.
Community (or perhaps, more accurately, "communitying") requires diverse
membership, divergent ideas, challenging voices, trickster energies—only then
will it continue to flourish. It is an ongoing, imperfect, ever-learning, and incomplete educational project at its very heart, and the community educator needs
to be able to lean in, roll with the seasons, and add care, heat, or pruning when
needed. These capacities of building relationship, of cultivating space for diver-

sity, of knowing when to plant and when to prune, of acting to protect from and translate for the mainstream and its threats, of leaning into change and the rich humus of possibility—all of these are going to be truly necessary for people going forward in our changing and uncertain world.

At the deepest level, the community educator is working toward *belonging, inclusion,* and *shared purpose* (that is, mutually beneficial flourishing), as these appear to be integral to both individual well-being and community vitality. Ecologizing communities are likely going to need to create and learn the values, skills, and rituals that foster and further their goals. At these schools, the best learning happens when the spaces are safe, diverse, open, with less direction by the human teacher or other centralized authority. By safe, we are not suggesting that these spaces should be passive, quiet, or strife-free or that all community members are assumed to be "on the same page." Those kinds of spaces often just ignore diversity for the sake of an artifice of harmony. Rather, these are places where work happens; where there is a commitment to each other and the process; where there is comfort in and celebration of diversity and discomfort; where mistakes can be made and biases expressed, discovered, named, and examined; and where the goal is never for some overarching homogeneity. Our farm doesn't want the beans to try to become adequate cucumbers but to be the best beans they can be. This is the community educator's challenge too—to *not* be the center, the expert, the singular being on whom the enterprise depends—for who knows being a bean better than a bean? Instead, the community educator is an important facilitator, supporter, and skilled communicator, who can create and protect these spaces and challenge the community to see their own vision and to acknowledge their ongoing problematic assumptions.

The Critically Engaged Ecologizing Educator

Most small-scale farms are filled with questions, experiments, and ongoing challenges. Why is the orchard dropping flowers just as they set fruit? Why are none of the brassicas growing well? The skills and orientations to the world that are involved in making these assessments parallel those of the critical educator—among them humility, curiosity, a willingness to ask questions and include oneself in the problems, and a desire to change and make the space fruitful for all. And yet many microfarms are also asking deeper questions, critiquing the accepted norms of agriculture, and positioning themselves as being different from mainstream ways of doing agriculture, land care, and even life. It is here, then, that the real parallel to the critically engaged ecologizing educator emerges.

As we have already discussed, to establish a safe, inclusive, and cohesive community in which culturally, racially, ethnically, and ecologically diverse people and beings can successfully work and grow, we need to acknowledge many unique histories, experiences, needs, voices, and contributions.[5] But we also need ask questions about the overall system, identify oppressions and marginalizations of various forms, and acknowledge the resulting violences and exclusions. Ecologizing educators are making decisions about how to *be* in the world, but this includes, as on the microfarm, deciding what *not* to be and how and why one is choosing to be different.

These "different" (that is, ecologizing) communities must find ways to name, bear witness to, and seek responses to eco-socio-historical-political issues, both past and present, which are impacting people and the more-than-human world. Furthermore, they must seek to do this without perpetuating the violences of systemic racism, instrumental resourcism, hyperactive capitalism, competitive, hierarchical isolationism, or any number of other systemic injustices—*and* without getting knocked offtrack by blind spots or obfuscatory strategies such as confrontation, anger, defensiveness, denial, or guilt.[6] After all, it doesn't really help to blame the broccoli, a brassica, if it doesn't grow. Instead, we need to figure out what is happening in the larger community that makes it impossible for the brassicas to thrive. Issues facing community members often have deep historical roots, and daily oppression thrives in judgment, silence, and invisibility.[7] This critical conversation also extends into human/more-than-human relations, especially in reference to modernity's coloniality.[8]

The bedrock of oppression is power inequity, which can be experienced at multiple levels. For example, society has constructed stories, or dominant cultural narratives, about disadvantaged or inferior groups.[9] This process of "othering," or objectifying, people and the natural world serves to maintain power imbalances. Often, these stories help those with more power and privilege to rationalize their position. These stories also become the status quo and the imaginative tools of future generations (as our "forts" example illustrates), which makes the work of the critical educator twofold: their task is not only to identify and name the challenges but also to offer other options to replace the problematic norms and narratives. After all, it isn't enough to just stand back and critique.

Listening to, acknowledging, and understanding stories, therefore, is a first step in repairing the damaging narratives that society has created about those who are "different" (read: lesser than). If we are truly looking through a critical lens, though, we will also notice that listening itself can be problematized. Who is being heard? How is listening happening? What is prioritized by any particular listener? Are the interpretations themselves layered in uncritical cultural problematics? Eco-social change and ecologizing education, then, often begins with empowerment, that is, addressing unjust psychological, sociopolitical, and structural circumstances through understanding, awareness, action—and getting out of the way.[10]

Ecologizing educators must then also consider how to do this across the species divide. What does it mean to listen to, acknowledge, and better understand the stories of Apple, Cabbage, Honeybee, Wren, and Earthworm? What work needs to be done to hear through to those stories from beyond the colonial narrative that positions humans as "better than" and nature as voiceless/rights-less? When individuals and collectives reclaim and recreate their history and continue to challenge destructive stories that serve to divide, communities can better understand and appreciate the resistance, resilience, and strengths of their members. Such reflexive and critical awarenesses and the work needed to teach and foster them are necessary in order for individuals to recognize the pathways of privilege, to shift the inertia of apathy, and to support communities in a move toward more just, respectful, and equitable relationships.

This kind of criticality is understood to be an important component of ecologizing education. Privileges and injustices need to be named, problematic assumptions explored, and diverse voices, ways of being, and doing sought out. Much of our critical work relates to issues of power, marginalization, and colonization, along with a commitment to finding ways to not recapitulate those forms. We understand power as operating at varying levels and as being embedded within language; this challenges us to think carefully before speaking and to notice how often seemingly comfortable pathways of speech are deeply antisocial and anti-ecological.

This is complex work, where we are prone to blind spots because—as we came to understand—epistemological, ontological, and even cosmological positions themselves are cultural creations. This, in turn, led us to seek insight from other-than-Western-knowing traditions and to engage with the global scholarship around issues of cognitive justice and the colonization of knowledge and knowing, writ large.[11] Perhaps this step is obvious now, but it was a specific blind spot in our seemingly radical design.

Our point here is that adopting criticality does not mean simply picking up a single critical discourse and assuming that it covers all of the community's needs. Individual communities might, because of their particular makeup or training, be better prepared to be critical in some areas, such as in matters of gender and class, and less prepared in others, say, ecological and global matters. For example, an eco-school might look to ecofeminists as it seeks to develop deep environmental commitments, robust language, practices, policies, and awarenesses regarding the more-than-human world and gender—yet, that theorizing might be less useful in examining issues relating to economic privilege, race, and Indigeneity.

Part of the work of the critically engaged ecologizing educator, then, is to help create internal, approved ways to extend the critical work of the community, while at the same time discovering their own, and the community's, under-examined areas. This can be done, for example, by seeking systems of team-building, inviting in diversity facilitators, or creating internal policies that might support the community to improve in myriad areas.

We see three important roles for the critically engaged ecologizing educator within the community. First, critical educators can help communities perceive themselves as incomplete and ever-in-process. For example, at Maple Ridge we saw ongoing educative experiences as essential because of our belief in human possibility, the assumption of fallibility, and a sense that this work is, by nature, never complete. Our experience also suggests that this process of employing the critical in order to change is not simply to be applied at the group, community, or institutional level. An active, vibrant, mutually influencing back and forth exists *between* community and the individual, and amongst individuals. Consequently, change at the community level might cause, inspire, or force change for individu-als, and those shifts might, in turn, lead to reconceptualizations and further changes at the community level. Second, critical educators are involved in the cre-ation of systems for ongoing critical self-examination because, based on our expe-rience, there is a tendency toward complacency, stasis, and stability. As such, we need to create formal processes to allow criticality to thrive. And third, critical educators are involved in discovering, suggesting, and supporting the implemen-tation of different ways of being, different systems of language, and different, more equitable, options for the community going forward. Just to critique is not enough. Communities need implementable options if they are really going to change.

This work also requires a recognition that intention and action are not mu-tually synonymous and that both are needed if change is actually to happen. We can offer one of our own experiences to illustrate this: We had committed to un-doing the anthropocentrism and species elitism of Western epistemology and in the public school system. Teachers, staff, and community members held gath-erings to explore this positioning of nature as co-teacher, then worked to define their goals, change their linguistic ways, evaluate their practices, and review their progress in light of this professed goal. But this process of critical self-reflection with the expressed purpose of "checking oneself and one's community" and "walking the talk" tended to vary quite a bit in terms of formality, consistency, and accuracy. Often there was little translation into practice even after good thoughts were shared in the gatherings. Thus, in order to move from good in-tentions to actions we sought out people who were to be responsible for holding us all to account. Finding ways to incorporate ongoing criticality into active official processes and procedures is important and requires a good facilitator, that is, a good critical ecologizing educator, or two, or three.

Ultimately, there is strength in difference. All rich and successful sustainable market gardens recognize this. Monocultures tend to destroy pollinators, overuse particular nutrients, and deaden the soil, whereas the self-sustaining market garden sees the value in the nitrogen fixer, the systems of pollinators, and in compost created from plants which might not have a direct role in human consumption, such as Borage or Yarrow. Microfarming\\s also tend to see the farm as a community, such that if something isn't flourishing—such as broccoli—perhaps something is not quite right with the entire system. Those somethings need to be located, named, and, hopefully, addressed, because every being is better for having a healthy orchard and happy brassicas.

Since fostering diversity is important for the health of all, this means that the ability to bring groups together, to challenge them critically, and to leverage diversity is an increasingly essential skill.[12] Diverse groups function better when they are differing but working together; that is, the focus is not on conformity but on leveraging the full talent or contributions of all their members: Earthworm, Green Mulch, Hoverfly, and Potassium. Individuals who are embedded in a network of supportive, authentic, and positive relationships are more likely to come into healing and also participate in political, social, and community life.[13] When groups work toward enacting a more just vision while overcoming discrimination, the resulting *transformation* that benefits everyone is a dynamic, imperfect, ongoing process. Being reflexive, actively critical, and transparent about one's actions is essential.

This brings us to one final point: in colonial Western society, a "neutral" stance simply doesn't exist, and in some ways, that is the key insight for the critical ecologizing educator. We live in a society where people can benefit from oppression without being overtly oppressive themselves. Thus, as we have noted, we also need to be critically aware that, in our determination to help or change the world, we can also unwittingly cause harm through our "good intentions" and blind spots. Communities who engage in regular individual and group self-reflexive practices—supported criticality—are often the most aware about addressing this directly.

The Care-Based Ecologizing Educator

Caring teachers are crucial in any education setting, but "care" in the context of the ecologizing educator goes beyond the students in the classroom and is about learning how to build, sustain, and restore relationships with myriad diverse others. This notion of care extends to include the natural world and the well-being of the ecosystems that sustain and support learners and schools.

The care-based ecologizing educator seeks to prioritize the healthy wholeness of the learners and the community. A lot of psychic dissonance and trauma exists in the larger culture. Indeed, environmental educators highlight multiple compounding issues impacting students: lack of a sense of belonging, stressful familial situations, feeling alienated from place or people, and experiencing pressure to be someone other than themselves. Mainstream educational systems are also recognizing this and now offer mindfulness training, trauma-informed practices, social-emotional learning programs, and mentoring with regard to building relationships. Yet, those steps may not be enough without more substantive change. Indigenous scholars point directly at colonization and the ongoing trauma of schooling as problematic contributors; at the same time, they look toward community, ceremony, traditions, and reconnections to Land as ways into well-being.[14]

One of the most striking challenges we encountered in our ecologizing education work, once we peeled back the layers, has been the depth of the pain throughout our communities. Although Western medicine is useful in many situations, the way it has tended to biomedicalize, individualize, and position health as simply the absence of disease does not appear to deal well with the shared pains of alienation, eco-anxiety, and the feelings of loss related to the destruction of more-than-human friends, neighbors, and places. For the care-based ecologizing educator, the question becomes, What happens to ideas of health, well-being, and love if one assumes relationality? That is, if the goal is flourishing and not simply the absence of disease, and if individual health is inextricably linked to context and community, then where and how might one begin? And, given that these kinds of challenges are becoming a regular part of the education system, what knowledge, attributes, and abilities might be usefully developed by educators who seek to teach from the heart?

Intriguingly, well-being overlaps with other practices that are central to ecologizing education. The quality of our relationships significantly impacts our well-being. Reinforcing a connection with Land and more-than-humans, for instance, generates a felt sense of belonging, meaning, and being cared for. Our work in ecologizing education not only addresses isolation and alienation but seems to propel many individuals into a mutually reinforcing experience of reciprocity. As they become more mindful, thoughtful, and caring toward others, they are more likely to experience how much the beings around them are, in fact, caring for and gifting the humans. This is a reciprocity that can never be fully repaid, given the extent of the gifts offered to each of us by the natural world. But we can certainly do much better.

These relation-building skills can be seen powerfully at work back on the microfarm. For example, the greenhouse at NEST has become a central hub for this kind of learning. In addition to lessons about planting, growing, and food, children learn to care for soil and seedlings, enjoying the gifts/fruits presented in return and experiencing the garden as a place of safety, respite, and refuge. The greenhouse has also become a source of fresh food for the larger community around the school. This connection between the social and the ecological appears to have supported some students into becoming stronger advocates for increased well-being and flourishing across the community. Those of us in ecologizing education believe that caring for and building relationships with others not only creates health and well-being, but also inspires a greater willingness to advocate and even fight for the natural world.

Change-Embracing Ecologizing Education

In some ways, our metaphor of the small sustainable farm is incomplete when we come to consider change-embracing ecologizing education. To make it work, we'll have to back up a bit into the history of our little farm. We start with a small group of humans interested in living closer to the land, growing their own good food, and *being* differently in the world. They have been looking for an appropriate piece of property and finally, one day, a 7.5-acre chunk of land comes on the market. It has a bit of a swale in it and a small copse of evergreens near the road, and it's been parceled off from a much larger property that has been farmed industrially for several generations. In the world of mass production, this little chunk of land is now considered marginal—it simply requires too much effort for too little return. The soil is tired and compacted from hard use. Some macronutrients are over-represented, while some micronutrients are limited because it has been monocultured all these years. Insect diversity is low due to reliance on pesticides. This Land has existed in one cultural way of doing farming for decades. Now, the project in front of those who are willing to hear the call is to cultivate a different culture, a heterogenous one—a more diverse, interconnected, interdependent, mutually beneficial and flourishing one.

Two of the most obvious, though at times under-acknowledged, challenges in moving toward an ecologizing education are these: (1) change tends not to be a central mandate for most formal education projects and (2) there is not much to work with. The soil fertility is gone, the lived and imaginative diversity is missing, and no one seems to know where to get water. The role of mass education—and, really, education in general—has been to bring the next generation into the norms, ways of being, structural systems, even cosmologies, of the dominant culture, or the culture that is designing the system as it currently stands. We might even make the case that North American public education is bringing its students into the culture *as it used to exist*; that is, we sometimes seem to be educating students for a 1950s version of the world, which hasn't existed for a long time.

Public education is, by its very nature, then, quite monoculture-ish and conservative. This is evidenced not so much in its left or right political positioning as in its focus on conserving traditions, on single, mass-applied ways of doing things, and on an oddly outdated vision of where the world is and where it will be when these young people become adults. Public education is not usually a site for cultural progressiveness, radicality, or even change activism. And yet, as suggested throughout this book, cultural change is necessarily a profoundly educational project. If we are going to change the world, education and educators are going to do much of the heavy lifting. Contemporary education exists, then, within a sort of push and pull dynamic: the pull of the historical aims of public education and its desire to stay the same, and the push of the urgent needs of the planet and questions of justice at large.

This work is not easy, we know that. Individual educators experience rising pressures as class sizes increase, as recognition of and the desire to respond to the diversity of learners grows, and as responsibilities expand. For example, as funding disappears for various mental health programs, the responsibility of meeting these needs is downloaded to classrooms, whether or not educators are ready for them. And yet, if our metaphor still holds some use, healing the depleted land involves healing for all—Soil, Broccoli, Wasp, and Child. To some extent, the farm works because there is a vision, plus patience, plus the ability to act when the moment (or the fruit) is ripe. Timing is important. No point putting seeds into frozen ground, but if the neighbor has a pile of good manure they want rid of, today is the day to shovel it (image and metaphor chosen intentionally). This visioning and responding to the opportunities of the moment, then, is part of the work of the ecologizing change educator. Take risks, try things out, have multiple projects on the go at the same time because often you don't know when, or even if, it will come together—until it does.

Change also calls for a creative energy—think of the trickster—as ecologizing educators are on the lookout for perspective-changing surprises from students or their more-than-human co-teachers. The forgotten compost produces abundant pumpkins, and the whole farm changes to align with what the orange gourd is asking and doing. Growing political diversity and polarization increasingly reveals that our efforts to maintain a "neutral" stance are problematic. It reveals more than that, though, because it also, importantly, exposes that assumed position of neutrality as the incongruous one it has *always* been.

Indeed, teachers are being told by some parents that climate change does not exist, that Indigenization is religious education, that eco-education is propaganda, that real learning happens indoors, and that politics has no place in the classroom. Our work has made clear, though, that the role of the teacher is *always* political and that—no matter what position one takes in the classroom and with respect to curriculum, pedagogy, and content—"neutral" simply doesn't exist. Educators are always inscribing ideas, priorities, and orientations to the world, even ways of being, on the lives of their students—no matter how neutral they may claim to be.

Maintaining the status quo reaffirms a commitment to "no change" and reinscribes systemic injustices and environmental problematics that are, at this point in history, untenable. If our little group of farmers tries to "use" the land in the way it has been used for the last fifty years, the whole project will fail. It is too expensive, it is not appropriate for the place and the times, and it won't fill the needs and possibilities of all involved. As such, the ecologizing change educator is, by definition, thrust into the position of activist and advocate for the world they would like to see and to be a part of. They are striving toward allyship, standing with those they deem unjustly marginalized. They also are positioned, necessarily, in the role of educator for parents and caregivers and the larger community too so that everyone understands how education is changing, and what it is becoming.

At the level of the school, the district, and the larger system, the same challenges exist. These are conservative operations, slow or unwilling to change, and often behind the times and out of step with the uncertain future that is approaching. Here, based on our interviews and research, the question becomes one of how to create policies, institutional spaces, lines of communication, cultures of openness, and the educational and fiscal supports such that vibrant, rich possibilities are allowed to emerge and flourish. Our experience suggests that although partnerships need to be made with those systems, often change happens in clandestine spaces—on the margins, in the cracks between immovable edifices, on small pieces of land surrounded by larger mega-operations. Thus, advocates for change are pushed to find allies, to look for opportunities from within, and to gird themselves for a fight. This impression is furthered by assumptions of permanent scarcity—change costs money, after all—and the prospect of pushing the Sisyphean boulder up an ever-growing slope. These problematic metaphors were questioned and critiqued by many in ecologizing school communities who see them as undermining the abundance and emergence of possible change and the wonders that are springing up all over the schools—and as continuing to position the status quo.

Change educators understand the challenges they are up against, but they don't see them as intractable. In fact, they actively seek ways to continually undo and redo. To have joy in the face of deep sadness. To see possibility rather than imaginative limits. To find abundance in the face of assumed scarcity. To notice emergence rather than hopelessness. And to let interdependence and diversity be the compost out of which their change pumpkins might arise.

Just like on the microfarm, ecologizing efforts can always go farther and do more. Admittedly, the work can be overwhelming at times. Sometimes the gardener leans on the fence—the not-yet-finished or starting-to-rot-out fence—to assess everything that needs doing. Ecologizing work is a verb, a process, filled with small, but still wonderful, successes. The pond holds water and the Muscovies produce a clutch. The three sisters—Corn, Bean, and Squash—have a banner year, and in so doing, declare their new home satisfactory and offer gifts to all. The diversity of songbirds increases. Garter Snake returns to the land and crosses the garden path.

We encourage readers to treasure the joys, the discoveries, the companionship, and the successes, however small, that appear in their efforts to change. Revel in children's insights into imagining and reimagining with the land. Remember that no matter the size of the project, from community garden to school district overhaul, this work takes time and mistakes will be made. Diversity helps. This book begins a conversation, but it's far from a final word. Our hope is that readers will keep the conversations, discoveries, and possibilities going. And let us know how things turn out.

Changing Times

At the end of this school year, Jodi, the most recent Maple Ridge principal, and one of their key educational assistants are retiring and leaving the school. With the fires, floods, and plagues this community has faced this year, it's a stressful transition out of long and meaningful work in eco-justice. In truth, these knowledge keepers, along with the original principal, Clayton Maitland, are irreplaceable. Their relational understandings of place and people and their abilities as ecologizing educators simply cannot be quickly or easily understood by someone else.

On the other hand, more and more students are joining and graduating from Maple Ridge and NEST every year. We hope these young, new knowledge keepers will continue the work we have started—and likely in richer ways than we have yet envisioned. These are big visions and big challenges aided by courage, a desire to get started, and a commitment to place and beings. It is a celebration of life throughout.

ECO RESOURCE LIST

This is just a short list of potential resources in and around the world of ecologizing education. Feel free to add/critique/change in whatever way is useful to you.[1]

Journals

Australian Journal of Environmental Education
https://www.aaee.org.au/get-involved/australian-journal-of-environmental
   -education/ https://www.cambridge.org/core/journals/australian-journal-of
   -environmental-education/latest-issue
Canadian Journal of Environmental Education
https://cjee.lakeheadu.ca/
Educational Theory Journal
https://edtheory.education.illinois.edu/
Environmental Education Research Journal
https://www.tandfonline.com/journals/ceer20
Environmental Humanities Journal
https://environmentalhumanities.org/
Experiential Learning & Teaching in Higher Education
https://journals.calstate.edu/elthe/index
Green Teacher Magazine
https://greenteacher.com/
Green Theory & Praxis Journal

http://greentheoryandpraxisjournal.org/
International Journal of Early Childhood Environmental Education
https://naaee.org/eepro/resources/international-journal-early-childhood
    -environmental-education-ijecee
Journal of Adventure Education and Outdoor Learning
https://www.outdoor-learning.org/Journal
Journal of Curriculum Theorizing
https://journal.jctonline.org/index.php/jct/index
Journal of Environmental Education
https://www.tandfonline.com/loi/vjee20?ai=2ep&mi=ffghu2&af=R
Journal of Experiential Education
https://www.aee.org/journal-of-experiential-education
Journal of Outdoor and Environmental Education
https://js.sagamorepub.com/jorel/article/view/8886
Ontario Journal of Outdoor Education
https://www.coeo.org/pathways-journal/
Studies in Philosophy of Education Journal
https://www.springer.com/journal/11217

Online Resources

Association for Experiential Education. *AEE Books and Publications.* 2023.
    https://www.aee.org/books-and-publications.
Back to Nature Network. *Resources & Research.* 2023. https://www.back2
    nature.ca/resources-research/
Common Worlds Research Collective. *Research Projects.* Accessed June 18,
    2023. https://www.commonworlds.net/research-projects.
Council of Outdoor Educators of Ontario. *Classroom Teacher Tools.* 2023.
    https://www.coeo.org/classroom-teacher-tools/.
Eco-Education. *Materials.* 2017. http://ecoed.org.au/materials/.
Eco Schools Canada. *Research and Publications.* 2022. https://ecoschools.ca
    /about/research-and-publications/.
North American Association for Environmental Education. *Resources.*
    Accessed June 18, 2023. https://eepro.naaee.org/resource.
Project Learning Tree. *Sample Student Activities.* 2019. https://www.plt.org
    /sample-lesson-plans.
Promise of Place. *Curricular Resources.* Accessed June 18, 2023. https://
    promiseofplace.org/curricular-resources.

Teton Science Schools. *Getting Started with Place-Based Education, Step-by-Step.* 2023. https://www.tetonscience.org/getting-started-with-place-based-education-step-by-step.

Wild Pedagogies. *Learning from More-Than-Human Voices.* 2023. https://wildpedagogies.com.

Zeni, Megan. *School Gardens: Outdoor Classrooms. Education Outdoors & Playful Learning.* 2023. https://meganzeni.com/.

Notes

INTRODUCING

1. Paulo Freire, *Pedagogy of the Oppressed* (New York: Continuum, 2000), 45.
2. Stan Rushworth, in discussion with author, May 2020.
3. David Abram, *The Spell of the Sensuous: Perception and Language in a More-Than-Human World* (New York: Vintage Books, 1997).
4. Matthew D. Lieberman, *Social: Why Our Brains Are Wired to Connect* (New York: Crown Publishers, 2013); Sue Gerhardt, *Why Love Matters: How Affection Shapes a Baby's Brain* (New York: Routledge, 2015).
5. Robert Stolorow and George E. Atwood, *Contexts of Being: Intersubjective Foundations of Psychological Life* (New York: Routledge, 1992).
6. Lieberman, *Social*.
7. Jean M. Twenge, "The Age of Anxiety? The Birth Cohort Change in Anxiety and Neuroticism, 1952–1993," *Journal of Personality and Social Psychology* 79, no. 6 (2000): 1007–21, https://doi.org/10.1037/0022-3514.79.6.1007.
8. "Depression in Teens," Mental Health America, accessed June 2018, https://mhanational.org/depression-teens-0.
9. Thomas R. Verny, *Pre-Parenting* (New York: Simon & Schuster, 2002), 207–8.
10. Gabor Maté, research notes in author's (Kuchta) possession, 2016.
11. John McMurtry, *The Cancer Stage of Capitalism* (Halifax, Nova Scotia: Fernwood Publishing, 2013), 37.
12. Stan Rushworth, correspondence with author, August 2021.
13. Alicia Kear, in discussion with author, September 2022.
14. "Anthropocene," *National Geographic*, accessed July 2020, https://www.nationalgeographic.org/encyclopedia/anthropocene/.
15. Stan Rushworth, in correspondence with authors, August 2021.
16. Sean Blenkinsop, Ramsey Affifi, Laura Piersol, and Michael De Danann Sitka-Sage, "Shut-Up and Listen: Implications and Possibilities of Albert Memmi's Characteristics of Colonization Upon the 'Natural World.'" *Studies in Philosophy and Education* 36, no. 3 (2017): 348–65.
17. Michael De Danann Sitka-Sage (Michael Derby), Laura Piersol, and Sean Blenkinsop, "Refusing to Settle for Pigeons and Parks: Urban Environmental Education in the Age of Neoliberalism," *Environmental Education Research* 21, no. 3 (2015): 378–89, https://doi.org/10.1080/13504622.2014.994166.

1. BEGINNING

1. Suzanne Simard, "How Trees Talk to Each Other," TED Talk, accessed July 4, 2023, YouTube video, 3:20 and 3:37, https://www.youtube.com/watch?v=dRSPy3ZwpBk.
2. See Michael Marker, "There Is No *Place of Nature*; There Is Only the *Nature of Place*: Animate Landscapes as Methodology for Inquiry in the Coast Salish Territory," *International Journal of Qualitative Studies in Education* 31, no. 6 (2018): 453–64, https://doi.org/10.1080/09518398.2018.1430391. See also Joe Sheridan and Roronhiakewen "He Clears the Sky" Dan Longboat, "The Haudenosaunee Imagination and the Ecology of

the Sacred," *Space and Culture* 9, no. 4 (2006): 365–81, https://doi.org/10.1177/1206331 206292503.

3. "Our Land: In the Beginning," Kwakiutl Band Council, accessed August 2021, https://www.kwakiutl.bc.ca/Our-Land.

4. For example, see W. H. Collison, *In the Wake of the War Canoe: A Stirring Record of Forty Years' Successful Labour, Peril & Adventure amongst the Savage Indian Tribes of the Pacific Coast, and the Piratical Head-Hunting Haidas of the Queen Charlotte Islands, B.C.* (England: Seeley, Service & Co., 1915).

5. Marker, "There Is No *Place of Nature*," 453.

6. "Alternatives to Conventional Clearcutting," BC Ministry of Forests, accessed August 2021, https://www.for.gov.bc.ca/hfp/publications/00217/atcc.htm.

7. Brant Ran, "How Much Old Growth Forest Remains in the US?" *The Understory, The Blog of Rainforest Action Network*, November 11, 2008, https://www.ran.org/the-understory /how_much_old_growth_forest_remains_in_the_us/#:~:text=According%20to%20 one%20estimate%2C%20stands,(USDA%2DFS%202000).&text=Since%201600%2C%20 90%25%20of%20the,states%20have%20been%20cleared%20away.

8. Lorna B. Williams, "Honoring All Life," in *Child Honoring: How to Turn This World Around*, ed. Raffi and Sharna Olfman (Westport, CT: Praeger Publishers, 2006), 87–94.

9. Williams, "Honoring All Life," 88.

10. Sheridan and Longboat, "The Haudenosaunee Imagination," 379.

11. Sheridan and Longboat, "The Haudenosaunee Imagination," 365.

12. Sheridan and Longboat, "The Haudenosaunee Imagination," 366.

13. Sheridan and Longboat, "The Haudenosaunee Imagination," 370.

14. Robin Wall Kimmerer, *Braiding Sweetgrass: Indigenous Wisdom, Scientific Knowledge and the Teachings of Plants* (Minneapolis, MN: Milkweed Editions, 2013), 22–32.

15. Such as Arne Naess, Val Plumwood, Karen Warren, David Greenwood, Leanne Betasamosake Simpson, Neil Evernden, Aldo Leopold, David Abram, Chet Bowers, and Robin Wall Kimmerer.

16. "Principles and Values," Maple Ridge Environmental School, accessed December 2020, https://es.sd42.ca/principles-and-values/.

17. Val Plumwood, *Feminism and the Mastery of Nature* (New York: Routledge, 2002), 21, https://doi.org/10.4324/9780203006757.

18. Jean-Paul Sartre, *Notebooks for an Ethics*, trans. David Pellauer (Chicago: University of Chicago Press, 1992).

19. For more information, see http://www.circe-sfu.ca/. Simon Fraser University, "Welcome to CIRCE," accessed July 4, 2023.

20. For more on this discussion, see Sean Blenkinsop, Clayton Maitland, and Jody MacQuarrie, "In Search of Policy That Supports Educational Innovation: Perspective of a Place- and Community-Based Elementary School," *Policy Futures* 17 (2019): 489–502.

21. Mark Fettes, in discussion with author, October 2020.

22. James Britton, *Language and Learning* (Coral Gables, FL: University of Miami Press, 1970).

23. Yi Chien Jade Ho, in discussion with author, May 2020.

24. School District 46 Sunshine Coast, B.C. "Nature Based Learning," accessed July 4, 2023. https://sd46.bc.ca/programs/alternative-ed/nest/.

25. Taiwan Panorama, "Setting Sail for the Future: Principal Aaron Huang," New Southbound Policy Portal, Ministry of Foreign Affairs, Republic of China (Taiwan), January 18, 2018, https://nspp.mofa.gov.tw/nsppe/news.php?post=127997&unit=410.

26. Yi Chien Jade Ho, in discussion with author, May 2020.

27. Clayton Maitland, in discussion with author, May 2020.

28. Rick Smith and Bruce Lourie, *Slow Death by Rubber Duck: The Secret Danger of Everyday Things* (Berkeley: Counterpoint, 2009).

29. Philippe Grandjean and Philip Landrigan, "Neurobehavioural Effects of Developmental Toxicity," *Lancet Neurology* 13, no. 3 (2014): 330, https://doi.org/10.1016/S1474-4422(13)70278-3.

30. H. A. Abdel-Rahman, "Fatal Suffocation by Rubber Balloons in Children: Mechanism and Prevention," *Forensic Science International* 108, no. 2 (2000): 97–105, https://doi.org/10.1016/S0379-0738(99)00143-7.

31. Cecil Adams, "Do Falling Pianos Really Kill People?" *Washington City Paper*, April 12, 2013, https://washingtoncitypaper.com/article/209447/straight-dope-do-falling-pianos-really-kill-people/.

32. Chris Beeman, "Wilding Liability in Education: Introducing the Concept of Wide Risk as Counterpoint to Narrow-Risk-Driven Educative Practice," *Policy Futures in Education* 19, no. 3 (2021): 324–38, https://doi.org/10.1177/1478210320978096.

33. Chris Beeman and Sean Blenkinsop, "Cassandras of a Second Kind," *Journal of Environmental Education* 52, no. 3 (2021): 162–73, https://doi.org/10.1080/00958964.2021.1922331.

2. RELATING

1. Yi-fu Tuan, *Topophilia: A Study of Environmental Perception, Attitudes, and Values* (New York: Columbia University Press, 1990), 4.

2. Theodore Roszak, *Where the Wasteland Ends: Politics and Transcendence in Postindustrial Society* (New York: Doubleday, 1972), 400.

3. Abraham Maslow, *A Theory of Human Motivation* (Radford, VA: Wilder Publications, 2018).

4. Deborah Blum, *Love at Goon Park: Harry Harlow and the Science of Affection* (New York: Perseus Publishing, 2002), 33–51.

5. L. Emmett Holt, *The Care and Feeding of Children: A Catechism for the Use of Mothers and Children's Nurses*, 4th ed. (New York: Appleton and Company, 1907), https://www.gutenberg.org/files/15484/15484-h/15484-h.htm#Sleep.

6. Blum, *Love at Goon Park*, 37.

7. Blum, *Love at Goon Park*, 37.

8. John B. Watson and Rosalie Alberta Rayner Watson, *Psychological Care of Infant and Child* (New York: W.W. Norton & Company, 1928), 76–80.

9. Watson and Watson, *Psychological Care of Infant and Child*, 85, 81.

10. Watson and Watson, *Psychological Care of Infant and Child*, 83–84.

11. See, for example, Sue Gerhardt, *Why Love Matters* (London: Brunner-Routledge, 2004), or various blogposts by Darcia Narvaez, *Psychology Today Blog: Moral Landscapes*, accessed June 2021, https://www.psychologytoday.com/ca/blog/moral-landscapes.

12. Darcia Narvaez, *Neurobiology and the Development of Human Morality: Evolution, Culture, and Wisdom* (New York: W. W. Norton, 2014).

13. Gerhardt, *Why Love Matters*.

14. Department of Economic and Social Affairs, "News: 68% of World Population Projected to Live in Urban Areas by 2050, says UN," United Nations, May 16, 2018, https://www.un.org/development/desa/en/news/population/2018-revision-of-world-urbanization-prospects.html.

15. Richard Louv, *Last Child in the Woods: Saving Our Children from Nature-Deficit Disorder* (New York: Workman Publishing, 2005), 16–19.

16. Narvaez, *Neurobiology and the Development of Human Morality*.

17. Narvaez, *Neurobiology and the Development of Human Morality*.

18. Frances E. "Ming" Kuo, "Nature-Deficit Disorder: Evidence, Dosage, and Treatment," *Journal of Policy Research in Tourism, Leisure and Events* 5, no. 2 (2013): 172–86, https://doi.org/10.1080/19407963.2013.793520.

19. Sue Gerhardt, *The Selfish Society: How We All Forgot to Love One Another and Made Money Instead* (New York: Simon & Schuster, 2010), 13.

20. Dennis Raphael, *Social Determinants of Health: Canadian,* 2nd ed. (Toronto: Canadian Scholar's Press, 2009).

21. See, for example, Darcia Narvaez, Kristin Valentino, Agustin Fuentes, James J. McKenna, and Peter Gray, eds., *Ancestral Landscapes in Human Evolution: Culture, Childrearing and Social Wellbeing* (Oxford, UK: Oxford University Press, 2014).

22. Michael J. Meaney, "Maternal Care, Gene Expression, and the Transmission of Individual Differences in Stress Reactivity across Generations," *Annual Review of Neuroscience* 24, no. 1 (2001): 1161–92, https://doi.org/10.1146/annurev.neuro.24.1.1161.

23. Narvaez et al., *Ancestral Landscapes in Human Evolution.*

24. Center on the Developing Child, "Serve and Return," Harvard University, accessed June 2022, https://developingchild.harvard.edu/science/key-concepts/serve-and-return/.

25. Narvaez, *Neurobiology and the Development of Human Morality.*

26. Ming Kuo, interview by Shankar Vedantam, "Our Better Nature: How the Great Outdoors Can Improve Your Life," *Hidden Brain,* podcast audio and transcript, NPR, September 10, 2018, https://www.npr.org/transcripts/646413667.

27. Kuo, "Our Better Nature"; Ming Kuo, "How Might Contact with Nature Promote Human Health? Promising Mechanisms and a Possible Central Pathway," *Frontiers in Psychology* 6 (2015): 1093, https://doi.org/10.3389/fpsyg.2015.01093.

28. For more on this topic, see Edward O. Wilson, *Biophilia: The Human Bond with Other Species* (Cambridge, MA: Harvard University Press, 1986).

29. Alfie Kohn, *No Contest: The Case against Competition.* (Boston, MA: Houghton-Mifflin Court, 1992).

30. Winona LaDuke, *All Our Relations: Native Struggles for Land and Life* (Chicago: Haymarket Books, 1999).

31. See Paul Shepard, *Nature and Madness* (Athens, GA: University of Georgia, 1998); and Neil Evernden, *The Natural Alien: Humankind and Environment* (Toronto, ON: University of Toronto, 1993).

32. Gabor Maté, with Daniel Maté, *The Myth of Normal: Trauma, Illness, and Healing in a Toxic Culture* (Toronto: Knopf Canada, 2022).

33. Robert D. Putnam, *Bowling Alone: The Collapse and Revival of American Community* (New York: Simon & Schuster, 2000).

34. Jean M. Twenge, "The Age of Anxiety? Birth Cohort Change in Anxiety and Neuroticism, 1952–1993," *Journal of Personality and Social Psychology* 79, no. 6 (2000): 1007–21, https://doi.org/10.1037/0022-3514.79.6.1007.

35. Narvaez, *Neurobiology and the Development of Human Morality*; Maté, *The Myth of Normal*; and Sue Gerhardt, "The Selfish Society: The Current State of Things," in *The Political Self: Understanding the Social Context for Mental Illness,* ed. Rod Tweedy (Abingdon, UK: Routledge, 2017), 69–86, https://doi.org/10.4324/9780429482762-4.

36. Robert Whitaker, *Anatomy of an Epidemic: Magic Bullets, Psychiatric Drugs and the Astonishing Rise of Mental Illness* (New York: Broadway Books, 2010).

37. Jared M. Diamond, *The World Until Yesterday: What Can We Learn from Traditional Societies?* (New York: Viking, 2012), 189–90.

38. Florence Williams, *The Nature Fix: Why Nature Makes Us Happier, Healthier and More Creative* (New York: W. W. Norton, 2017).

39. Philippe Grandjean and Philip Landrigan, "Neurobehavioural Effects of Developmental Toxicity," *Lancet Neurology* 13, no. 3 (2014): 330–38, https://doi.org/10.1016/S1474-4422(13)70278-3.

40. Grandjean and Landrigan, "Neurobehavioural Effects."

41. Columbia University's Mailman School of Public Health, "Prenatal Exposure to Air Pollution Linked to Impulsivity, Emotional Problems in Children," March 17, 2016, https://www.publichealth.columbia.edu/public-health-now/news/prenatal-exposure-air-pollution-linked-impulsivity-emotional-problems-children; Grandjean and Landrigan, "Neurobehavioural Effects."

42. Jennifer T. Wolstenholme, Michelle Edwards, Savera R. J. Shetty, Jessica D. Gatewood, Julia A. Taylor, Emilie F. Rissman, and Jessica J. Connelly, "Gestational Exposure to Bisphenol A Produces Transgenerational Changes in Behaviors and Gene Expression," *Endocrinology* 153, no. 8 (2012): 3828–38, https://doi.org/10.1210/en.2012-1195.

43. Felice Wyndham, personal communication, October 2006.

44. John Caldwell Holt, *How Children Fail* (New York: Dell, 1970).

45. Vandana Shiva, "Schooling the World," Schooling the World, accessed July 2019, http://schoolingtheworld.org/people/vandana/.

46. Kohn, *No Contest.*

47. Kohn, *No Contest.*

48. Matthew D. Lieberman, *Social: Why Our Brains Are Wired to Connect* (New York: Crown Publishers, 2013), 43.

49. Narvaez, *Neurobiology and the Development of Human Morality.*

50. Diamond, *The World until Yesterday.*

51. Carol Gilligan, "In a Different Voice: Women's Conceptions of Self and of Morality," *Harvard Educational Review* 47, no. 4 (1977): 482. https://doi.org/10.17763/haer.47.4.g6167429416hg5l0.

52. Sean Blenkinsop, Laura Piersol, and Michael De Danann Sitka-Sage, "Boys Being Boys: Eco-Double Consciousness, Splash Violence, and Environmental Education," *Journal of Environmental Education* 49, no. 4 (2018): 350–56, https://doi.org/10.1080/00958964.2017.1364213.

53. Sean Blenkinsop, "Martin Buber: Educating for Relationship," *Ethics, Place and Environment* 8, no. 3 (2005): 285–307, https://doi.org/10.1080/13668790500348232.

54. Blenkinsop, "Martin Buber."

55. Native Languages of the Americas website. "Native American Nature Spirits of Myth and Legend," accessed July 3, 2019, http://www.native-languages.org/nature-spirits.htm.

56. Robin Wall Kimmerer, "The Grammar of Animacy," *Anthropology of Consciousness* 28, no. 2 (2017): 131.

57. Lev Vygotsky, *Mind in Society: The Development of Higher Psychological Processes*, ed. Michael Cole, Vera John-Steiner, Sylvia Scribner, and Ellen Souberman (Cambridge, MA: Harvard University Press, 1980), 23, 32.

58. For a longer discussion of this linguistic point see: Estella Kuchta and Sean Blenkinsop, "Toward a More Eco-Relational English," *Canadian Journal of Environmental Education* (in press).

59. Sean Blenkinsop and Laura Piersol, "Listening to the Literal: Orientations Towards How Nature Communicates," *Phenomenology & Practice* 7, no. 2 (2013): 51–56, https://doi.org/10.29173/pandpr21167.

60. Blenkinsop and Piersol, "Listening to the Literal," 56.

61. Chris Beeman and Sean Blenkinsop, "Dwelling Telling: Literalness and Ontology," *Paideusis* (Saskatoon) 17, no. 1 (2008): 13.

62. Beeman and Blenkinsop, "Dwelling Telling,"

63. Bob Jickling, Sean Blenkinsop, Nora Timmerman, and Michael De Danann Sitka-Sage, *Wild Pedagogies: Touchstones for Re-Negotiating Education and the Environment in the Anthropocene* (Cham, Switzerland: Palgrave-MacMillan, 2018).

64. Blenkinsop and Piersol, "Listening to the Literal," 54.

65. Sean Blenkinsop, "Four Slogans for Cultural Change: An Evolving Place-Based, Imaginative and Ecological Learning Experience," *Journal of Moral Education* 41, no. 3 (2012): 356, https://doi.org/10.1080/03057240.2012.691634.

66. Van Matre, S., *The Earth Speaks*. Bradford Woods: Institute for Earth Education, 1983: v.

3. HEALING

1. Mary Lister, "13 of the Most Persuasive Ads We've Ever Seen." Wordstream: By LocaliQ, last modified December 27, 2021, https://www.wordstream.com/blog/ws/2019/08/13/persuasive-ads.

2. McDonald's Corporation, "Happy Meal," accessed December 2022, https://www.mcdonalds.com/ca/en-ca/full-menu/happy-meal.html.

3. Rhonda Bryne, *The Secret* (Miami, FL: Atria Publishing, 2006).

4. Michele M. Tugade, Barbara L. Fredrickson, and Lisa Feldman Barrett, "Psychological Resilience and Positive Emotional Granularity: Examining the Benefits of Positive Emotions on Coping and Health," *Journal of Personality* 72, no. 6 (2004): 1161–90, https://doi.org/10.1111/j.1467-6494.2004.00294.x.

5. Rosalind Gill and Shani Orgad, "The Amazing Bounce-Backable Woman: Resilience and the Psychological Turn in Neoliberalism," *Sociological Research Online* 23, no. 2 (2018): 477, https://doi.org/10.1177/1360780418769673.

6. Edgar Cabanas, "Rekindling Individualism, Consuming Emotions: Constructing 'Psytizens' in the Age of Happiness," *Culture & Psychology* 22, no. 3 (2016): 467, https://doi.org/10.1177/1354067X16655459.

7. Cabanas, "Rekindling Individualism," 476.

8. For more on these discussions, see Carl Cederström and Andre Spicer, *The Wellness Syndrome* (Oxford, UK: Wiley, 2015); Sue Gerhardt, "The Selfish Society: The Current State of Things," in *The Political Self*, ed. Roderick Tweedy, 69–86 (Abingdon, OX: Routledge, 2017), https://doi.org/10.4324/9780429482762-4; and Barbara Ehrenreich, *Bright-Sided: How the Relentless Promotion of Positive Thinking Has Undermined America* (New York: Metropolitan Books, 2009).

9. See Lauren Gail Berlant, *Cruel Optimism* (Durham, NC: Duke University Press, 2011).

10. Helga Dittmar, Rod Bond, Megan Hurst, and Tim Kasser, "The Relationship between Materialism and Personal Wellbeing: A Meta-Analysis," *Journal of Personality and Social Psychology* 107, no. 5 (2014): 879–924, https://doi.org/10.1037/a0037409.

11. Kaveri, "18 Meditation Devices and Apps for a More Mindful 2022," Geekflare, November 30, 2022, https://geekflare.com/meditation-gadgets-apps/.

12. Jean M. Twenge, Brittany Gentile, C. Nathan DeWall, Debbie Ma, Katharine Lacefield, and David R. Schurtz, "Birth Cohort Increases in Psychopathology among Young Americans, 1938–2007: A Cross-Temporal Meta-Analysis of the MMPI," *Clinical Psychology Review* 30, no. 2 (2010): 145–54, https://doi.org/10.1016/j.cpr.2009.10.005.

13. Johann Hari, "Cause Three: Disconnection from Meaningful Values," in *Lost Connections* (New York: Bloomsbury Circus, 2018), 91–105.

14. Cederström and Spicer, *The Wellness Syndrome*, 3–4.

15. Cederström and Spicer, *The Wellness Syndrome*, 2.

16. Alenka Zupančič, *The Odd One In: On Comedy* (Cambridge, MA: MIT Press, 2008), 5.

17. Timothy J. Legg, "What to Know about Eco-Anxiety," Medical News Today, Health-line Media, December 19, 2019, https://www.medicalnewstoday.com/articles/327354.

18. Mark Fettes (Professor of Imaginative Education at Simon Fraser University), in conversation with the author, October 2020.

19. Joanna Macy, "Despair Work," in *Peace Movements Worldwide*, ed. Marc Pilisuk and Michael N. Nagler (Westport, CT: Praeger, 2010), 285.

20. David Ludden, "East West Cultural Differences in Depression," Talking Apes Blog, Psychologytoday.com, November 20, 2017, https://www.psychologytoday.com/ca/blog /talking-apes/201711/east-west-cultural-differences-in-depression.

21. See, for example, WebMD, "Holistic Medicine," March 18, 2020, https://www .webmd.com/balance/guide/what-is-holistic-medicine.

22. See, for example, Isabella Tree, *Wilding: The Return of Nature to a British Farm* (London, UK: Picador, 2018).

23. Gabor Maté with Daniel Maté, *The Myth of Normal: Illness and Health in an In-sane Culture* (Toronto: Knopf Canada, 2022).

24. *The Wisdom of Trauma*, directed by Maurizio Benazzo and Zaya Benazzo (Oak-land, CA: The Hive Studios, 2021), https://thewisdomoftrauma.com/portfolio-item/about -the-film/.

25. Michael T. Hernke and Rian J. Podein, "Sustainability, Health and Precautionary Perspectives on Lawn Pesticides, and Alternatives," *EcoHealth* 8, no. 2 (2011): 223–32, https://doi.org/10.1007/s10393-011-0697-7.

26. A. R. Ravishankara, John S. Daniel, and Robert W. Portmann, "Nitrous Oxide (N$_2$O): The Dominant Ozone-Depleting Substance Emitted in the 21st Century," *Science (American Association for the Advancement of Science)* 326, no. 5949 (2009): 123–25, https://doi.org/10.1126/science.1176985.

27. Jean-Pierre Gattuso and Lina Hansson, *Ocean Acidification* (Oxford, UK: Oxford University Press, 2011).

28. Ju Hwan Kim, Jin-Koo Lee, Hyung-Gun Kim, Kyu-Bong Kim, and Hak Rim Kim, "Possible Effects of Radiofrequency Electromagnetic Field Exposure on Central Nerve System," *Biomolecules & Therapeutics* 27, no. 3 (2019): 265–75, https://doi.org/10.4062 /biomolther.2018.152.

29. For an exception, see Maté, *The Myth of Normal*.

30. Joanna Moncrieff, Ruth E. Cooper, Tom Stockmann, Simone Amendola, Mi-chael P. Hengartner, and Mark A. Horowitz, "The Serotonin Theory of Depression: A Systematic Umbrella Review of the Evidence," *Molecular Psychiatry* (2022), https://doi .org/10.1038/s41380-022-01661-0.

31. For example, see Thomas Insel, *Healing: Our Path from Mental Illness to Mental Health* (New York: Penguin, 2022); and Robert Whitaker, *Anatomy of an Epidemic* (New York: Broadway Books, 2010).

32. Hari, *Lost Connections*.

33. Nidya Diaz-Camal, Jesús Daniel Cardoso-Vera, Hariz Islas-Flores, Leobardo Man-uel Gómez-Oliván, and Alejandro Mejía-García, "Consumption and Occurrence of Antidepressants (SSRIs) in Pre- and Post-COVID-19 Pandemic, Their Environmental Impact and Innovative Removal Methods: A Review," *The Science of the Total Environ-ment* 829 (2022): 4, https://doi.org/10.1016/j.scitotenv.2022.154656.

34. Diaz-Camal, *The Science of the Total Environment*.

35. Ed Yong, "What Happens When Americans Can Finally Exhale?" *The Atlantic*, May 20, 2021, https://www.theatlantic.com/health/archive/2021/05/pandemic-trauma -summer/618934/.

36. Sara Platto, Jinfeng Zhou, Yanqing Wang, Huo Wang, and Ernesto Carafoli, "Bio-diversity Loss and COVID-19 Pandemic: The Role of Bats in the Origin and the Spreading

of the Disease," *Biochemical and Biophysical Research Communications* 538 (2021): 2–13, https://doi.org/10.1016/j.bbrc.2020.10.028.

37. "The Covid Pandemic from a Global Environmental Perspective," Global Environmental Health Newsletter, National Institute of Environmental Health Sciences, June 1, 2020, https://www.niehs.nih.gov/research/programs/geh/geh_newsletter/2020/6/articles /the_covid19_pandemic_from_a_global_environmental_health_perspective.cfm.

38. For example, see Samuel Wilson, Lovell Jones, Christine Coussens, and Kathi Hanna, eds., *Cancer and the Environment: Gene-Environment Interaction,* Roundtable of Environmental Health Sciences, Research, and Medicine, Board on Health Sciences Policy, Institute of Medicine (Washington, DC: National Academy Press, 2002), https://doi .org/10.17226/10464; Sandra Steingraber, *Living Downstream: An Ecologist's Personal Investigation of Cancer and the Environment* (New York: Hachette Books, 2010); and P. Nicolopoulou-Stamati, L. Hens, C. V. Howard and N. Van Larebeke, eds., *Cancer as an Environmental Disease* (Norwell, MA: Kluwer Academic Publishers, 2004), https://link .springer.com/content/pdf/bfm:978-0-306-48513-8/1.

39. *The Wisdom of Trauma.*

40. Maté, *The Myth of Normal.*

41. Susan Clayton, Christie Manning, Kirra Krygsman, and Meighen Speiser, *Mental Health and Our Changing Climate: Impacts, Implications, and Guidance* (Washington, DC: American Psychology Association and ecoAmerica, 2017), 7, https://www.apa.org /news/press/releases/2017/03/mental-health-climate.pdf.

42. Jodi MacQuarrie, in discussion with author, September 2019.

43. Drawn from Jon Young, *What the Robin Knows: How Birds Reveal the Secrets of the Natural World* (Boston, MA: Mariner Books, 2013).

44. Kristine Engemann, Carsten Bøcker Pedersen, Lars Arge, Jens-Christian Svenning, "Residential Green Space in Childhood Is Associated with Lower Risk of Psychiatric Disorders from Adolescence into Adulthood," *Proceedings of the National Academy of Sciences (PNAS)* 116, no. 11 (2019): 5188–93, https://doi.org/10.1073/pnas.1807504116.

45. Christoffer van Tulleken, Michael Tipton, Heather Massey, and C Mark Harper, "Open Water Swimming as a Treatment for Major Depressive Disorder," *BMJ Case Reports* (2018): 1–3, https://doi.org/10.1136/bcr-2018-225007; Jane Clatworthy, Joe Hinds, and Paul M. Camic, "Gardening as a Mental Health Intervention: A Review," *Mental Health Review Journal* 18, no. 4 (2013): 214–25, https://doi.org/10.1108/MHRJ-02-2013 -0007.

46. Masashi Soga, Kevin J. Gaston, and Yuichi Yamaura, "Gardening Is Beneficial for Health: A Meta-Analysis," *Preventive Medicine Reports* 5, no. C (2016): 92, https://doi.org /10.1016/j.pmedr.2016.11.007.

47. Ming Kuo, "How Might Contact with Nature Promote Human Health? Promising Mechanisms and a Possible Central Pathway," *Frontiers in Psychology* 6 (2015): 1, https://doi.org/10.3389/fpsyg.2015.01093.

48. Lara S. Franco, Danielle F. Shanahan, and Richard A. Fuller, "A Review of the Benefits of Nature Experiences: More Than Meets the Eye," *International Journal of Environmental Research and Public Health* 14, no. 8 (2017): 864, https://doi.org/10.3390 /ijerph14080864.

49. Kuo, "How Might Contact with Nature Promote Human Health?" 6.

50. Caroline Hägerhäll, Richard Taylor, Gunnar Cerwén, Greg Watts, Matilda van den Bosch, Daniel Press, and Steven Minta, "Biological Mechanisms and Neurophysiological Responses to Sensory Impact from Nature," in *Oxford Textbook of Nature and Public Health,* ed. Matilda van den Bosch and William Bird (Oxford, UK: Oxford University, 2018), 81.

51. Hägerhäll et al., "Biological Mechanisms," 83–84.

52. Alessandra Della Vecchia, Federico Mucci, Andrea Pozza, Donatella Marazziti, "Negative Air Ions in Neuropsychiatric Disorders," *Current Medicinal Chemistry* 28, no. 13 (2021): 2521–39, https://doi.org/10.2174/0929867327666200630104550.

53. Qing Li, "Effect of Forest Bathing Trips on Human Immune Function," *Environmental Health and Preventive Medicine* 15, no. 1 (2010): 9–17, https://doi.org/10.1007/s12199-008-0068-3.

54. Wilson Da Silva, "How Adding Microbial Diversity to Urban Environments Improves Health," *Australian Geographic*, November 25, 2019, https://www.australiangeographic.com.au/topics/science-environment/2019/11/how-adding-microbial-diversity-to-urban-environments-improves-health/.

55. Winfried E. H. Blum, Sophie Zechmeister-Boltenstern, and Katharina M. Keiblinger, "Does Soil Contribute to the Human Gut Microbiome?" *Microorganisms* 7, no. 9 (2019): 287, https://doi.org/10.3390/microorganisms7090287.

56. Kuo, "How Might Contact with Nature Promote Human Health?" 4.

57. John Barrat, "A Poison Ivy Primer," Smithsonian Institute, August 12, 2014, https://www.si.edu/stories/poison-ivy-primer.

58. Natural History of Orange County, "Toxicodendron Diversilobum," June 12, 2005, http://nathistoc.bio.uci.edu/Plants%20of%20Upper%20Newport%20Bay%20(Robert%20De%20Ruff)/Anacardiaceae/Toxicodendron%20diversilobum.htm.

59. Michael Pollan, *The Botany of Desire: A Plant's-Eye View of the World* (New York: Random House, 2001).

60. Joe Sheridan and Roronhiakewen "He Clears the Sky" Dan Longboat, "The Haudenosaunee Imagination and the Ecology of the Sacred," *Space and Culture* 9, no. 4 (2006): 365–81, https://doi.org/10.1177/1206331206292503.

61. Robin Wall Kimmerer, *Braiding Sweetgrass. Indigenous Wisdom, Scientific Knowledge and the Teachings of Plants* (Minneapolis, MN: Milkweed Editions, 2013), 16.

62. Kimmerer, *Braiding Sweetgrass*, 24.

63. Kimmerer, *Braiding Sweetgrass*, 28.

64. Kimmerer, *Braiding Sweetgrass*, 28.

65. Robin Wall Kimmerer, "Mishkos Kenomagwen: The Teachings of Grass," posted by the Bioneers, November 15, 2014, https://www.youtube.com/watch?v=cumEQcRMY3c.

66. Jordan Peterson, *12 Rules for Living* (Toronto, ON: Random House, 2018), 16.

67. Robyn Maynard, "Reading Black Resistance through Afrofuturism: Notes on Post-Apocalyptic Blackness and Black Rebel Cyborgs in Canada," *Topia* 39 (2018): 29.

68. Susan Laird, "Learning to Live in the Anthropocene: Our Children and Ourselves," *Studies in Philosophy and Education* 36 (2017): 265–82.

69. Michelle Alexander, *The New Jim Crow: Mass Incarceration in the Age of Colorblindness* (New York: New Press, 2010).

70. Rodney A. Brooks, "African Americans Struggle with Disproportionate COVID Death Toll," *National Geographic*, April 24, 2020, https://www.nationalgeographic.com/history/2020/04/coronavirus-disproportionately-impacts-african-americans/.

71. Gianna Melillo, "Recognizing the Role of Systemic Racism in Diabetes Disparities," *AJMC*, February 2, 2021, https://www.ajmc.com/view/recognizing-the-role-of-systemic-racism-in-diabetes-disparities.

72. Audience participant in Tobias C. Van Veen presentation, "Afro-Futurism & Anthropocene: Strategies for Imagining Other Worlds," *Afrocentrism Conference*, September 21–22, 2019, Vancouver, BC.

73. *Stan Rushworth Interview*, directed by Katie Teague, uploaded Friday, March 20, 2020 (Santa Cruz, CA: Katie Teague Minute, Vimeo), 6:20, https://vimeo.com/399323963.

74. See Elizabeth Kolbert, *The Sixth Extinction: An Unnatural History* (New York: Henry Holt and Company, 2014); Gerardo Ceballos, Paul R. Ehrlich, Anthony D. Barnosky, Andrés

García, Robert M. Pringle, and Todd M. Palmer, "Accelerated Modern Human-Induced Species Losses: Entering the Sixth Mass Extinction," *Science Advances* 1, no. 5 (2015): e1400253–e1400253, https://doi.org/10.1126/sciadv.1400253; and Anthony D. Barnosky, Nicholas Matzke, Ben Mersey, Elizabeth A. Ferrer, Susumu Tomiya, Guinevere O. U. Wogan, Brian Swartz, et al., "Has the Earth's Sixth Mass Extinction Already Arrived?" *Nature (London)* 471, no. 7336 (2011): 51–57, https://doi.org/10.1038/nature09678.

75. Naomi Klein, *No Is Not Enough: Resisting Trump's Shock Politics and Winning the World We Need* (Chicago, IL: Haymarket Books, 2017).

76. Stan Rushworth, in discussion with author, May 2020.

77. Bayo Akomolafe, "When You Meet the Monster, Anoint Its Feet," *Emergence Magazine*, October 16, 2018, https://emergencemagazine.org/story/when-you-meet-the-monster/.

78. Tobias C. Van Veen and Reynaldo Anderson, "Future Movements: Black Lives, Black Politics, Black Futures—An Introduction," *TOPIA: Canadian Journal of Cultural Studies* 39 (2018): 8.

79. Tobias C. Van Veen, "Afro-Futurism & Anthropocene: Strategies for Imagining Other Worlds," *Afrocentrism Conference*, September 21–22, 2019, Vancouver, BC.

80. John Broadway, "Sankofa: Lessons in Returning to Our Roots," Public Allies website, February 18, 2022, https://www.uis.edu/africanamericanstudies/students/sankofa/.

81. Stan Rushworth, in discussion with author, May 2020.

82. Val Plumwood, *Feminism and the Mastery of Nature* (Milton Park, OX: Taylor and Francis, 2002), 29, https://doi.org/10.4324/9780203006757.

83. Carol Gilligan and Naomi Snider, *Why Does Patriarchy Persist?* (Cambridge, UK: Polity Press, 2018).

84. Gilligan and Snider, *Why Does Patriarchy Persist?*, 33.

85. Sean Blenkinsop, Laura Piersol, and Michael De Danann Sitka-Sage, "Boys Being Boys: Eco-Double Consciousness, Splash Violence, and Environmental Education," *The Journal of Environmental Education* 49, no. 4 (2018): 350–56, https://doi.org/10.1080/00958964.2017.1364213.

86. Nicholas A. Groth and H. Jean Birnbaum, *Men Who Rape: The Psychology of the Offender* (New York: Plenum Press, 1979).

87. Gillian Greensite, *Support for Survivors: Training for Sexual Assault Counsellors* (California Coalition Against Sexual Assault, 2008), https://evawintl.org/wp-content/uploads/CALCASA-2008-Support-for-Survivors-TrainingforSACounselors.pdf.

88. William F. McKibbin, Todd K. Shackelford, Aaron T. Goetz, and Valerie G. Starratt, "Why Do Men Rape? An Evolutionary Psychological Perspective," *Review of General Psychology* 12, no. 1 (2008): 86–97, https://doi.org/10.1037/1089-2680.12.1.86.

89. Gilligan and Snider, *Why Does Patriarchy Persist?*, 7.

90. Maté, *The Myth of Normal*.

91. Stan Rushworth, in discussion with author, May 2020.

92. Stefano Harney and Fred Moten, *The Undercommons: Fugitive Planning & Black Study* (New York: Minor Compositions, 2013), 10.

93. Maxwell Rickus (Estella's son), in discussion with author, June 2020.

94. Rasunah Marsden, "The World Pattern of Process" (PhD diss., University of British Columbia, 2019), 141, http://dx.doi.org/10.14288/1.0378038.

95. Angela Ka-yee Leung, William W. Maddux, Adam D. Galinsky, and Chi-yue Chiu, "Multicultural Experience Enhances Creativity," *The American Psychologist* 63, no. 3 (2008): 169–81, https://doi.org/10.1037/0003-066X.63.3.169.

4. THEORIZING

1. Mendocino Pygmy Forest, "Pygmy-Forest.com," accessed July 4, 2023, http://pygmy-forest.com.

2. For more information, see https://eleducation.org/. EL Education, "Educating for a Better World," accessed July 4, 2023, https://eleducation.org/.

3. Gilles Deleuze and Félix Guattari, *A Thousand Plateaus: Capitalism and Schizophrenia,* trans. Brian Massumi (Minneapolis, MN: University of Minnesota Press, 1987).

4. Cheryl Bartlett, Murdena Marshall, and Albert Marshall, "Two-Eyed Seeing and Other Lessons Learned within a Co-Learning Journey of Bringing Together Indigenous and Mainstream Knowledges and Ways of Knowing," *Journal of Environmental Studies and Sciences* 2 (2012): 331–40.

5. Albert Camus, *The Rebel: An Essay on Man in Revolt,* trans. Anthony Bower (New York: Vintage Books, 1992).

6. Albert Camus, banquet speech, NobelPrize.org, Nobel Prize Outreach AB 2023, January 22, 2023, https://www.nobelprize.org/prizes/literature/1957/camus/speech/.

7. Michel Serres, *The Natural Contract,* trans. Elizabeth MacArthur and William Paulson (Ann Arbor, MI: Michigan University Press, 1995).

8. Merlin Sheldrake, *The Entangled Life: How Fungi Make Our Worlds, Change Our Minds, and Shape Our Futures* (London, UK: Random House, 2021).

9. See Agustín Fuentes, "Naturalcultural Encounters in Bali: Monkeys, Temples, Tourists, and Ethnoprimatology," *Cultural Anthropology* 25 (2010): 600–24; and Donna J. Haraway, *The Companion Species Manifesto: Dogs, People, and Significant Otherness* (Chicago: Prickly Paradigm Press, 2003).

10. See Marie J. Hall et al., *The Collected Works of L. S. Vygotsky: Problems of General Psychology, Including the Volume Thinking and Speech* (Netherlands: Plenum, 1987).

11. Thomas King, *The Truth about Stories: A Native Narrative* (Toronto: House of Anansi, 2003).

12. Luce Irigaray, *In the Beginning, She Was* (New York: Bloomsbury, 2013).

13. Deborah Bird Rose, "Connectivity Thinking, Animism, and the Pursuit of Liveliness," *Educational Theory* 67, no. 4 (2018): 491–508.

14. Paul Kingsnorth, *Confessions of a Recovering Environmentalist and Other Essays* (Minneapolis, MN: Graywolf Press, 2017).

15. The names in this story have been invented.

16. There are lots of resources that explore the gendered nature of our relationship with the natural world, the role of violence in colonial and hierarchical relationships, and the insights and limitations of various psychological frameworks. This vignette is explored in more depth later in the chapter.

17. W. E. B. DuBois, *The Souls of Black Folks* (New York: Penguin Classics, 1996).

5. PRACTICING

1. In fact, much curriculum has already been developed that is profoundly ecologizing and offers very rich learning experiences. See Appendix for examples.

2. Other theorists have worked with similar ideas, such as the "touchstones" found in *Wild Pedagogies.* This is unsurprising, given our shared aims of cultural and educational change, our commitments to issues of eco-social justice, and the roles we, the authors of this book, have played in the development and enunciation of wild pedagogies. See Bob Jickling, Sean Blenkinsop, Nora Timmerman, & Michael De Danann Sitka-Sage, *Wild Pedagogies: Touchstones for Re-negotiating Education and the Environment in the Anthropocene* (Cham, Switzerland: Palgrave-MacMillan, 2018).

3. Ralph Tyler, *Basic Principles of Curriculum and Instruction* (Chicago: University of Chicago Press, 1949).

4. See, for example, Francis Hunkins and Patricia Hammill, "Beyond Tyler and Taba: Reconceptualizing the Curriculum Process," *Peabody Journal of Education* 69, no. 3 (1994): 4–18, doi:10.1080/01619569409538774; James Fogarty, "The Tyler Rationale: Support and Criticism," *Educational Technology* 16, no. 3 (1976): 28–32; and Thabo Msibi, "Queering Curriculum Studies in South Africa: A Call for Reconceptualisation?" in *Disrupting Higher Education Curriculum: Undoing Cognitive Damage*, ed. Michael Samuel, Rubby Dhunpath, and Nina Amin (Rotterdam: SensePublishers, 2016), 213–28.

5. For more on lateral thinking, see Sean Blenkinsop, John Telford, and Marcus Morse, "A Surprising Discovery: Five Pedagogical Skills Outdoor and Experiential Educators Have to Offer More Mainstream Educators in This Time of Change," *Journal of Adventure Education and Outdoor Leadership* 16, no. 4 (2016): 346–58.

6. Aldo Leopold was a natural historian and writer who has had a great deal of influence on environmental movements in North America. He was also a university professor, and one of his well-known pedagogical practices was to place undergraduates in natural places around the campus for a few days and have them use their observational skills, their scientific knowledge, and their understanding of relationships to answer three questions: "What has happened here?" "What is happening here?" "And what should happen here?" The first two involve examining plants, animals, soils, and so on in order to find clues that point to land use, succession, fertility, and more. The final question challenges the students to place those findings into a political and axiological context. Interesting stuff.

7. Joe Sheridan and Roronhiakewen "He Clears the Sky" Dan Longboat, "The Haudenosaunee Imagination and the Ecology of the Sacred," *Space and Culture* 9, no. 4 (2006): 365, https://doi.org/10.1177/1206331206292503.

8. See Vanessa Watts, "Indigenous Place-Thought and Agency amongst Humans and Non-Humans (First Woman and Sky Woman Go on a European World Tour)," *Decolonization: Indigeneity, Education, and Society* 2, no. 1 (2013): 20–34.

9. Sheridan and Longboat, "The Haudenosaunee Imagination," 368.

10. Keith Basso, *Wisdom Sits in Places: Landscape and Language among the Western Apache,* (Albuquerque, NM: University of New Mexico Press, 1996).

11. Sheridan and Longboat, "The Haudenosaunee Imagination," 369.

12. See Sean Blenkinsop and Laura Piersol, "Listening to the Literal: Orientations towards How Nature Communicates," *Phenomenology and Practice* 7, no. 2 (2013): 41–60.

13. Martin Buber, *Between Man and Man*, trans. Ronald G. Smith (New York: Macmillan, 1968).

14. Michel Foucault, "On the Genealogy of Ethics: An Overview of Work in Progress," in *Michel Foucault: Beyond Structuralism and Hermeneutics*, ed. Hubert Dreyfus and Paul Rabinow (Chicago: University of Chicago Press, 1983), 229–64.

15. See, for example, Greta Gaard, "Toward a Queer Ecofeminism," *Hypatia* 12, no. 1 (1997): 114–37; and Catriona Mortimer-Sandilands and Bruce Erickson, eds., *Queer Ecologies: Sex, Nature, Politics, Desire* (Indianapolis, IN: Indiana University Press, 2010).

16. Carl Safina, *Beyond Words: What Animals Think and Feel* (New York: Henry Holt and Company, 2015).

17. Wade Davis, *The Wayfinders: Why Ancient Wisdom Matters in the Modern World* (Toronto, ON: House of Anansi, 2009).

18. See Sean Blenkinsop, "Four Slogans for Cultural Change: An Evolving Place-based, Imaginative, and Ecological Learning Experience," *Journal of Moral Education* 41, no. 3 (2012): 353–68.

19. See David Sobel, *Children's Special Places: Exploring the Role of Forts, Dens, and Bush Houses in Middle Childhood* (Detroit, MI: Wayne State University Press, 2001).

20. Jickling et al., *Wild Pedagogies*.

21. C. A. Bowers, *Education, Cultural Myths, and the Ecological Crisis: Toward Deep Changes* (Albany, NY: SUNY Press, 1993).

CHANGING CULTURE

1. Jodi MacQuarrie, personal interview with author, December 17, 2021.

2. Jodi MacQuarrie, personal interview with author, December 17, 2021.

3. See Wendell Berry, *The Unsettling of America: Culture and Agriculture* (Berkeley, CA: Counterpoint Publishing, 2004); Vandana Shiva, *Who Really Feeds the World?: The Failures of Agribusiness and the Promise of Agroecology* (Berkeley, CA: North Atlantic Books, 2016); and Janisse Ray, *The Seed Underground: A Growing Revolution to Save Food* (White River Junction, VT: Chelsea Green Publishing, 2014).

4. This chapter is influenced by and builds out of a long report completed under the auspices of a Knowledge Synthesis Grant from the Social Sciences and Humanities Research Council of Canada (http://www.circesfu.ca/wp-content/uploads/2021/06/Final -Report-Blenkinsop-Fettes.pdf). The rich work that was done over the course of a year is deeply salient here for our purposes, so Skylar Sage, Mark Fettes, Chloe Humphries, Lindsey Cole, and David Chang can all be considered co-cogitators, co-producers, co-cultivators, co-authors.

5. Cheryl Charles, and Bob Samples, *Coming Home: Community, Creativity, and Consciousness* (Fawnskin, CA: Personhood Press, 2004); Geoffrey Nelson and Isaac Prilleltensky, *Community Psychology: In Pursuit of Liberation and Wellbeing* (London: Palgrave MacMillan, 2010).

6. Paul Kivel, *Uprooting Racism: How White People Can Work for Racial Justice* (Gabriola Island, BC: New Society Publishers, 2017).

7. Nelson and Prilleltensky, *Community Psychology*.

8. Sean Blenkinsop, Ramsey Affifi, Laura Piersol, and Michael De Danann Sitka-Sage, "Shut-Up and Listen: Implications and Possibilities of Albert Memmi's Characteristics of Colonization upon the 'Natural World,'" *Studies in Philosophy and Education* 36, no. 3 (2017): 349–65.

9. Kivel, *Uprooting Racism*.

10. Nelson and Prilleltensky, *Community Psychology*.

11. Michalinos Zembylas, "The Quest for Cognitive Justice: Towards a Pluriversal Human Rights Education," *Globalisation, Societies and Education* 15, no. 4 (2017): 397–409, https://doi.org/10.1080/14767724.2017.1357462.

12. Kivel, *Uprooting Racism*.

13. Nelson and Prilleltensky, *Community Psychology*.

14. See Leanne Betasamosake Simpson, *As We Have Always Done: Indigenous Freedom through Radical Resistances* (Minneapolis: Minnesota University Press, 2017).

APPENDIX

1. Many thanks to Megan Tucker and Aaron Lefler for creating and maintaining the Eco Resource List.

References

Abdel-Rahman, H. A. "Fatal Suffocation by Rubber Balloons in Children: Mechanism and Prevention." *Forensic Science International* 108, no. 2 (2000): 97–105. https://doi.org/10.1016/S0379-0738(99)00143-7.

Abraham, A., K. Sommerhalder, and T. Abel. "Landscape and Well-Being: A Scoping Study on the Health-Promoting Impact of Outdoor Environments." *International Journal of Public Health* 55, no. 1 (2010): 59–69.

Abram, David. *The Spell of the Sensuous: Perception and Language in a More-Than-Human World*. New York: Vintage Books, 1997.

Abram, David. *Becoming Animal*. New York: Vintage, 2010.

Acampora, R. R. *Corporeal Compassion*. Pittsburgh: University of Pittsburgh Press, 2006.

Adams, Cecil. "Do Falling Pianos Really Kill People?" *Washington City Paper*. April 12, 2013. https://washingtoncitypaper.com/article/209447/straight-dope-do-falling-pianos-really-kill-people/.

Affifi, R. "What Weston's Spider and My Shorebirds Might Mean for Bateson's Mind: Some Educational Wanderings in Interspecies Curricula." *Canadian Journal of Environmental Education* 16 (2011): 46–58.

Affifi, R. "The Metabolic Core of Environmental Education." *Studies in Philosophy and Education* 36 (2016): 315–32.

Affifi, R. "Engaging the Adaptive Subject: Learning Evolution beyond the Cell Walls." *Biological Theory* 15 (2020): 121–35.

Affifi, R. "Ecologizing Education beyond Angels and Villains." *Environmental Education Research* (2022). https://doi.org/10.1080/13504622.2022.2108768.

Affifi, R., S. Blenkinsop, C. Humphreys, and C. W. Joldersma. "Introduction to Ecologizing Philosophy of Education." *Studies in Philosophy and Education* 36, no. 3 (2017): 1–13.

Akomolafe, Bayo. "When You Meet the Monster, Anoint Its Feet." *Emergence Magazine*. October 16, 2018. https://emergencemagazine.org/story/when-you-meet-the-monster/.

Alaimo, S. "Trans-Corporal Feminisms and the Ethical Space of Nature." In *Material Feminisms,* edited by S. Alaimo and S. Heckman, pp. 237–64. Bloomington, IN: Indiana University Press, 2008.

Alexander, Michelle. *The New Jim Crow: Mass Incarceration in the Age of Colorblindness*. New York: New Press, 2010.

"Alternatives to Conventional Clearcutting." BC Ministry of Forests. Accessed August 2021. https://www.for.gov.bc.ca/hfp/publications/00217/atcc.htm.

Anderson, S. *Bringing Life to School: Place-Based Education across the Curriculum*. Lanham: Rowman & Littlefield, 2017.

Andrzejewski, J., H. Pedersen, and F. Wicklund. "Interspecies Education for Humans, Animals, and the Earth." In *Social justice, peace, and environmental education: Transformative Standards,* pp. 136–154. Philadelphia: Routledge, 2009.

"Anthropocene," *National Geographic*. Accessed July 2020. https://www.nationalgeographic.org/encyclopedia/anthropocene/.

Arnold, E. H., F. G. Cohen, and A. Warner. "Youth and Environmental Action: Perspective of Young Environmental Leaders on Their Formative Influences." *The Journal of Environmental Education* 40, no. 3 (2009): 27–36.

Asfeldt, M., and S. Beames "Trusting the Journey: Embracing the Unpredictable and Difficult to Measure Nature of Wilderness Educational Expeditions." *Journal of Experiential Education* 40, no. 1 (2017): 72–86.

Asfeldt, M., R. Purc-Stephenson, M. Rawleigh, and S. Thackeray. "Outdoor Education in Canada: A Qualitative Investigation." *Journal of Adventure Education and Outdoor Learning* 21, no. 4 (2021): 297–310.

Asfeldt, M., I. Urberg, and B. Henderson. "Wolves, Ptarmigan and Lake Trout: Critical Elements of a Northern Canadian Place-Conscious Pedagogy." *Canadian Journal of Environmental Education* 14 (2009): 33–41.

Assadourian, E., L. Mastny, and Worldwatch Institute. *EarthEd: Rethinking Education on a Changing Planet.* Washington, DC: Island Press, 2017.

Atweh, B., S. Kemmis, and P. Weeks. *Action Research in Practice: Partnerships for Social Justice in Education.* Philadelphia, PA: Routledge, 1998.

Bai, H. "Reanimating the Universe." In *Fields of Green: Restorying Culture, Environment, and Education,* edited by Marcia McKenzie, Paul Hart, Heesoon Bai, and Bob Jickling. New York: Hampton Press, 2009.

Bai, H., and G. Scutt. "Touching the Earth with the Heart of Enlightened Mind: The Buddhist Practice of Mindfulness for Environmental Education." *Canadian Journal of Environmental Education* 14 (2009): 92–106.

Bailey, A. W., and H. Kang. "Modeling the Impact of Wilderness Orientation Programs on First-Year Academic Success and Life Purpose." *Journal of Adventure Education and Outdoor Learning* 15, no. 3 (2015), 209–23.

Barad, K. *Meeting the Universe Half-way.* Durham, NC: Duke Press, 2007.

Barnosky, Anthony D., Nicholas Matzke, Ben Mersey, Elizabeth A. Ferrer, Susumu Tomiya, Guinevere O. U. Wogan, Brian Swartz, et al. "Has the Earth's Sixth Mass Extinction Already Arrived?" *Nature (London)* 471, no. 7336 (2011): 51–57. https://doi.org/10.1038/nature09678.

Barrat, John. "A Poison Ivy Primer." Smithsonian Institute. August 12, 2014. https://www.si.edu/stories/poison-ivy-primer.

Bartlett, Cheryl, Murdena Marshall, and Albert Marshall. "Two-Eyed Seeing and Other Lessons Learned within a Co-Learning Journey of Bringing Together Indigenous and Mainstream Knowledges and Ways of Knowing." *Journal of Environmental Studies and Sciences* 2 (2012): 331–40.

Basso, Keith. *Wisdom Sits in Places: Landscape and Language among the Western Apache.* Albuquerque, NM: University of New Mexico Press, 1996.

Bates, C. "Rewilding Education? Exploring an Imagined and Experienced Outdoor Learning Space." *Children's Geographies* 18, no. 3 (2020): 364–74.

Battiste, M. "Indigenous Knowledge and Pedagogy in First Nations Education: A Literature Review with Recommendations." *National Working Group on Education* (2002).

Battiste, M., M. Bell, I. Findlay, L. Findlay, and J. S. Youngblood Henderson. "Thinking Place: Animating the Indigenous Humanities in Education." *Australian Journal of Indigenous Education* 34 (2005): 7–19.

Becker, L. G., S. Spengler, U. Dettweiler, and F. Mess. "Effects of Regular Classes in Outdoor Education Settings: A Systematic Review on Students' Learning, Social and Health Dimensions." *International Journal of Environmental Research and Public Health* 14, no. 5 (2017): 485.

Beeman, Chris. "Wilding Liability in Education: Introducing the Concept of Wide Risk as Counterpoint to Narrow-Risk-Driven Educative Practice." *Policy Futures in Education* 19, no. 3 (2021): 324–38. https://doi.org/10.1177/1478210320978096.

Beeman, Chris, and Sean Blenkinsop. "Cassandras of a Second Kind." *Journal of Environmental Education* 52, no. 3 (2021): 162–73. https://doi.org/10.1080/00958964.2021.1922331.

Beeman, Chris, and Sean Blenkinsop. "Dwelling Telling: Literalness and Ontology." *Paideusis* (Saskatoon) 17, no. 1 (2008): 13.

Beery, T. H., & D. Wolf-Watz. "Nature to Place: Rethinking the Environmental Connectedness Perspective." *Journal of Environmental Psychology* 40 (2014): 198–205.

Beightol, J., J. Jevertson, S. Gray, S. Carter, and M. Gass. "The Effect of an Experiential Adventure-Based 'Anti-Bullying Initiative' on Levels of Resilience: A Mixed Method Study." *Journal of Experiential Education* 31, no. 3 (2009): 420–424.

Bell, A., and C. Russell. "Beyond Human, beyond Words: Anthropocentrism, Critical Pedagogy, and the Poststructuralist Turn." *Canadian Journal of Education* 25, no. 3 (2000): 188–203.

Bell, B. J., M. A. Gass, C. S. Nafziger, and J. D. Starbuck, J. D. "The State of Knowledge of Outdoor Orientation Programs: Current Practices, Research, and Theory." *Journal of Experiential Education* 37, no. 1 (2014): 31–45.

Berlant, Lauren Gail. *Cruel Optimism*. Durham, NC: Duke University Press, 2011.

Berman, M. G., J. Jonides, and S. Kaplan. "The Cognitive Benefits of Interacting with Nature." *Psychological Science* 19 (2008): 1207–12.

Berry, Wendell. *The Unsettling of America: Culture and Agriculture*. Berkeley, CA: Counterpoint Publishing, 2004.

Biesta, G. (2010). *Good Education in an Age of Measurement: Ethics, Politics, Democracy*. Baltimore: Paradigm Publishers.

Bird Rose, Deborah. "Connectivity Thinking, Animism, and the Pursuit of Liveliness." *Educational Theory* 67, no. 4 (2018): 491–508.

Bjørgen, K. "Children's Well-Being and Involvement in Physically Active Outdoors Play in Norwegian Kindergarten: Playful Sharing of Physical Experiences." *Child Care in Practice* 21, no. 4 (2015): 305–23.

Blackie, S. "David Abram (No. 10)" [Audio podcast episode]. *In the Mythic Life*. October 4, 2019. Society and Culture, Apple podcast.

Blair, D. "The Child in the Garden: An Evaluative Review of the Benefits of School Gardening." *Journal of Environmental Education* 40, no. 2 (2009): 15–38.

Blenkinsop, S., C. Nolan, J. Hunt, P. Stonehouse, and J. Telford. "The Lecture as Experiential Education: The Cucumber in 17th-Century Flemish Art." *Journal of Experiential Education* 39, no. 2 (2016): 101–14.

Blenkinsop, S., J. Telford, and M. Morse. "A Surprising Discovery: Five Pedagogical Skills Outdoor and Experiential Educators Might Offer More Mainstream Educators in This Time of Change." *Journal of Adventure Education and Outdoor Learning* 16, no. 4 (2016): 346–58.

Blenkinsop, Sean. "Martin Buber: Educating for Relationship." *Ethics, Place and Environment* 8, no. 3 (2005): 285–307. https://doi.org/10.1080/13668790500348232.

Blenkinsop, Sean. "Imaginative Ecological Education: Six Necessary Components." In *Teaching 360°: Effective Learning through the Imagination*, 147–56. Rotterdam, Netherlands: Sense, 2008.

Blenkinsop, Sean. "Four Slogans for Cultural Change: An Evolving Place-Based, Imaginative and Ecological Learning Experience." *Journal of Moral Education* 41, no. 3 (2012): 356. https://doi.org/10.1080/03057240.2012.691634.

Blenkinsop, Sean. "In Search of the Eco-Teacher: Public School Edition." *Canadian Journal of Environmental Education* 19 (2014): 145–59.

Blenkinsop, Sean, Ramsey Affifi, Laura Piersol, and Michael De Danann Sitka-Sage. "Shut-Up and Listen: Implications and Possibilities of Albert Memmi's Characteristics of Colonization upon the 'Natural World.'" *Studies in Philosophy and Education* 36 (2016): 349–65.

Blenkinsop, Sean, and C. Beeman. "The World as Co-Teacher: Learning to Work with a Peerless Colleague." *Trumpeter* 26, no. 3 (2010): 26–39.

Blenkinsop, Sean, and M. Fettes. "Developing the Scientific Imagination: A Key to Sustainability?" In *Sustainable Communities, Sustainable Environments,* edited by D. Zandlviet and D. Fisher, 37–47. Rotterdam, Netherlands: Sense, 2007.

Blenkinsop, Sean, Clayton Maitland, and Jody MacQuarrie. "In Search of Policy That Supports Educational Innovation: Perspective of a Place- and Community-Based Elementary School." *Policy Futures* 17 (2019): 489–502.

Blenkinsop, Sean, and Laura Piersol. "Listening to the Literal: Orientations towards How Nature Communicates." *Phenomenology and Practice* 7, no. 1 (2013): 41–60.

Blenkinsop, Sean, Laura Piersol, and Michael De Danann Sitka-Sage. "Boys Being Boys: Eco-Double Consciousness, Splash Violence, and Environmental Education." *Journal of Environmental Education* 49, no. 4 (2018): 350–56. https://doi.org/10.1080/00958964.2017.1364213.

Blum, Deborah. *Love at Goon Park: Harry Harlow and the Science of Affection.* New York: Perseus Publishing, 2002.

Blum, Winfried E. H., Sophie Zechmeister-Boltenstern, and Katharina M. Keiblinger. "Does Soil Contribute to the Human Gut Microbiome?" *Microorganisms* 7, no. 9 (2019): 287. https://doi.org/10.3390/microorganisms7090287.

Bocarro, J., and A. Richards. "Experiential Research At-Risk: The Challenge of Shifting Traditional Research Paradigms." *Journal of Experiential Education* 21, no. 2 (1998): 102–7.

Bølling, O., P. Elsborg, G. Nielsen, and P. Bentsen. "The Association between Education outside the Classroom and Students' School Motivation: Results from a One-School-Year Quasi-Experiment." *International Journal of Educational Research* 89 (2018): 22–35.

Bonnett, M. *Retrieving Nature. Education for a Post-Humanist Age.* Hoboken, NJ: Blackwell, 2004.

Bonnett, M. "Environmental Consciousness, Sustainability, and the Character of Philosophy of Education." *Studies in Philosophy and Education* 36, no. 3 (2017): 333–47.

Bonnett, M. "Towards an Ecologization of Education." *Journal of Environmental Education* 50, no. 4–6 (2019): 251–58.

Bonnett, M. "Environmental Consciousness, Nature, and the Philosophy of Education: Some Key Themes." *Environmental Education Research* (2021). https://doi.org/10.1080/13504622.2021.1951174.

Bowers. C. A. *Education, Cultural Myths, and the Ecological Crisis: Toward Deep Changes.* Albany, NY: SUNY Press, 1993.

Bowers, C. A. *Educating for an Ecologically Sustainable Culture: Rethinking Moral Education, Creativity, Intelligence, and Other Modern Orthodoxies.* Albany, NY: SUNY Press, 1995.

Bowers, C. A. *The Culture of Denial: Why the Environmental Movement Needs a Strategy for Reforming Universities and Public Schools.* Albany, NY: SUNY Press, 1997.

Bowler, D. E., L. M. Buyung-Ali, T. M. Knight, and A. S. Pullin. "A Systematic Review of Evidence for the Added Benefits to Health of Exposure to Natural Environments." *BioMed Central BM* 10, no. 1 (2010): 1–10.

Bratman G. N., J. P. Hamilton, and G. C. Daily G. C. "The Impacts of Nature Experience on Human Cognitive Function and Mental Health." *Annals of the New York Academy of Sciences* 1249 (2012): 118–36.

Braun, B. "Environmental Issues: Writing a More-Than-Human Urban Geography." *Progress in Human Geography* 29, no. 5 (2005): 635–50.

Britton, James. *Language and Learning.* Coral Gables, FL: University of Miami Press, 1970.

Broadway, John. "Sankofa: Lessons in Returning to Our Roots." Public Allies website. February 18, 2022. https://www.uis.edu/africanamericanstudies/students/sankofa/.

Brooks, Rodney A. "African Americans Struggle with Disproportionate COVID Death Toll." *National Geographic.* April 24, 2020. https://www.nationalgeographic.com/history/2020/04/coronavirus-disproportionately-impacts-african-americans/.

Brosius, J. P. "Analyses and Interventions: Anthropological Engagements with Environmentalists." *Current Anthropology* 40, no. 3 (1999): 277–309.

Brugger, A., F. G. Kaiser, and N. Roczen. "One for All? Connectedness to Nature, Inclusion of Nature Environmental Identity, and Implicit Association with Nature." *European Psychologist* 16, no. 4 (2011): 324–33.

Brussoni, M., R. Gibbons, C. Gray, T. Ishikawa, E. Sandseter, A. Bienenstock, M. Tremblay. "What Is the Relationship between Risky Outdoor Play and Health in Children? A Systematic Review. *International Journal of Environmental Research and Public Health* 12, no. 6 (2015): 6423.

Buber, Martin. *Between Man and Man.* Translated by Ronald G. Smith. New York: Macmillan, 1968.

Buldur, B., E. Yalcin, and E. Yucel. "The Impact of an Outdoor Education Project on Middle School Students' Perceptions and Awareness of the Renewable Energy." *Renewable & Sustainable Energy Reviews* 134 (2020): 110364.

Bundy, A. C., G. Naughton, P. Tranter, S. Wyver, L. Baur, W. Schiller, and J. Brentnall. "The Sydney Playground Project: Popping the Bubble Wrap—Unleashing the Power of Play: A Cluster Randomized Controlled Trial of a Primary School Playground-Based Intervention Aiming to Increase Children's Physical Activity and Social Skills." *BMC Public Health 11* (2011): 680.

Bryne, Rhonda. *The Secret.* Miami, FL: Atria Publishing, 2006.

Cabanas, Edgar. "Rekindling Individualism, Consuming Emotions: Constructing 'Psytizens' in the Age of Happiness." *Culture & Psychology* 22, no. 3 (2016): 467. https://doi.org/10.1177/1354067X16655459.

Cajete, G. *Look to the Mountain: An Ecology of Indigenous Education.* Durango, CO: Kivaki Press, 1994.

Cajete, G. "Indigenous Education and the Development of Indigenous Community Leaders." *Leadership* 12, no. 3 (2016): 364–76.

Came, K. "Risky Outdoor Play Positively Impacts Children's Health: UBC Study News." UBC News, June 2015. http://news.ubc.ca/2015/06/09/risky-outdoor-play-positively-impacts-childrens-health-ubc-study/

Camus, Albert. *The Rebel: An Essay on Man in Revolt.* Translated by Anthony Bower. New York: Vintage Books, 1992.

Camus, Albert. Banquet speech, NobelPrize.org, Nobel Prize Outreach AB 2023. January 22, 2023. https://www.nobelprize.org/prizes/literature/1957/camus/speech/.

Ceballos, Gerardo, Paul R. Ehrlich, Anthony D. Barnosky, Andrés García, Robert M. Pringle, and Todd M. Palmer. "Accelerated Modern Human-Induced Species Losses: Entering the Sixth Mass Extinction." *Science Advances* 1, no. 5 (2015): e1400253–e1400253. https://doi.org/10.1126/sciadv.1400253.

Cederström, Carl, and Andre Spicer. *The Wellness Syndrome.* Oxford, UK: Wiley, 2015.

Center on the Developing Child, Harvard University. "Serve and Return." Accessed June 2022. https://developingchild.harvard.edu/science/key-concepts/serve-and -return/.

Chang, D. "Holding the Pieces: Pedagogy beyond Disruptive Environmental Education." *Philosophy of Education* 73 (2017): 507–20.

Charles, Cheryl, and Bob Samples. *Coming Home: Community, Creativity, and Consciousness*. Fawnskin, CA: Personhood Press, 2004.

Chawla, L. "Childhood Place Attachments." In *Place attachment,* edited by I. Altman and S. Low, 63–86. New York: Plenum Press, 1992.

Chawla, L. "Benefits of Nature Contact for Children." *Journal of Planning Literature* 30, no. 4 (2015): 433–52.

Chawla L., K. Keena, I. Pevec, and E. Stanley. "Green Schoolyards as Havens from Stress and Resources for Resilience in Childhood and Adolescence." *Health and Place* 28 (2014): 1–13.

Christian, D., and R. Wong, eds. *Downstream: Reimagining Water*. Waterloo, ON: Wilfrid Laurier University Press, 2016.

Clarke, D. "The Potential of Animism: Experiential Outdoor Education in the Ecological Education Paradigm. *Pathways: Ontario Journal of Outdoor Education* 26, no. 2 (2014): 13–17.

Clarke, D. A. G., and J. McPhie. "Becoming Animate in Education: Immanent Materiality and Outdoor Learning for Sustainability." *Journal of Adventure Education and Outdoor Learning* 14, no. 3 (2014): 198–216.

Clatworthy, Jane, Joe Hinds, and Paul M. Camic. "Gardening as a Mental Health Intervention: A Review." *Mental Health Review Journal* 18, no. 4 (2013): 214–25. https://doi.org/10.1108/MHRJ-02-2013-0007.

Clayton, Susan, Christie Manning, Kirra Krygsman, and Meighen Speiser. *Mental Health and Our Changing Climate: Impacts, Implications, and Guidance*. Washington, DC: American Psychology Association and ecoAmerica, 2017. https:// www.apa.org/news/press/releases/2017/03/mental-health-climate.pdf.

Cohen, J. J., and L. Duckert, eds. *Veer Ecology: A Companion for Environmental Thinking*. Minneapolis: University of Minnesota Press.

Cole, P., & P. O'Riley. "Coyote & Raven (P)re-visit Environmental Education, Sustainability, and Runaway Capitalism." *Canadian Journal of Environmental Education* 15 (2010): 25–46.

Collison, W. H. *In the Wake of the War Canoe: A Stirring Record of Forty Years' Successful Labour, Peril & Adventure amongst the Savage Indian Tribes of the Pacific Coast, and the Piratical Head-Hunting Haidas of the Queen Charlotte Islands, B.C.* England: Seeley, Service & Co., 1915.

Columbia University's Mailman School of Public Health. "Prenatal Exposure to Air Pollution Linked to Impulsivity, Emotional Problems in Children." March 17, 2016, https://www.publichealth.columbia.edu/public-health-now/news/prenatal -exposure-air-pollution-linked-impulsivity-emotional-problems-children.

Constable. *The Outdoor Classroom Ages 3–7*. Philadelphia: Routledge, 2012.

Curthoys, L. P. "Finding a Place of One's Own." *Canadian Journal of Environmental Education* 12, no. 1 (2007): 68–79.

Da Silva, Wilson. "How Adding Microbial Diversity to Urban Environments Improves Health." *Australian Geographic*, November 25, 2019. https://www.australiangeo graphic.com.au/topics/science-environment/2019/11/how-adding-microbial -diversity-to-urban-environments-improves-health/.

Davis, Wade. *The Wayfinders: Why Ancient Wisdom Matters in the Modern World*. Toronto: House of Anansi, 2009.

Deleuze, Gilles, and Félix Guattari. *A Thousand Plateaus: Capitalism and Schizophrenia.* Translated by Brian Massumi. Minneapolis, MN: University of Minnesota Press, 1987.

Della Vecchia, Alessandra, Federico Mucci, Andrea Pozza, Donatella Marazziti. "Negative Air Ions in Neuropsychiatric Disorders." *Current Medicinal Chemistry* 28, no. 13 (2021): 2521–39. https://doi.org/10.2174/0929867327666200630104550.

Department of Economic and Social Affairs. "News: 68% of World Population Projected to Live in Urban Areas by 2050, Says UN." United Nations. May 16, 2018. https://www.un.org/development/desa/en/news/population/2018-revision-of -world-urbanization-prospects.html.

Derby, M. *Place, Being, Resonance: Towards a Critical Ecohermeneutic Education.* Bern, Switzerland: Peter Lang, 2015.

Despret, V. "Responding Bodies and Partial Affinities in Human-Animal Worlds." *Theory, Culture and Society* 30, no. 7/8 (2013): 5–75.

Diamond, Jared M. *The World until Yesterday: What Can We Learn from Traditional Societies?* New York: Viking, 2012.

Diaz-Camal, Nidya, Jesús Daniel Cardoso-Vera, Hariz Islas-Flores, Leobardo Manuel Gómez-Oliván, and Alejandro Mejía-García. "Consumption and Occurrence of Antidepressants (SSRIs) in Pre- and Post-COVID-19 Pandemic, Their Environmental Impact and Innovative Removal Methods: A Review." *The Science of the Total Environment* 829 (2022): 4. https://doi.org/10.1016/j.scitotenv.2022.154656.

District of Maple Ridge. "Corporate Strategic Plan: Implementing Sustainability Principles." District of Maple Ridge, 2007.

Dittmar, Helga, Rod Bond, Megan Hurst, and Tim Kasser. "The Relationship between Materialism and Personal Wellbeing: A Meta-Analysis." *Journal of Personality and Social Psychology* 107, no. 5 (2014): 879–924, https://doi.org/10.1037/a0037409.

DuBois, W. E. B. *The Souls of Black Folks.* New York: Penguin Classics, 1996.

Duerden, D. M, and A. P. Witt. "The Impact of Direct and Indirect Experiences on the Development of Environmental Knowledge, Attitudes, and Behaviour." *Journal of Environmental Psychology* 30 (2010): 379–92.

Dutcher D. D., J. C. Finely, A. E. Luloff, and J. Buttolph Johnson. "Connectivity with Nature as a Measure of Environmental Values." *Environment and Behavior* 39, no. 4 (2007): 474–93.

Egan, K. *Teaching as Storytelling.* London, ON: The Althouse Press, 1986.

Egan, K. *Primary Understanding: Education in Early Childhood.* Philadelphia: Routledge, 1988.

Egan, K. *Romantic Understanding: The Development of Rationality and Imagination, Ages 8–15.* Philadelphia: Routledge, 1990.

Egan, K. *Imagination in Teaching and Learning.* Chicago: University of Chicago Press, 1992.

Egan, K. *The Educated Mind: How Cognitive Tools Shape Our Understanding.* Chicago: University of Chicago Press, 1997.

Egan, K. *An Imaginative Approach to Teaching.* Hoboken, NJ: Jossey-Bass, 2005.

Egan, K., M. Stout, and K. Takaya, eds. *Teaching and Learning outside the Box: Inspiring Imagination across the Curriculum.* New York: Teachers' College Press, 2007.

Ehrenreich, Barbara. *Bright-Sided: How the Relentless Promotion of Positive Thinking Has Undermined America.* New York: Metropolitan Books, 2009.

EL Education. "Educating for a Better World." Accessed July 4, 2023. https://eleducation .org/.

Elliott, S., ed. *The Outdoor Playspace Naturally for Children Birth to Five Years.* New South Wales, AU: Pademelon Press, 2008.

Engemann, Kristine, Carsten Bøcker Pedersen, Lars Arge, Jens-Christian Svenning. "Residential Green Space in Childhood Is Associated with Lower Risk of Psychiatric Disorders from Adolescence into Adulthood." *Proceedings of the National Academy of Sciences (PNAS)* 116, no. 11 (2019): 5188–93. https://doi.org/10.1073/pnas.1807504116.

Environmental School. Maple Ridge, BC. 2022. https://es.sd42.ca/

Erickson, D. M., and J. A. Ernst. "The Real Benefits of Nature Play Everyday." *Exchange* 33, no. 4 (2011): 97–99.

Ernst, J. "Early Childhood Educators' Use of Natural Outdoor Settings as Learning Environments: An Exploratory Study of Beliefs, Practices, and Barriers." *Environmental Education Research* 20, no. 6 (2014): 735–52.

Evergreen. "Outdoor Classrooms: An Unexpected Public Health Solution?" June 9, 2020. https://www.evergreen.ca/blog/entry/outdoor-classrooms-an-unexpected-public-health-solution/.

Fang, L., D. Gill, S. Liu, T. Chyi, and B. Chen. A Systematic Review and Meta-Analysis of the Effects of Outdoor Education Programs on Adolescents' Self-Efficacy." *Perceptual and Motor Skills* 128, no. 5 (2021): 1932–58.

Farrier, D. *Anthropocene Poetics: Deep Time, Sacrifice Zones, and Extinction.* Minneapolis: University of Minnesota Press, 2019.

Fawcett, L. "Children's Wild Animal Stories: Questioning Interspecies Bonds." *Canadian Journal of Environmental Education* 7, no. 2 (2002) 125–39.

Fawcett, L. "Bioregional Teaching: How to Climb, Eat, Fall, and Learn from Porcupines." In *Teaching as Activism: Equity Meets Environmentalism,* edited by L. J. Muzzin and P. Tripp, 269–80. Montreal: McGill-Queen's Press, 2005.

Fawcett, L. "Kinship Imaginaries: Children's Stories of Wild Friendships, Fear, and Freedom." In *Routledge Handbook of Human-Animal Studies,* 259–74. Philadelphia: Routledge, 2014.

Fernandes, A. *The Wholesome Benefits of Nature-Based Education.* Inkspire. November 3. 2020. https://inkspire.org/post/the-wholesome-benefits-of-nature-based-education/-MI4dArziO2Umbgqn7Kf.

Ferrando, F. *Philosophical Posthumanism.* London: Bloomsbury, 2020.

Fettes, M. "Mid-Term Report, Building Culturally Inclusive Schools through Imaginative education (The LUCID Project)." Report to Community-University Research Alliances, Social Sciences and Humanities Research Council of Canada, June 23, 2006.

Fettes, M. "Culture and Imagination in the Science Classroom." In *Teaching 360a: Effective Learning through the Imagination,* edited by G. Judson, 97–106. Rotterdam, Netherlands: Sense, 2008.

Flouri, E., E. Midouhas, and H. Joshi. "The Role of Urban Neighborhood Green Space in Children's Emotional and Behavioural Resilience." *Journal of Environmental Psychology,* 40 (2014): 179–86.

Fogarty, James. "The Tyler Rationale: Support and Criticism." *Educational Technology* 16, no. 3 (1976): 28–32.

Forest and Nature School in Canada. Forest School Canada. June 2014.

Foucault, Michel. "On the Genealogy of Ethics: An Overview of Work in Progress." In *Michel Foucault: Beyond Structuralism and Hermeneutics,* edited by Hubert Dreyfus and Paul Rabinow, 229–64. Chicago: University of Chicago Press, 1983.

Franco, Lara S., Danielle F. Shanahan, and Richard A. Fuller. "A Review of the Benefits of Nature Experiences: More Than Meets the Eye." *International Journal of Environmental Research and Public Health* 14, no. 8 (2017): 864. https://doi.org/10.3390/ijerph14080864.

Freebody, P. *Qualitative Research in Education: Interaction and Practice*. London: Sage, 2003.

Freire, Paulo. *Pedagogy of the Oppressed*. New York: Continuum, 2000.

Fuentes, Agustín. "Naturalcultural Encounters in Bali: Monkeys, Temples, Tourists, and Ethnoprimatology." *Cultural Anthropology* 25 (2010): 600–24.

Gaard, Greta. "Toward a Queer Ecofeminism." *Hypatia* 12, no. 1 (1997): 114–37.

Gair, N. P. *Outdoor Education: Theory and Practice*. London: Cassell, 1997.

Gattuso, Jean-Pierre, and Lina Hansson. *Ocean Acidification*. Oxford, UK: Oxford University Press, 2011.

Gerhardt, Sue. *The Selfish Society: How We All Forgot to Love One Another and Made Money Instead*. New York: Simon & Schuster, 2010.

Gerhardt, Sue. *Why Love Matters: How Affection Shapes a Baby's Brain*. New York: Routledge, 2015.

Gerhardt, Sue. "The Selfish Society: The Current State of Things." In *The Political Self: Understanding the Social Context for Mental Illness*, edited by Rod Tweedy, 69–86. Abingdon, UK: Routledge, 2017. https://doi.org/10.4324/9780429482762-4.

Gill, Rosalind, and Shani Orgad. "The Amazing Bounce-Backable Woman: Resilience and the Psychological Turn in Neoliberalism," *Sociological Research Online* 23, no. 2 (2018): 477. https://doi.org/10.1177/1360780418769673.

Gilligan, Carol. "In a Different Voice: Women's Conceptions of Self and of Morality." *Harvard Educational Review* 47, no. 4 (1977): 482.

Gilligan, Carol, and Naomi Snider. *Why Does Patriarchy Persist?* Cambridge, UK: Polity Press, 2018.

Giroux, H. *Ideology, Culture, and the Process of Schooling*. Philadelphia: Temple University Press, 1981.

Glover, S. K. "Walking alongside My Relations: A Transdisciplinary Exploration of Interconnectedness." *Simon Fraser University Educational Review* 11, no. 1 (2019): 83–105.

Grandjean, Philippe, and Philip Landrigan. "Neurobehavioural Effects of Developmental Toxicity." *Lancet Neurology* 13, no. 3 (2014): 330. https://doi.org/10.1016/S1474-4422(13)70278-3.

Graveline, F. J. *Circle Works: Transforming Eurocentric Consciousness*. Black Point, NS: Fernwood Press, 1998.

Gray, C., R. Gibbons, R. Larouche, E. Sandseter, A. Bienenstock, M. Brussoni, and M. Tremblay. "What Is the Relationship between Outdoor Time and Physical Activity, Sedentary Behaviour, and Physical Fitness in Children? A Systematic Review." *International Journal of Environmental Research and Public Health* 12, no. 6 (2015): 6455.

Gray, T. "The 'F' Word: Feminism in Outdoor Education." *Journal of Outdoor and Environmental Education* 19, no. 2 (2016): 25–41.

Green, B., and N. Hopgood. *The Body in Professional Practice, Learning and Education*. New York: Springer, 2015.

Green School. 2022. https://www.greenschool.org/about-us/.

Greene, M. *Releasing the Imagination: Essays on Education, the Arts, and Social Change*. Hoboken, NJ: Jossey-Bass, 1995.

Greensite, Gillian. *Support for Survivors: Training for Sexual Assault Counsellors*. California Coalition Against Sexual Assault. 2008. https://evawintl.org/wp-content/uploads/CALCASA-2008-Support-for-Survivors-TrainingforSACounselors.pdf.

Groth, Nicholas A., and H. Jean Birnbaum. *Men Who Rape: The Psychology of the Offender*. New York: Plenum Press, 1979.

Gruenewald, D., and G. Smith, eds. *Place-Based Education in the Global Age: Local Diversity*. Lawrence Erlbaum, 2008.

Gruenewald, D. A. "The Best of Both Worlds: A Critical Pedagogy of Place." *Educational Researcher* 32, no. 4 (2003): 3–12.

Gruenewald, D. A. "Foundations of Place: A Multidisciplinary Framework for Place-Conscious Education." *American Educational Research Journal* 40, no. 3 (2003): 619–54.

Gurholt, K. P. "Joy of Nature, 'Friluftsliv' Education and Self: Combining Narrative and Cultural-Ecological Approaches to Environmental Sustainability." *Journal of Adventure Education and Outdoor Learning* 14, no. 3 (2014): 233–46.

Hägerhäll, Caroline, Richard Taylor, Gunnar Cerwén, Greg Watts, Matilda van den Bosch, Daniel Press, and Steven Minta. "Biological Mechanisms and Neurophysiological Responses to Sensory Impact from Nature." In *Oxford Textbook of Nature and Public Health*, edited by Matilda van den Bosch and William Bird. Oxford, UK: Oxford University, 2018.

Hall, Marie J., et al. *The Collected Works of L. S. Vygotsky: Problems of General Psychology, Including the Volume Thinking and Speech.* Netherlands: Plenum, 1987.

Hanley, P. "'Holistic yet Tangible': Embracing the Challenge of Complexity for Education for Sustainable Development." *Current Issues in Comparative Education* 7, no. 2 (2005): 85–93.

Haraway, D. J. *When Species Meet.* Minneapolis: University of Minnesota Press, 2008.

Haraway, D. J. "Anthropocene, Capitalocene, Plantationocene, Chthulucene: Making Kin." *Environmental Humanities* 6, no. 1 (2015): 159–65.

Haraway, D. J. *Staying with the* Trouble, Making Kin *in the* Chthulucene. Durham, NC: Duke, 2016.

Haraway, Donna J. *The Companion Species Manifesto: Dogs, People, and Significant Otherness.* Chicago: Prickly Paradigm Press, 2003.

Hari, Johann. *Lost Connections.* New York: Bloomsbury Circus, 2018.

Harney, Stefano, and Fred Moten. *The Undercommons: Fugitive Planning & Black Study.* New York: Minor Compositions, 2013.

Harris, F. "Outdoor Learning Spaces: The Case of Forest School." *Area* 50, no. 2 (2018): 222–31.

Harris, F. "Developing a Relationship with Nature and Place: The Potential Role of Forest School." *Environmental Education Research* 27, no. 8 (2021): 1214–28.

Harrison, S. "'Why Are We Here?' Taking 'Place' into Account in UK Outdoor Environmental Education. *Journal of Adventure Education and Outdoor Learning* 10, no. 1 (2010): 3–18.

Hart, P. *Teachers' Thinking in Environmental Education: Consciousness and Responsibility.* New York: Peter Lang, 2003.

Hartmeyer, R., and E. Mygind. "A Retrospective Study of Social Relations in a Danish Primary School Class Taught in 'Udeskole.'" *Journal of Adventure Education and Outdoor Learning* 16, no. 1 (2016): 78–89.

Hatch, A. "The View from All Fours: A Look at an Animal-Assisted Activity Program from the Animals' Perspective." *Anthrozoös* 20 no. 1 (2007): 37–50.

Hay, R. "Sense of Place in Developmental Context." *Journal of Environmental Psychology* 18 (1998): 5–29.

Heintzman, P. "Spirituality and the Outdoors." In *International Handbook of Outdoor Studies*, edited by H. Prince, K. Henderson, and B. Humberstone, 388–397. Philadelphia: Routledge, 2016.

Hernke, Michael T., and Rian J. Podein. "Sustainability, Health and Precautionary Perspectives on Lawn Pesticides, and Alternatives." *EcoHealth* 8, no. 2 (2011): 223–32. https://doi.org/10.1007/s10393-011-0697-7.

Higgins, P. "Into the Big Wide World: Sustainable Experiential Education for the 21st Century." *Journal of Experiential Education* 32, no. 1 (2009): 44–60.

Hirtenfelder, C. *The Animal Turn*. 2020–2022. IRoar.

Holt, John Caldwell. *How Children Fail*. New York: Dell, 1970.

Holt, L. Emmett. *The Care and Feeding of Children: A Catechism for the Use of Mothers and Children's Nurses*. 4th ed. New York: Appleton and Company, 1907. https://www.gutenberg.org/files/15484/15484-h/15484-h.htm#Sleep.

Honig, A. S. *Experiencing Nature with Young Children*. New York: National Association for the Education of Young Children, 2015.

Honig, A. S. "Outdoors in Nature: Special Spaces for Young Children's Learning." *Early Child Development and Care* 189, no. 4 (2019): 659–69.

hooks, b. *Teaching Critical Thinking: Practical Wisdom*. Philadelphia: Routledge, 2009.

Horwood, B. "Tasting the Berries: Deep Ecology and Experiential Education." *The Journal of Experiential Education* 14, no. 3 (1991): 23–26.

Howard, R. A., T. S. O'Connell, and A. H. Lathrop. "Community Development, Transitional Value, and Institutional Affinity: Outdoor Orientation Program Impacts." *Journal of Experiential Education* 39, no. 1 (2016): 45–58.

Humberstone. B. "Embodiment and Social and Environmental Action in Nature-Based Sport: Spiritual Spaces." *Leisure Studies 30*, no. 4 (2011): 495–512.

Humes, B. "Moving toward a Liberatory Pedagogy for All Species: Mapping the Need for Dialogue between Humane and Anti-Oppressive Education." *Green Theory & Praxis Journal* 4, no. 1 (2008): 65–85.

Hunkins, Francis, and Patricia Hammill. "Beyond Tyler and Taba: Reconceptualizing the Curriculum Process." *Peabody Journal of Education* 69, no. 3 (1994): 4–18. https://doi.org/10.1080/01619569409538774.

Ingold, T. *Being Alive: Essays on Movement, Knowledge, and Description*. Philadelphia: Routledge, 2011.

Ingold, T. *Anthropology and/as Education*. Philadelphia: Routledge, 2017.

Insel, Thomas. *Healing: Our Path from Mental Illness to Mental Health*. New York: Penguin, 2022.

Irigaray, Luce. *In the Beginning, She Was*. New York: Bloomsbury, 2013.

Jardine, D. *To Dwell with a Boundless Heart: Essays in Curriculum Theory, Hermeneutics, and the Ecological Imagination*. New York: Peter Lang Publishing, 1998.

Jickling, B., and S. Sterling, eds. *Post-Sustainability and Environmental Education: Remaking Education for the Future*. Cham, Switzerland: Palgrave Macmillan, 2017.

Jickling, Bob, Sean Blenkinsop, Nora Timmerman, and Michael De Danann Sitka-Sage. *Wild Pedagogies: Touchstones for Re-Negotiating Education and the Environment in the Anthropocene*. Cham, Switzerland: Palgrave-MacMillan, 2018.

Joldersma, C. W., and Sean Blenkinsop. "Ecologizing Education: Philosophy, Place, and Possibility." *Educational Theory* 67 (2017): 371–77.

Kahn, R. "From Education for Sustainable Development to Eco-Pedagogy: Sustaining Capitalism or Sustaining Life?" *Green Theory and Praxis: The Journal of Ecopedagogy* 4, no. 1 (2008): 1–14.

Kahn, R. *Critical Pedagogy, Ecoliteracy, & Planetary Crisis: The Ecopedagogy Movement*. New York: Peter Lang, 2010.

Kals, E., D. Schumacher, and L. Montada. Emotional Affinity toward Nature as a Motivational Basis to Protect Nature. *Environment and Behavior* 31, no. 2 (1999): 178–202.

Kaplan, S. "Human Nature and Environmentally Responsible Behavior." *Journal of Social Issues* 56 (2000): 491–508.

Kaplan, S., and J. F. Talbot. "Psychological Benefits of a Wilderness Experience." In *Behavior and the Natural Environment*, edited by I. Altman and J. F. Wohlwill, 163–203. New York: Plenum, 1983.

Kaveri. "18 Meditation Devices and Apps for a More Mindful 2022." Geekflare. November 30, 2022. https://geekflare.com/meditation-gadgets-apps/.

Kellert, S. R. *Building for Life: Designing and Understanding the Human-Nature Connection*. Washington, DC: Island Press, 2005.

Kim, Ju Hwan, Jin-Koo Lee, Hyung-Gun Kim, Kyu-Bong Kim, and Hak Rim Kim. "Possible Effects of Radiofrequency Electromagnetic Field Exposure on Central Nerve System." *Biomolecules & Therapeutics* 27, no. 3 (2019): 265–75. https://doi.org/10.4062/biomolther.2018.152.

Kimmerer, Robin Wall. *Braiding Sweetgrass: Indigenous Wisdom, Scientific Knowledge and the Teachings of Plants*. Minneapolis, MN: Milkweed Editions, 2013.

Kimmerer, Robin Wall. "Mishkos Kenomagwen: The Teachings of Grass." Posted by the Bioneers. November 15, 2014. https://www.youtube.com/watch?v=cumEQcRMY3c.

Kimmerer, Robin Wall. "The Grammar of Animacy." *Anthropology of Consciousness* 28, no. 2 (2017): 131.

King, Thomas. *The Truth about Stories: A Native Narrative*. Toronto: House of Anansi, 2003.

Kingsnorth, Paul. *Confessions of a Recovering Environmentalist and Other Essays*. Minneapolis, MN: Graywolf Press, 2017.

Kivel. Paul. *Uprooting Racism: How White People Can Work for Racial Justice*. Gabriola Island, British Columbia: New Society Publishers, 2017.

Klein, Naomi. *No Is Not Enough: Resisting Trump's Shock Politics and Winning the World We Need*. Chicago, IL: Haymarket Books, 2017.

Knight, S. *Risk and Adventure in Early Years Outdoor Play: Learning from Forest Schools*. London: Sage, 2011.

Kohn, Alfie. *No Contest: The Case against Competition*. San Francisco: Harperone Press, 1992.

Kohn, Eduardo. *How Forests Think: Toward an Anthropology beyond the Human*. Oakland: University of California Press, 2013.

Kolbert, Elizabeth. *The Sixth Extinction: An Unnatural History*. New York: Henry Holt and Company, 2014.

Kollmus, A., and J. Ageyman, "Mind the Gap: Why Do People Act Environmentally and What Are the Barriers to Pro-Environmental Behavior?" *Environmental Education Research* 8, no. 3 (2002): 239–60.

Kreutz, A. *Children and the Environment in an Australian Indigenous Community*. Philadelphia: Routledge, 2015.

Kuby, C. R. "(Re)thinking and (Re)imagining Social(ing) with a More-Than-Human Ontology Given the Limits of (Re)(con)straining Language." *Sage Publications* 19, no. 2 (2019): 126–43.

Kuchta, E., and S. Blenkinsop, "Toward a More Eco-Relational English," *Canadian Journal of Environmental Education* (in press).

Kuhl, G. "Representing Animal-Others in Educational Research." *Canadian Journal of Environmental Education* 16 (2011): 106–22.

Kuo, F. E., and A. Faber Taylor. "A Potential Natural Treatment for Attention Deficit/Hyperactivity Disorder: Evidence from a National Study." *American Journal of Public Health* 94, no. 9 (2004): 1580–86.

Kuo, Frances E. "Ming." "Nature-Deficit Disorder: Evidence, Dosage, and Treatment." *Journal of Policy Research in Tourism, Leisure and Events* 5, no. 2 (2013): 172–86. https://doi.org/10.1080/19407963.2013.793520.

Kuo, Ming. "How Might Contact with Nature Promote Human Health? Promising Mechanisms and a Possible Central Pathway," *Frontiers in Psychology* 6 (2015): 1093. https://doi.org/10.3389/fpsyg.2015.01093.

Kuo, Ming. "Our Better Nature: How the Great Outdoors Can Improve Your Life." By Shankar Vedantam. *Hidden Brain*. NPR, September 10, 2018. https://www.npr.org/transcripts/646413667.

Laird, Susan. "Learning to Live in the Anthropocene: Our Children and Ourselves." *Studies in Philosophy and Education* 36 (2017): 265–82.

Larimore, R. "Preschool beyond Walls: Blending Early Childhood Education and Nature-Based Learning." *Philosophy and Education* 36, no. 3 (2019): 1–18.

Lavrysen, A., E. Bertrands, L. Leyssen, L. Smets, A. Vanderspikken, and P. De Graef. "Risky-Play at School: Facilitating Risk Perception and Competence in Young Children." *European Early Childhood Education Research Journal* 25, no. 1 (2015): 89–105.

Lee, C. K., and P. Ensel Bailie "Nature-Based Education: Using Nature Trails as a Tool to Promote Inquiry-Based Science and Math Learning in Young Children. *Science Activities* 56, no. 4 (2019): 147–58.

Legg, Timothy J. "What to Know about Eco-Anxiety." Medical News Today, Healthline Media, December 19, 2019. https://www.medicalnewstoday.com/articles/327354.

Leung, Angela Ka-yee, William W. Maddux, Adam D. Galinsky, and Chi-yue Chiu. "Multicultural Experience Enhances Creativity." *The American Psychologist* 63, no. 3 (2008): 169–81. https://doi.org/10.1037/0003-066X.63.3.169.

Li, Qing. "Effect of Forest Bathing Trips on Human Immune Function." *Environmental Health and Preventive Medicine* 15, no. 1 (2010): 9–17. https://doi.org/10.1007/s12199-008-0068-3.

Lieberman, G. *Education and the Environment Creating Standards-Based Programs in Schools and Districts*. Cambridge, MA: Harvard Education Press, 2013.

Lieberman, Matthew D. *Social: Why Our Brains Are Wired to Connect*. New York: Crown Publishers, 2013.

Lindgren, N., & J. Öhman. "A Posthuman Approach to Human-Animal Relationships: Advocating Critical Pluralism." *Environmental Education Research* 25, no. 8 (2018): 1200–15.

Lister, Mary. "13 of the Most Persuasive Ads We've Ever Seen." Wordstream: By LocaliQ. Last modified December 27, 2021. https://www.wordstream.com/blog/ws/2019/08/13/persuasive-ads.

Lloro-Bidart, T. "A Feminist Posthumanist Political Ecology of Education for Theorizing Human-Animal Relations/Relationships." *Environmental Education Research* 23, no. 1 (2017): 111–30.

Lloro-Bidart, T. "A Feminist Posthumanist Ecopedagogy in/for/with Animalscapes." *Journal of Environmental Education* 49, no. 2 (2018): 152–63.

Louv, R. *Vitamin N: The Essential Guide to a Nature-Rich Life*. New York: Workman Publishing, 2016.

Louv, R. *Our Wild Calling: How Connecting with Animals Can Transform Our Lives and Save Theirs Too*. Chapel Hill: Algonquin Books, 2019.

Louv, Richard. *Last Child in the Woods: Saving Our Children from Nature-Deficit Disorder*. New York: Workman Publishing, 2005.

Lowan, G. "Exploring Place from an Aboriginal Perspective: Considerations for Outdoor and Environmental Education. *Canadian Journal of Environmental Education* 14, no. 1 (2009): 42–58.

Lowan, G. "Ecological Métissage: Exploring the Third Space in Outdoor and Environmental Education." *Pathways: The Ontario Journal of Outdoor Education* 23, no. 2 (2011): 10–15.

Lowan-Trudeau, G. "Considering Ecological Métissage: To Blend or Not to Blend?" *Journal of Experiential Education* 37, no. 4 (2014): 351–66.

Lowell, D., and J. J. Cohen. *Elemental Ecocriticism.* Minneapolis: University of Minnesota Press, 2015.

Lubbock, J. *Guide to the Growing World of Nature-Based Learning.* Childhood by Nature. Accessed June 18, 2023. https://www.childhoodbynature.com/guide-to-the -growing-world-of-nature-based-learning/.

Ludden, David. "East West Cultural Differences in Depression." Talking Apes Blog, Psychologytoday.com. November 20, 2017. https://www.psychologytoday.com /ca/blog/talking-apes/201711/east-west-cultural-differences-in-depression.

Lundvall, S., and N. Maivorsdotter. "Environing as Embodied Experience—a Study of Outdoor Education as Part of Physical Education." *Frontiers in Sports and Active Living* 3 (2021).

Lupinacci, J., and A. Happel-Parkins. "(Un)learning anthropocentrism: An ecojustice framework for teaching to resist human-supremacy in schools." In *The Educational Significance of Human and Non-Human Animal Interactions,* edited by S. Rice and A. G. Rud, 13–30. Cham, Switzerland: Palgrave Macmillan, 2016.

Lyman, K. "Lessons from a Garden Spider: How Charlotte Transformed My Classroom." In *A People's Curriculum for the Earth,* edited by B. Bigelow and T. Swinehart, 48–51. Milwaukee, WI: Rethinking Schools, 2014.

MacQuarrie, S., Nugent, C., and C. Warden. "Learning with Nature and Learning from Others: Nature as Setting and Resource for Early Childhood Education." *Journal of Adventure Education and Outdoor Learning* 15, no. 1 (2015): 1–23.

Macy, Joanna. "Despair Work." In *Peace Movements Worldwide,* edited by Marc Pilisuk and Michael N. Nagler. Westport, CT: Praeger, 2010.

Malone, K. "Reconsidering Children's Encounters with Nature and Place Using Posthumanism." *Australian Journal of Environmental Education* 32, no. 1 (2016): 42–56.

Mammen, G., and G. Faulkner. "Physical Activity and the Prevention of Depression: A Systematic Review of Prospective Studies." *American Journal of Preventive Medicine* 45 (2013): 605–23.

Manzo, L. C. "Beyond House and Haven: Toward a Revisioning of Emotional Relationships with Places." *Journal of Environmental Psychology* 23 (2003): 47–61.

Marker, Michael. "There Is No *Place of Nature*; There Is Only the *Nature of Place*: Animate Landscapes as Methodology for Inquiry in the Coast Salish Territory." *International Journal of Qualitative Studies in Education* 31, no. 6 (2018): 453–64. https://doi.org/10.1080/09518398.2018.1430391.

Marsden, Rasunah. "The World Pattern of Process." PhD diss., University of British Columbia, 2019. http://dx.doi.org/10.14288/1.0378038.

Martin, P. "Outdoor Adventure in Promoting Relationships with Nature." *Journal of Outdoor and Environmental Education* 8 (2004): 20–28.

Martin, P. "Human to Nature Relationships through Outdoor Education." In *Outdoor and Experiential Learning: Views from the Top,* edited by T. J. Dickson and T. Gray, 28–53. Dunedin, NZ: Otago University Press, 2005.

Martin, P., and S. Ho. "Seeking Resilience and Sustainability: Outdoor Education in Singapore." *Journal of Adventure Education and Outdoor Learning* 9, no. 1 (2009): 79–92.

Marvin, G., and S. McHugh, eds. *Routledge Handbook of Human-Animal Studies.* Milton Park, UK: Taylor and Francis, 2014.

Maslow, Abraham. *A Theory of Human Motivation.* Radford, VA: Wilder Publications, 2018.

Mason, L., A. Ronconi, S. Scrimin, and F. Pazzaglia. "Short-Term Exposure to Nature and Benefits for Students' Cognitive Performance: A Review." *Educational Psychology Review* 34, no. 2 (2021): 609–47.

Maté, Gabor, with Daniel Maté. *The Myth of Normal: Trauma, Illness, and Healing in a Toxic Culture*. Toronto: Knopf Canada, 2022.

Matsuoka, R. H. "Student Performance and High School Landscapes." *Landscape and Urban Planning* 97, no. 4 (2010): 273–82.

Maynard, Robyn. "Reading Black Resistance through Afrofuturism: Notes on Post-Apocalyptic Blackness and Black Rebel Cyborgs in Canada," *Topia* 39 (2018): 29.

McClennen, N., E. Liebtag, and T. Vander Ark. *The Power of Place: Authentic Learning through Place-Based Education*. Alexandria, VA: ASCD, 2020.

McDonald's Corporation. "Happy Meal." Accessed December 2022. https://www.mcdonalds.com/ca/en-ca/full-menu/happy-meal.html.

McKibbin, William F., Todd K. Shackelford, Aaron T. Goetz, and Valerie G. Starratt. "Why Do Men Rape? An Evolutionary Psychological Perspective." *Review of General Psychology* 12, no. 1 (2008): 86–97. https://doi.org/10.1037/1089-2680.12.1.86.

McMurtry, John. *The Cancer Stage of Capitalism*. Halifax, NS: Fernwood Publishing, 2013.

Meaney, Michael J. "Maternal Care, Gene Expression, and the Transmission of Individual Differences in Stress Reactivity across Generations." *Annual Review of Neuroscience* 24, no. 1 (2001): 1161–92. https://doi.org/10.1146/annurev.neuro.24.1.1161.

Mendocino Pygmy Forest. "Pygmy-Forest.com." Accessed July 4, 2023. http://pygmy-forest.com.

Melillo, Gianna. "Recognizing the Role of Systemic Racism in Diabetes Disparities." *AJMC*. February 2, 2021. https://www.ajmc.com/view/recognizing-the-role-of-systemic-racism-in-diabetes-disparities.

Mikaels, J., and M. Asfeldt. "Becoming-Crocus, Becoming-River, Becoming-Bear: A Relational Materialist Exploration of Place(s)." *Journal of Outdoor and Environmental Education* 20, no. 2 (2016).

Moncrieff, Joanna, Ruth E. Cooper, Tom Stockmann, Simone Amendola, Michael P. Hengartner, and Mark A. Horowitz. "The Serotonin Theory of Depression: A Systematic Umbrella Review of the Evidence." *Molecular Psychiatry* (2022). https://doi.org/10.1038/s41380-022-01661-0.

Moore, J. "Barriers and Pathways to Creating Sustainability Education Programs: Policy, Rhetoric, and Reality." *Environmental Education Research* 11, no. 5 (2005): 537–55.

Mortimer-Sandilands, Catriona, and Bruce Erickson, eds. *Queer Ecologies: Sex, Nature, Politics, Desire*. Indianapolis, IN: Indiana University Press, 2010.

Msibi, Thabo. "Queering Curriculum Studies in South Africa: A Call for Reconceptualisation?" In *Disrupting Higher Education Curriculum: Undoing Cognitive Damage*, edited by Michael Samuel, Rubby Dhunpath, and Nina Amin, 213–28. Rotterdam: SensePublishers, 2016.

Mullins, P. M. "Living Stories of the Landscape: Perception of Place through Canoeing in Canada's North." *Tourism Geographies* 11, no. 2 (2009), 233–255.

Mutz, M., and J. Müller. "Mental Health Benefits of Outdoor Adventures: Results from Two Pilot Studies." *Journal of Adolescence* 49 (2016): 105–14.

Mygind, E. "A Comparison of Children's Statements about Social Relations and Teaching in the Classroom and in the Outdoor Environment." *Journal of Adventure Education and Outdoor Learning* 9, no. 2 (2009): 151–69.

Naess, A. "The Shallow and Deep Range Ecology Movement: A Summary." *Inquiry* 16 (1973): 95–100.

Narvaez, Darcia. *Neurobiology and the Development of Human Morality: Evolution, Culture, and Wisdom*. New York: W. W. Norton, 2014.

Narvaez, Darcia. *Psychology Today Blog: Moral Landscapes*. Accessed June 2021. https://www.psychologytoday.com/ca/blog/moral-landscapes.

Narvaez, Darcia, Kristin Valentino, Agustin Fuentes, James J. McKenna, and Peter Gray, eds. *Ancestral Landscapes in Human Evolution: Culture, Childrearing and Social Wellbeing*. Oxford, UK: Oxford University Press, 2014.

Native Languages of the Americas website. "Native American Nature Spirits of Myth and Legend." Accessed July 3, 2019. http://www.native-languages.org/nature-spirits.htm.

Natural History of Orange County. "Toxicodendron Diversilobum." June 12, 2005. http://nathistoc.bio.uci.edu/Plants%20of%20Upper%20Newport%20Bay%20(Robert%20De%20Ruff)/Anacardiaceae/Toxicodendron%20diversilobum.htm.

Neimanis, A., ed. *Bodies of Water: Posthuman Feminist Phenomenology*. London: Bloomsbury Publishing, 2019.

Nelson, Geoffrey, and Isaac Prilleltensky. *Community Psychology: In Pursuit of Liberation and Wellbeing*. London: Palgrave MacMillan, 2010.

Nicol, R. "Entering the Fray: The Role of Outdoor Education in Providing Nature-Based Experiences That Matter." *Educational Philosophy and Theory* 46, no. 5 (2014): 449–61.

Nicolopoulou-Stamati, P., L. Hens, C. V. Howard, and N. Van Larebeke, eds. *Cancer as an Environmental Disease*. Norwell, MA: Kluwer Academic Publishers, 2004. https://link.springer.com/content/pdf/bfm:978-0-306-48513-8/1.

Nisbet, E. K., and J. M. Zelenski. "Underestimating Nearby Nature: Affective Forecasting Errors Obscure the Happy Path to Sustainability." *Psychological Science* 22 (2011): 1101–6.

Nisbet, E. K., J. M. Zelenski, and S. A. Murphy. "The Nature Relatedness Scale: Linking Individuals' Connection with Nature to Environmental Concern and Behavior." *Environment and Behavior* 41, no. 5 (2009): 715–40.

Nussbaum, M. C. *Creating Capabilities*. Cambridge, MA: Harvard University Press, 2011.

Nxumalo, F., and V. Pacini-Ketchabaw. "Staying with the Trouble in Child-Insect-Educator Common Worlds." *Environmental Education Research* 23, no. 10 (2017): 1414–26.

Oakley, J., G. P. L. Watson, C. L. Russell, A. Cutter-Mackenzie, L. Fawcett, G. Kuhl, J. Russell, M. van der Waal, and T. Warkentin. "Animal Encounters in Environmental Education Research: Responding to the Question of the Animal." *Canadian Journal of Environmental Education* 15 (2010): 86–102.

O'Brien, L., and R. Murray. "Forest School and Its Impacts on Young Children: Case Studies in Britain." *Urban Forestry & Urban Greening* 6, no. 4 (2007): 249–65.

Orr, D. W. *Ecological Literacy: Education and the Transition to a Postmodern World*. Albany: State University of New York Press, 1992.

Orr, D. W. *Earth in Mind*. Washington, DC: Island Press, 1994.

O'Sullivan, S. *Knowing Animals*. 2015–2022. Sydney, AU: Sydney University Press.

Otte, C., M. Bølling, M. P. Stevenson, N. Ejbye-Ernst, G. Nielsen, and P. Bentsen. "Education outside the Classroom Increases Children's Reading Performance: Results from a One-Year Quasi-Experimental Study." *International Journal of Educational Research* 94 (2019): 42–51.

Otto, S., and P. Pensini. "Nature-Based Environmental Education of Children: Environmental Knowledge, and Connectedness to Nature, Together, Are Related to Ecological Behaviour." *Global Environmental Change* 47 (2017): 88–94.

"Our Land: In the Beginning," Kwakiutl Band Council. Accessed August 2021. https://www.kwakiutl.bc.ca/Our-Land.

Pacini-Ketchabaw, V., and F. Nxumalo. "Unruly Raccoons and Troubled Educators: Nature/Culture Divides in a Childcare Centre." *Environmental Humanities* 7 (2015): 151–68.

Pacini-Ketchabaw, V., A. Taylor, and M. Blaise. "Decentering the Human in Multispecies Ethnographies." In *Posthuman Research Practices*, edited by C. Taylor and C. Hughes, 149–167. Cham, Switzerland: Palgrave Macmillan, 2016.

Palmer, J. A. *Environmental Education in the 21st Century: Theory, Practice, Progress, and Promise.* Philadelphia: Routledge, 1998

Palmer, J. A., and J. Suggate. "Influences and Experiences Affecting the Pro-Environmental Behaviour of Educators." *Environmental Education Research* 2, no. 1 (1996): 109–21.

Payne, P., and B. Wattchow. "Phenomenological Deconstruction, Slow Pedagogy, and the Corporeal Turn in Wild Environmental/Outdoor Education." *Canadian Journal of Environmental Education* 14, no. 1 (2009): 15–32.

Pedersen, H. "Schools, Speciesism, and Hidden Curricula: The Role of Critical Pedagogy for Human Education Futures." *Journal of Futures Studies* 8, no. 4 (2004): 1–14.

Pelo, A. *The Goodness of Rain: Developing an Early Ecological Identity in Young Children.* Lincoln, NE: Exchange Press, 2013.

Perkins, H. E. "Measuring Love and Care for Nature." *Journal of Environmental Psychology* 30, no. 4 (2010): 455–63.

Peterson, Jordan. *12 Rules for Living.* Toronto: Random House, 2018.

Piersol, L. "Listening Place." *Australian Journal of Outdoor Education* 17, no. 2 (2014): 43–53.

Pirchio, S., Y. Passiatore, A. Panno, M. Cipparone, and G. Carrus. "The Effects of Contact with Nature during Outdoor Environmental Education on Students' Wellbeing, Connectedness to Nature and Pro-Sociality." *Frontiers in Psychology* 12 (2021): 648458.

Platto, Sara, Jinfeng Zhou, Yanqing Wang, Huo Wang, and Ernesto Carafoli. "Biodiversity Loss and COVID-19 Pandemic: The Role of Bats in the Origin and the Spreading of the Disease." *Biochemical and Biophysical Research Communications* 538 (2021): 2–13. https://doi.org/10.1016/j.bbrc.2020.10.028.

Plumwood, Val. *Feminism and the Mastery of Nature.* New York: Routledge, 2002. https://doi.org/10.4324/9780203006757.

Pollan, Michael. *The Botany of Desire: A Plant's-Eye View of the World.* New York: Random House, 2001.

Pooley, J. A., and M. O'Connor. "Environmental Education and Attitudes: Emotions and Beliefs Are What Is Needed." *Environment and Behavior* 32, no. 5 (2000): 711–23.

Postma, D., and P. Smeyers. "Like a Swallow, Moving Forward in Circles: On the Future Dimension of Environmental Care and Education." *Journal of Moral Education* 41, no. 3 (2012): 399–412.

Prabawa-Sear, K., and C. Baudains. "Asking the Participants: Students' Views on Their Environmental Attitudes, Behaviours, Motivators, and Barriers." *Australian Journal of Environmental Education* 27, no. 2 (2011): 219–28.

"Principles and Values." Maple Ridge Environmental School. Accessed December 2020. https://es.sd42.ca/principles-and-values/.

Pulkki, J., B. Dahlin, and V. Varri. "Environmental Education as a Lived-Body Practice? A Contemplative Pedagogy Perspective. *Journal of Philosophy of Education* 51 (2016): 214–29.

Putnam, Robert D. *Bowling Alone: The Collapse and Revival of American Community.* New York: Simon & Schuster, 2000.

Ran, Brant. "How Much Old Growth Forest Remains in the US?" *The Understory, The Blog of Rainforest Action Network.* November 11, 2008. https://www.ran.org/the

-understory/how_much_old_growth_forest_remains_in_the_us/#:~:text
=According%20to%20one%20estimate%2C%20stands,(USDA%2DFS%202000)
.&text=Since%201600%2C%2090%25%20of%20the,states%20have%20been%20
cleared%20away.

Raphael, Dennis. *Social Determinants of Health: Canadian.* 2nd ed. Toronto: Canadian Scholar's Press, 2009.

Rasmussen D., and T. Akulukjuk. "My Father Was Told to Talk to the Environment First before Anything Else. In *Fields of Green,* edited by M. Mckenzie, P. Hart, H. Bai, and Bob Jickling. New York: Hampton Press, 2009.

Ravishankara, A. R., John S. Daniel, and Robert W. Portmann. "Nitrous Oxide (N_2O): The Dominant Ozone-Depleting Substance Emitted in the 21st Century." *Science (American Association for the Advancement of Science)* 326, no. 5949 (2009): 123–25. https://doi.org/10.1126/science.1176985.

Ray, Janisse. *The Seed Underground: A Growing Revolution to Save Food.* White River Junction, VT: Chelsea Green Publishing, 2014.

Rice, S., and A. G. Rud, eds. *The educational significance of human and nonhuman animal interactions.* Cham, Switzerland: Palgrave, 2015.

Ritchie, S. D., M. J. Wabano, R. G. Corbiere, B. Restoule, K. Russell, and N. L. "Young. Connecting to the Good Life through Outdoor Adventure Leadership Experiences." *Journal of Adventure Education & Outdoor Learning* 15, no. 4 (2015): 350–70.

Roberts, J. (2012). *Beyond Learning by Doing: Theoretical Currents in Experiential Education.* Philadelphia: Routledge.

Roe, J., and P. Aspinall. "The Restorative Outcomes of Forest School and Conventional School in Young People with Good and Poor Behavior." *Urban Forestry and Urban Greening* 10, no. 3 (2011): 205–12.

Rorty, R. *Philosophy and the Mirror of Nature.* Hoboken, NJ: Blackwell, 1994.

Rosa, C. D., C. C. Profice, and S. Collado, S. "Nature Experiences and Adults' Self-Reported Pro-Environmental Behaviors: The Role of Connectedness to Nature and Childhood Nature Experiences." *Frontiers in Psychology* (2018): 9.

Roszak, Theodore. *Where the Wasteland Ends: Politics and Transcendence in Postindustrial Society.* New York: Doubleday, 1972.

Russell, C., and J. Oakley. "Engaging the Emotional Dimensions of Environmental Education." *Canadian Journal of Environmental Education* 21 (2016): 13–22.

Russell, J., and L. Fawcett, L. "Childhood Animalness: Relationality, Vulnerabilities, and Conviviality." In *Research Handbook on Childhood Nature,* edited by A. Cutter-Mackenzie-Knowles, K. Malone, and E. Barratt Hacking. Rotterdam, Netherlands: Springer International Handbooks of Education, 2020.

Richardson, R. *Creating a Space to Grow: Developing Your Enabling Environment Outdoors.* Philadelphia: Routledge, 2017.

Safina, Carl. *Beyond Words: What Animals Think and Feel.* New York: Henry Holt and Company, 2015.

Sandseter, E. B. H., and L. E. O. Kennair. "Children's Risky Play from an Evolutionary Perspective: The Antiphobic Effects of Thrilling Experiences." *Evolutionary Psychology* 9, no. 2 (2011): 257–84.

Sartre, Jean-Paul. *Notebooks for an Ethics.* Translated by David Pellauer. Chicago: University of Chicago Press, 1992.

School District 42 (Maple Ridge–Pitt Meadows). "Mission, Vision, and Values Statement." 2008. http://www.sd42.ca/pdf/080410-vision.pdf.

School District 46 Sunshine Coast, B.C. "Nature Based Learning." Accessed July 4, 2023. https://sd46.bc.ca/programs/alternative-ed/nest/.

School Spaces: Innovative Outdoor Solutions. "The School Yard Space. 2022. https://outdoorspaces.ie/the-schoolyard-space/.

Schultz, P. W. "The Structure of Environmental Concern: Concern for the Self, Other People, and the Biosphere." *Journal of Environmental Psychology* 21, no. 4 (2001): 327–39.

Schultz, P. W. "Inclusion in Nature: The Psychology of Human-Nature Relations. In Schmuck, P. & Schultz, P. W. (Eds.), *Psychology of Sustainable Development* (pp. 61–78). Philadelphia: Kluwer Academic Publishers, 2002.

Serres, Michel. *The Natural Contract.* Translated by Elizabeth MacArthur and William Paulson. Ann Arbor, MI: Michigan University Press, 1995.

Sheldrake, Merlin. *The Entangled Life: How Fungi Make Our Worlds, Change Our Minds, and Shape Our Futures.* London: Random House, 2021.

Sheridan, Joe, and Roronhiakewen "He Clears the Sky" Dan Longboat. "The Haudenosaunee Imagination and the Ecology of the Sacred," *Space and Culture* 9, no. 4 (2006): 365–81. https://doi.org/10.1177/1206331206292503.

Shiva, Vandana. *Who Really Feeds the World?: The Failures of Agribusiness and the Promise of Agroecology.* Berkeley, CA: North Atlantic Books, 2016.

Shiva, Vandana. "Schooling the World." Schooling the World. Accessed July 2019. http://schoolingtheworld.org/people/vandana/.

Simard, Suzanne "How Trees Talk to Each Other." TED Talk filmed August 30, 2016, in Banff, Canada. YouTube video, 18:24. https://www.youtube.com/watch?v=Un2yBgIAxYs.

Simon Fraser University. "Welcome to CIRCE." Accessed July 4, 2023. http://www.circe-sfu.ca/.

Simpson, L. "Land as Pedagogy: Nishnaabeg Intelligence and Rebellious Transformation." *Decolonization: Indigeneity, Education & Society* 3, no. 3 (2014): 1–25.

Simpson, Leanne Betasamosake. *As We Have Always Done: Indigenous Freedom through Radical Resistances.* Minneapolis, MN: Minnesota University Press, 2017.

Sitka-Sage, M. D., H. Kopnina, S. Blenkinsop, and L. Piersol. "Rewilding Education in Troubled Times; or, Getting Back to the Wrong Post Nature." *Visions for Sustainability* 8 (2017): 20–37.

Sitka-Sage, Michael De Danann (Michael Derby), Laura Piersol, and Sean Blenkinsop. "Refusing to Settle for Pigeons and Parks: Urban Environmental Education in the Age of Neoliberalism." *Environmental Education Research* 21, no. 3 (2015): 378–89. https://doi.org/10.1080/13504622.2014.994166.

Skilbeck, A., and J. Stickney. "Section 5 Indigenous Land-Based, Forest School and Place Based Education. *Journal of Philosophy of Education* 54, no. 4 (2020): 1032.

Smith, G., and D. Williams, eds. *Ecological Education in Action: On Weaving Education, Culture, and the Environment.* Albany, NY: SUNY Press, 1999.

Smith, G. "Going Local." *Educational Leadership* 60, no. 1 (2000): 30–33.

Smith, G. "Place-Based Education: Learning to Be Where We Are." *Phi Delta Kappan* 83, no. 8 (2000), 584–594.

Smith, M., A. Dunhill, and G. W. Scott. "Fostering Children's Relationship with Nature: Exploring the Potential of Forest School." *Education 3-13* 46, no. 5 (2018): 525–34.

Smith, Rick, and Bruce Lourie. *Slow Death by Rubber Duck: The Secret Danger of Everyday Things.* Berkeley: Counterpoint, 2009.

Snaza, N., P. Appelbaum, S. Bayne, D. Carlson, and M. Morris. "Toward a Posthuman Education." *Journal of Curriculum Theorizing* 30, no. 2 (2014): 39–55.

Snaza, N., and A. J. Weaver, eds. *Posthumanism and Educational Research.* New York: Routledge, 2015.

Sobel, D. *Place-Based Education: Connecting Classrooms and Communities.* Great Barrington, MA: The Orion Society, 2005.

Sobel, D. *Children and Nature: Design Principles for Educators.* Portsmouth, NH: Stenhouse Publishers, 2008.

Sobel, David. *Children's Special Places: Exploring the Role of Forts, Dens, and Bush Houses in Middle Childhood.* Detroit, MI: Wayne State University Press, 2001.

Soga, Masashi, Kevin J. Gaston, and Yuichi Yamaura. "Gardening Is Beneficial for Health: A Meta-Analysis." *Preventive Medicine Reports* 5, no. C (2016): 92. https://doi.org/10.1016/j.pmedr.2016.11.007.

Spannring, R. "Animals in Environmental Education Research." *Environmental Education Research* 23, no. 1 (2017): 63–74.

Stan Rushworth Interview. Directed by Katie Teague. Uploaded Friday, March 20, 2020. Santa Cruz, CA: Katie Teague Minute, Vimeo. 6:20. https://vimeo.com/399323963.

Stedman, R. C. "Toward a Social Psychology of Place: Predicting Behavior from Place-Based Cognitions, Attitude, and Identity." *Environment and Behavior* 34, no. 5 (2002): 561–81.

Stedman, R. C. "Is It Really Just a Social Construction?: The Contributions of the Physical Environment to Sense of Place." *Society and Natural Resources* 16 (2003): 671–85.

Steingraber, Sandra. *Living Downstream: An Ecologist's Personal Investigation of Cancer and the Environment.* New York: Hachette Books, 2010.

Stevenson, K. T., N. M. Peterson, J. S. Carrier, L. R. Strnad, and D. H. Bondell. "Role of Significant Life Experiences in Building Environmental Knowledge and Behaviour among Middle School Students." *The Journal of Environmental Education* 45, no. 3 (2014): 163–77.

Stewart, A. "Decolonising Encounters with the Murray River: Building Place Responsive Outdoor Education." *Australian Journal of Outdoor Education* 8, no. 2 (2004): 46–56.

Stewart, A. *Developing Place-Responsive Pedagogy in Outdoor Environmental Education.* Rotterdam, Netherlands: Springer International Publishing, 2020.

Stolorow, Robert, and George E. Atwood. *Contexts of Being: Intersubjective Foundations of Psychological Life.* New York: Routledge, 1992.

Stratford, R. "Educational Philosophy, Ecology, and the Anthropocene." *Educational Philosophy and Theory* (2017): 149–152.

Taiwan Panorama. "Setting Sail for the Future: Principal Aaron Huang." New Southbound Policy Portal, Ministry of Foreign Affairs, Republic of China (Taiwan). January 18, 2018. https://nspp.mofa.gov.tw/nsppe/news.php?post=127997&unit=410.

Takano, T., P. Higgins, and P. McLaughlin. "Connecting with Place: Implications of Integrating Cultural Values into the School Curriculum in Alaska." *Environmental Education Research* 15, 3 (2009): 343–70.

Taylor, A., and V. Pacini-Ketchabaw. Learning with Children, Ants, and Worms in the Anthropocene: Toward a Common World Pedagogy of Multispecies Vulnerability." *Pedagogy, Culture, and Society* 23, no. 4 (2015): 507–29.

Tiplady, L., and H. Menter. "Forest School for Wellbeing: An Environment in which Young People Can 'Take What They Need.'" *Journal of Adventure Education and Outdoor Learning* 21, no. 2 (2021): 99–114.

Tooth, R., and P. Renshaw. "Reflections on Pedagogy and Place: A Journey into Learning for Sustainability through Environmental Narrative and Deep Attentive Reflection." *Australian Journal of Environmental Education* 25 (2012): 95–104.

Torkar, G. "Learning Experiences That Produce Environmentally Active and Informed Minds." *NJAS: Wageningen Journal of Life Sciences* 69, no. 1 (2012): 49–55.

Tsing, A. *The Mushroom at the End of the World: On the Possibility of Life in Capitalist Ruins*. Princeton, NJ: Princeton University Press, 2017.

Tuan, Yi-fu. *Topophilia: A Study of Environmental Perception, Attitudes, and Values*. New York: Columbia University Press, 1990.

Tugade, Michele M., Barbara L. Fredrickson, and Lisa Feldman Barrett. "Psychological Resilience and Positive Emotional Granularity: Examining the Benefits of Positive Emotions on Coping and Health." *Journal of Personality* 72, no. 6 (2004): 1161–90. https://doi.org/10.1111/j.1467-6494.2004.00294.x.

Tree, Isabella. *Wilding: The Return of Nature to a British Farm*. London: Picador, 2018.

Twenge, Jean M. "The Age of Anxiety? The Birth Cohort Change in Anxiety and Neuroticism, 1952–1993." *Journal of Personality and Social Psychology* 79, no. 6 (2000): 1007–21. https://doi.org/10.1037/0022-3514.79.6.1007.

Twenge, Jean M., Brittany Gentile, C. Nathan DeWall, Debbie Ma, Katharine Lacefield, and David R. Schurtz. "Birth Cohort Increases in Psychopathology among Young Americans, 1938–2007: A Cross-Temporal Meta-Analysis of the MMPI." *Clinical Psychology Review* 30, no. 2 (2010): 145–54. https://doi.org/10.1016/j.cpr.2009.10.005.

Tyler, Ralph. *Basic Principles of Curriculum and Instruction*. Chicago: University of Chicago Press, 1949.

Ungar, M., C. Dumont, and W. MacDonald. "Risk, Resilience, and Outdoor Programming for at Risk Children." *Journal of Social Work* 5, no. 3 (2005): 319–38.

van den Berg, A. E., and C. G. van den Berg. "A Comparison of Children with ADHD in a Natural and Built Setting." *Child: Care, Health, and Development* 37, no. 3 (2011): 430–439.

Van Horn, G., R. Wall Kimmerer, and J. Hausdoerffer. *Kinship: Belonging in a World of Relations*. Chicago: Center for Humans & Nature, 2021.

Van Matre, S. *Earth Education: A New Beginning*. Bradford Woods, PA: Institute for Earth Education, 1983.

van Tulleken, Christoffer, Michael Tipton, Heather Massey, and C. Mark Harper. "Open Water Swimming as a Treatment for Major Depressive Disorder." *BMJ Case Reports* (2018): 1–3. https://doi.org/10.1136/bcr-2018-225007.

Van Veen, Tobias C. "Afro-Futurism & Anthropocene: Strategies for Imagining Other Worlds." *Afrocentrism Conference*. September 21–22, 2019, Vancouver, BC.

Van Veen, Tobias C., and Reynaldo Anderson. "Future Movements: Black Lives, Black Politics, Black Futures—An Introduction." *TOPIA: Canadian Journal of Cultural Studies* 39 (2018): 8.

Vasconcelos, C., and C. S. C. Calheiros. *Enhancing Environmental Education through Nature-Based Solutions*. Rotterdam, Netherlands: Springer International Publishing AG, 2022.

Verny, Thomas R. *Pre-Parenting*. New York: Simon & Schuster, 2002.

Vygotsky, Lev. *Mind in Society: The Development of Higher Psychological Processes*, edited by Michael Cole, Vera John-Steiner, Sylvia Scribner, and Ellen Souberman. Cambridge, MA: Harvard University Press, 1980.

Waite, S. "'Knowing Your Place in the World': How Place and Culture Support and Obstruct Educational Aims." *Cambridge Journal of Education* 43, no. 4 (2013): 413–33.

Warren, K., N. Roberts, M. Breunig, and A. Alvarez. "Social Justice in Experiential Education: Past, Present, and Future." *Journal of Experiential Education* 37 no. 1 (2014): 89–103.

Watson, John B., and Rosalie Alberta Rayner Watson. *Psychological Care of Infant and Child*. New York: W.W. Norton & Company, 1928.

Wattchow, B., and M. Brown. *A Pedagogy of Place: Outdoor Education for a Changing World*. Melbourne, AU: Monash University, 2020.

Watts, Vanessa. "Indigenous Place-Thought and Agency amongst Humans and Non-Humans (First Woman and Sky Woman Go on a European World Tour)." *Decolonization: Indigeneity, Education, and Society* 2, no. 1 (2013): 20–34.

WebMD. "Holistic Medicine." March 18, 2020. https://www.webmd.com/balance/guide/what-is-holistic-medicine.

Wells, N., and G. Evans. "Nearby Nature: A Buffer of Life Stress among Rural Children." *Environment and Behavior* 35, no. 3 (2003): 311–30.

Weston, A. "What If Teaching Went Wild." *Canadian Journal of Environmental Education* 9 (2004): 40–52.

Wigglesworth, J., and P. Heintzman. "A Qualitative Study of the Perceived Significant Life Impacts of a University Summer Outdoor Education Course." *Journal of Adventure Education and Outdoor Learning* 21, no. 4 (2020): 385–97.

Williams, Florence. *The Nature Fix: Why Nature Makes Us Happier, Healthier and More Creative.* New York: W. W. Norton, 2017.

Williams, Lorna B. "Honoring All Life." In *Child Honoring: How to Turn This World Around,* edited by Raffi and Sharna Olfman, 87–94. Westport, CT: Praeger Publishers, 2006.

Willis, A. "Re-Storying Wilderness and Adventure Therapies: Healing Places and Selves in an Era of Environmental Crises." *Journal of Adventure Education & Outdoor Learning* 11, no. 2 (2011): 91–108.

Whitaker, Robert. *Anatomy of an Epidemic.* New York: Broadway Books, 2010.

White, R., and V. Stoecklin. "Children's Outdoor Play & Learning Environments: Returning to Nature." *Early Childhood News* 10, no. 2 (1998): 24–30.

Whittington, A., J. Aspelmeier, and N. Budbill. "Promoting Resiliency in Adolescent Girls through Adventure Programming." *Journal of Adventure Education and Outdoor Learning* 16, no. 1 (2016): 1–14.

Whittington, A., and N. Budbill, N. "Breaking the Mold: Impacts of Adventure Education on Girls." *Journal of Outdoor Recreation, Education and Leadership* 5, no. 1 (2013): 37–53.

Wilson, Edward O. *Biophilia: The Human Bond with Other Species.* Cambridge, MA: Harvard University Press, 1986.

Wilson, R. *Fostering a Sense of Wonder during the Early Childhood Years.* Greyden Press, 1993.

Wilson, R. *Nature and Young Children: Encouraging Creative Play and Learning in Natural Environments.* Routledge, 2020.

Wilson, Samuel, Lovell Jones, Christine Coussens, and Kathi Hanna, eds. *Cancer and the Environment: Gene-Environment Interaction.* Roundtable of Environmental Health Sciences, Research, and Medicine, Board on Health Sciences Policy, Institute of Medicine. Washington, DC: National Academy Press, 2002. https://doi.org/10.17226/10464.

The Wisdom of Trauma, directed by Maurizio Benazzo and Zaya Benazzo. Oakland, CA: The Hive Studios, 2021. https://thewisdomoftrauma.com/portfolio-item/about-the-film/.

Wolstenholme, Jennifer T., Michelle Edwards, Savera R. J. Shetty, Jessica D. Gatewood, Julia A. Taylor, Emilie F. Rissman, and Jessica J. Connelly. "Gestational Exposure to Bisphenol A Produces Transgenerational Changes in Behaviors and Gene Expression." *Endocrinology* 153, no. 8 (2012): 3828–38. https://doi.org/10.1210/en.2012-1195.

Wood, D. *Thinking Plant Animal Human, Encounters with Communities of Difference.* Minneapolis: University of Minnesota Press, 2020.

Wu, C.-D., E. McNeely, J. G. Cedeño-Laurent, W. C. Pan, G. Adamkiewicz, F. Dominici, C. S. Lung, H. Jen-Su, and J. D. Spengler. "Linking Student Performance in Massachusetts Elementary Schools with the 'Greenness' of School Surroundings Using Remote Sensing." *PloS One* 9, no. 10 (2014).

Yong, Ed. "What Happens When Americans Can Finally Exhale?" *The Atlantic*. May 20, 2021. https://www.theatlantic.com/health/archive/2021/05/pandemic-trauma-summer/618934/.

Young, Jon. *What the Robin Knows: How Birds Reveal the Secrets of the Natural World*. Boston, MA: Mariner Books, 2013.

Zelenski, J. M., and E. K. Nisbet. "Happiness and Feeling Connected: The Distinct Role of Nature Connectedness." *Environment and Behaviour* 46, no. 1 (2014): 3–23.

Zembylas, Michalinos. "The Quest for Cognitive Justice: Towards a Pluriversal Human Rights Education." *Globalisation, Societies and Education* 15, no. 4 (2017): 397–409. https://doi.org/10.1080/14767724.2017.1357462.

Zupančič, Alenka. *The Odd One In: On Comedy*. Cambridge, MA: MIT Press, 2008.

Index

Abrams, David, 10
activism, 8, 41, 85, 146–50, 163–64
Adam (creation story figure), 119–20
addiction, 12, 79
advocacy, 22, 149
African Americans, 85, 87
Afrofuturism, 87–88
Akomolafe, Bayo, 86
alienation, 17, 55, 57, 90, 174; disease and, 14, 80; healing and, 12, 16; hyperactive pessimism and, 152; independence and, 51; more-than-human concept and, 10; "myth of the isolated mind" and, 11; neoliberalism and, 79; undoing, 115–16. *See also* isolation
allergies, 83
Anthropocene, 15, 46, 87, 111
anthropocentrism, 52, 131, 137; in Camus, 109; cosmology and, 120; of culture, 92–94, 129, 163; epistemology and, 172; marginalization and, 6; more-than-human concept and, 10, 55; pedagogy and, 133; of schools, 58, 72; teachers and, 106, 142
anxiety, 74, 80–81; biochemical model of, 78; eco-, 174; increases in, 12, 57, 77–79; individualism and, 162; relational capacity and, 63
assault, 90–91
assumptions, knowledge and, 105–6
asthma, 79, 83
attentive receptivity, 67
Atwood, George, 11
autochthony, 144
autonomy, 51–53, 99, 128–29, 143
axiology, 99, 107–12

Beeman, Chris, 46–48
belonging, 20, 39, 49, 69, 80, 96, 169
Between Man and Man (Buber), 147
biases, 6, 14–15, 55, 63, 81
binaries, 116–17, 193n16
bio-morality, 73
biophilia, 55
bipolar disorder, 57, 82
Bird Rose, Deborah, 119–20
Blenkinsop, Sean, 16, 22–23, 27, 41

bonding, 62–63, 69–70
Botany of Desire, The (Pollan), 83
BPA, 57
Braiding Sweetgrass (Kimmerer), 83–84
Britton, James, 36
Buber, Martin, 64, 147
bullying, 122–25

Cabanas, Edgar, 72
Camus, Albert, 107–10, 129
Cancer Stages of Capitalism, The (McMurtry), 13
capitalism, 15, 72, 84, 158, 170
caregivers, 34–35
Cederström, Carl, 73
child-rearing, 51–52, 62
citizenship, 132, 143
climate change, 13, 80, 84–86, 176
cognitive structures, of standard education, 25–27
colonialism, 16, 19–20, 94, 112, 164, 193n16
community: axiology and, 107; -based lessons, 141; building, 39, 45, 150, 162–63, 165; cultivation and, 5; -focused ecologizing educator, 166–69; gardening and, 82; as guiding principle/value, 29; Indigenous, 24, 91; integration, 31–32
competition, 5, 18, 56, 60, 84, 118, 158
conformity, 21, 60, 71, 88, 93–94, 126–27
cosmology, 118–21
courage, 94, 110, 178
COVID-19 pandemic, 37, 79, 85, 111, 162
creation stories, 119–20
criminal justice, 92–93
Crutzen, Paul, 15
cultural change, 14–17, 98–129, 156–59, 164–78
culture(s), 5–6; of detachment, 52; foundational stories and, 119–21; gift economy, 20; of happiness, 72; health and, 77; literacy-based, 120–21; of positivity, 74; power and, 96; rapacious, 13, 16; substrates of, 99; Western, 16
curriculum: design, 60, 138, 150; guidelines, 20; hidden, 74; implicit, 61; integration, 31; inverted, 141–42; mandated, 3; standard, 35, 131